THE CHOSEN
WILL BECOME HERDS

THE CHOSEN WILL BECOME HERDS

Studies in Twentieth-Century Kabbalah

JONATHAN GARB

Translated by

Yaffah Berkovits-Murciano

YALE UNIVERSITY PRESS / NEW HAVEN & LONDON

Published with assistance from the Lucius N. Littauer Foundation

Originally published as *Yeḥidei Ha-Segulot Yihyu La-'Adarim: 'Iyunim Be-Kabbalat Ha-Meah Ha-'Esrim*, © 2005 by the Shalom Hartman Institute and Carmel Press, Jerusalem.

Set in Quadraat type by Keystone Typesetting, Inc.
Printed in the United States of America.

Library of Congress Cataloging-in-Publication Data
Garb, Jonathan.
[Yehide ha-segulot yihyu la-'adarim. English]
The chosen will become herds : studies in twentieth-century kabbalah / Jonathan Garb ; translated by Yaffah Berkovits-Murciano.
p. cm.
Includes bibliographical references and index.
ISBN 978-0-300-12394-4 (paperback : alk. paper)
1. Cabala—History—20th century. I. Title.
BM525.G3613 2009
296.1'6—dc22
2008054918

A catalogue record for this book is available from the British Library.

This paper meets the requirements of ANSI/NISO Z39.48-1992 (Permanence of Paper).
It contains 30 percent postconsumer waste (PCW) and is certified by the Forest Stewardship Council (FSC).

10 9 8 7 6 5 4 3 2 1

This book is dedicated to my dear parents,
Aryeh Leib (Louis) and Erica (Hanna),
who instilled in me both love of Torah and love of Western culture

CONTENTS

PREFACE

This book is based partly on a series of articles that I published on twentieth-century Kabbalah, and partly on original and as yet unpublished research. The articles have not been copied verbatim but have rather been woven into the text alongside new findings. Readers interested in further research may consult former articles of mine on this topic. My interest in twentieth-century Kabbalah was triggered by my early exposure to the writings of R. Avraham Yizḥaq Ha-Kohen Kook. My in-depth study of his works led me, while a student at the Hebrew University, to participate in a research project conducted by Professor Tamar Rappaport into sociocultural processes in the Religious-Zionist world. Since then, my research has expanded to include other kabbalistic movements, and it is that research that forms the underpinnings of this book. This study of twentieth-century Kabbalah has allowed me to combine my interest in Kabbalah and comparative mysticism with my interest in postmodern culture.

It is incumbent on researchers studying the present or the recent past to try to narrow the distance between themselves and the phenomena they are studying, as well as the distance between themselves and their readers. I will, therefore, share with my readers some of the dilemmas and conflicts I encountered in researching twentieth-century Kabbalah. Clearly, my interest in the transformations that the world of Kabbalah has undergone in recent generations is related to the fact that I myself was exposed to these shifts, first as a Yeshiva student and later as a university researcher. My geocultural status also explains my focus on processes that took place in Israel.

As I predicted in the postscript to the Hebrew edition of this book, a great deal has happened in the world of contemporary Kabbalah even in the short time since that edition was published. At that time, I argued that the main obstacle facing researchers of twentieth-century Kabbalah was the fact that many important works remained in manuscript or circulated within closed circles. Fortunately, this state of affairs has greatly improved, for in the past couple of years works by almost all of the important late kabbalists mentioned in the book have been published.

In addition to these texts, we have seen over the past few years the publication of new and interesting works by many of the living figures discussed here (such as R. Ginsburgh, Ohad Ezraḥi, Michael Laitman, R. Moshe Shapira, and R. Tau), the extraordinary appearance of extremely esoteric works (such as the *Scroll of Secrets* by R. Naḥman of Bratzlav, published by Zvi Mark), and the emergence of intriguing new figures (such as R. Itamar Schwartz, author of the multivolume *Bi-Lvavi Mishkan Evne*). Naturally, recent events in Israel, such as the disengagement from the Gaza Strip and the Second Lebanon War, have also prompted fresh kabbalistic discourses, by R. Ginsburgh and R. Yitzḥaq Maier Morgenstern, respectively. Finally, the emergent field of twentieth-century Kabbalah research has produced a spate of new and important studies, such as those by Yoram Bilu, Smadar Cherlow, Shlomo Fischer, Boaz Huss, Jonatan Meir, Ḥaviva Pedaya, Avinoam Rosenak, Philip Wexler, and others.

These bibliographical developments, discussions with the colleagues mentioned below, and the further development of my own thought have alerted me to several issues that are only partly addressed in the present volume, and that I hope will be expanded on in future studies, whether my own or those of other scholars. These include the proliferation and development of Hasidic mystical music; the evolving synthesis between Mussar and Hasidism exemplified in the extremely influential works and discourses of R. Tzevi Maier Zilberberg; and the ideological and halakhic opposition to the spread of Kabbalah in more conservative circles, especially in some Sephardic Yeshivas. On the technical level, I have added a short glossary of names and terms for the benefit of the English reader, as well as some bibliographical additions and updates.

I would like to thank Professor Moshe Idel for important insights relating to contemporary Kabbalah. Special thanks also go to Professor Philip Wexler, a pioneer of sociological research into contemporary mysticism, for the many conversations we had on this topic and for joining me in setting up a research group dedicated to this topic at the Institute of Advanced Studies in Jerusalem. Likewise, I offer my heartfelt thanks to my colleagues Daniel Abrams, Eli'ezer Baumgarten, Yoram Bilu, Yaron Ezrahi, Shlomo Fischer, Boaz Huss, Yehudah Liebes, Ron Margolin, Zvi Mark, Jonatan Meir, Edwin Serrousi, and Elliot R. Wolfson for our creative discussions on contemporary mysticism.

My affiliation with the Hebrew University of Jerusalem enabled me to write this book. I am especially grateful for the grant I received from the Committee for the Promotion of Innovative Research headed by the Vice President of R&D, which facilitated the writing of this book, as well as a further grant from the Authority for R&D, which assisted the translation into English. I also owe a debt of gratitude to my students Yair Halevi, Patrick Koch, and Netanel Yeḥieli, whose contributions inspired some of the insights in the book. My sincere thanks to Carmel Press, which published the Hebrew edition. Sections of the book were presented at seminars at the Shalom Hartman Institute, which participated in the publication of the Hebrew edition, and I would like to thank the members of the institute, particularly Professor David Hartman and Professor Moshe Halbertal, for their valuable comments during the earlier stages of this research. Profound thanks are due to Maurice Kriegel, for inviting me to lecture on this book, and to the scholars at the École des hautes études en sciences sociales in Paris, for their valuable comments. I wish to thank the staff at Yale University Press and especially Jack Borrebach, William Frucht, and Jessie Hunnicutt for their courteous and effective assistance. Warm thanks are also due to Martin Peretz for his support. Finally, I wish to thank Yaffah Murciano for her sensitive, swift, and fluent translation of the book into English.

This book owes a great debt to my friends who are affiliated with the world of mysticism and who strive to preserve the quality of spiritual practice in a world overtaken by commercialization and popularization. I especially wish to thank Dan Russell Sensai, director of the School of Hypnotherapy in Carlisle, England, and Orit Sen-Gupta, head of the Vijnana Yoga method in Israel. Finally, my deepest thanks go to my beloved wife, Ronna, for our many discussions on contemporary culture, postmodernism, and globalization, and particularly for sharing the wonderful experience of raising our sons, Evyatar David and Ariel.

INTRODUCTION

The Study of Twentieth-Century Kabbalah: Dilemmas and Possibilities

The proliferation of mystical and magical ideas and practices has characterized cultural life in the past few decades. The Internet, the fashion world, the cinema, and literature are steeped in symbols, metaphors, and terms that derive from mystical and occult traditions. The sensational literary and cinematic success of the *Lord of the Rings* and *Harry Potter* series testifies to this unusual interest in the occult.[1] In these and similar works, the magician with supernatural powers has become a cultural icon of sorts.

I would like to begin by clarifying that I have adopted the cultural studies methodology in this book. In other words, my study encompasses phenomena associated with "popular culture" as well as those generally associated with "high culture." In this way, I hope to obtain a comprehensive picture of cultural processes. One of the prominent features of twentieth-century cultural and economic life has been the growing influence of the popular entertainment industry. In my opinion, we cannot understand spiritual life in this century without referring to popular culture.

The growth of mysticism is not merely a cultural phenomenon: it is part of an increasingly prevalent social phenomenon commonly known as the New Age.[2] As a number of researchers have already pointed out, the New Age, as a social movement, lacks a recognized leader, a clear platform, and central institutions.[3] Rather, it consists of a network of ties between a vast range of organizations, publications, schools, businesses, festivals, and even localities.[4] In this social sense, the New Age movement is a postmodern one.

The world of Kabbalah plays a central role in this movement. Over the past century, particularly in recent decades, kabbalistic symbols and images have proliferated beyond the boundaries of the orthodox Jewish world and become extremely commonplace. The use of metaphors derived from the world of Kabbalah by superstars such as Madonna is merely the tip of the iceberg.[5] Even the term *Kabbalah* has become a kind of logo promoting various ideological and even commercial agendas. For many, the word has become synonymous with the mysterious, the miraculous, and the magical.

In this book, I will not be discussing Kabbalah as merely a popular and superficial phenomenon. Over the past century, the world of Kabbalah itself has experienced an unprecedented revival, and kabbalistic literature is being disseminated and studied on a far larger scale than in the thirteenth and sixteenth centuries—the golden ages of Kabbalah. Moreover, the proliferation of different kabbalistic currents in the past century has stimulated new kabbalistic activity that differs from the classical activity of previous centuries. Twentieth-century Kabbalah has a distinctly modern (and perhaps even postmodern) flavor, and it is this that accounts for the contemporary assimilation and influence of Kabbalah. I have therefore drawn a distinction throughout the book between "classical Kabbalah," namely kabbalistic literature predating the twentieth century, and "modern Kabbalah," or twentieth-century Kabbalah.

This distinction does not imply that twentieth-century Kabbalah lacks continuity but is intended rather to highlight its stylistic and even substantive innovations. It is this innovative quality that is the focal point of book. As Michel Foucault wrote, we must relinquish our emphasis on the "infinite continuity" of discourse in favor of the "sudden eruption" of moments of discourse.[6] The focus on the innovative in twentieth-century Kabbalah, however, does not imply that classical Kabbalah is homogeneous. On the contrary, classical Kabbalah is itself characterized by a variety of currents and paradigms.

I believe that this juncture, toward the end of the first decade of the twenty-first century—when far-reaching environmental, political, social, and technological changes are taking place that may distinguish the twenty-first century from the previous one—is a good time for reviewing twentieth-century Kabbalah and its place in the current cultural and social context. Some might argue that we lack the necessary perspective for studying recent and contemporary phenomena. Indeed, this belief in the need for perspective has been responsible, inter alia, for the dearth of comprehensive and in-depth research into twentieth-century Kabbalah and the new mysticism in general.[7] In my opinion, however, there is no single perspective that provides an objective picture of the past. According to the distinguished twentieth-century theoretician Hans Gadamer, each generation is situated within its own "horizon," from which it interprets the past. The way twentieth-century Kabbalah will be interpreted in the next century will be different (but not necessarily better) than the way it is interpreted now, just as Safedian Kabbalah is interpreted differently (but not necessarily better) in this century than in the previous one. I do not share the modernist belief in linear "progress"; instead, I hold the view of the historian of science, Thomas Kuhn, that the evolution of theories does not necessarily signify progress but rather signifies the transition between paradigms, or different research languages.

The desire for perspective and objectivity is one of the motives that has deterred researchers from studying twentieth-century Kabbalah. Boaz Huss, who documented prevailing attitudes toward research of contemporary Kabbalah, proposed other, more hidden motives, including Zionist ideology, which identified Jewish mysticism as a movement that had outlived its function as a survival mechanism in the Diaspora period; a modernist approach that sees the traditional forms of religion as phenomena that are increasingly losing their public significance in the modern world; and an "Orientalist" approach that associates Kabbalah with the "Orient"—the "source of archaic knowledge" that today exists in a "frozen, atrophied and backward" form.[8]

In addition to the causes mentioned above, the lack of research into contemporary Kabbalah is due to the stigma of popularism, superficiality, and even charlatanism associated with some contemporary kabbalistic works.[9] Also, researchers who wish to avoid being labeled kabbalists or journalists will naturally gravitate toward more distant historical research.

The researcher's reluctance to focus on contemporary phenomena may be motivated by a desire for social distinction, in the sense implied by the noted sociologist Pierre Bourdieu. Just as people consider themselves more "cultured" because they prefer classical music to rap, so may researchers perceive themselves as more "authentic" because they study thirteenth-century Spanish manuscripts rather than contemporary kabbalistic works published in the small Israeli town of Bet Shemesh, for example. I believe, however, that the study of thirteenth- or sixteenth-century manuscripts does not preclude research into the present or the recent past. On the contrary, Foucault advocated recording the "history of the present" and even researching the past from the perspective of the present, as he himself did. Foucault's practice was to study the roots of contemporary phenomena until the discontinuity between contemporary phenomena and earlier phenomena surfaced. To a large extent this is the methodology used here.

In addition to these possible explanations for the paucity of research into contemporary Kabbalah, there is another, more technical obstacle. Many contemporary kabbalistic works have not yet been published, either because they have not been committed to paper (as with some of the teachings of the French kabbalist R. Yehuda Léon Ashkenazy, for example) or because they were censored by kabbalist circles themselves (as with some of the diaries of R. Avraham Yizḥaq Ha-Kohen Kook or R. Yehuda Leib Ha-Levi Ashlag, the "Ba'al Ha-Sulam," for example).[10] It is, therefore, entirely possible that contemporary studies will need to be rewritten once these as yet unpublished manuscripts become available. Although this problem exists in the research of classical Kabbalah, too, the popularity of Kabbalah in our times, the reopening of Eastern Europe, and the development of advanced information technologies have led to the discovery and publication of many classical kabbalistic manuscripts.

A study of contemporary manuscripts is an important complement to the study of kabbalistic writing throughout the generations.[11] Indeed, our temporal proximity to the works we are studying enables us to carry out a kind of rescue dig, by preserving texts that might otherwise sink into oblivion. Had academic research into Kabbalah existed in the thirteenth century, several additional kabbalistic works would have been preserved, greatly enhancing the research of this period. One of the objectives of this book is to preserve contemporary kabbalistic traditions, an effort that researchers and libraries have so far largely failed to undertake.

The search for contemporary kabbalistic material, which is frequently hard to access, forces the researcher to abandon the library or office for the field in order to collect texts or oral traditions, which are sometimes even more valuable than texts.[12] This approach is even more valid with research into social practices and processes rather than merely ideas and symbols. Yet contact with contemporary kabbalists fuels the concern that researchers might lose their identity and, hence, their objectivity.[13] Indeed, contemporary kabbalists have attempted to enlist researchers for their own agendas. According to Yoram Bilu, this situation typifies research in the postmodern era (see the "new anthropology," for example), which advocates "participatory observation."[14]

Recently, the boundary between researcher and kabbalist (to borrow the title of R. Moshe Ḥayyim Luzzatto's book, *Ḥoker Ve-Mequbal*, or Researcher and Kabbalist) has become blurred. Some researchers practice Kabbalah and mysticism and even have mystical experiences, while many kabbalists publish increasingly scientific editions of manuscripts.[15] Some of these kabbalists are extremely au fait with the world of research and have no qualms about meeting researchers (even female ones). Evidently, kabbalistic research and the dissemination of Kabbalah go hand in hand. Given these factors, safeguarding the quality of academic research and protecting it against outside interests cannot be achieved through isolation or erecting rigid barriers. There is a growing recognition in contemporary society that even the definition of the term *research* is fluid and dynamic. Students of the positivistic "Wissenschaft des Judentums" (*Ḥokhmat Yisra'el*, or Science of Judaism) in nineteenth-century Germany would almost certainly consider contemporary researchers to be overly empathetic toward the subject of their research. No doubt researchers of the coming century will also view their predecessors in a different light.

Despite the general lack of contemporary research into twentieth-century Kabbalah, such research has recently experienced a revival as part of the "new directions" in kabbalistic research introduced by researchers such as Yehuda Liebes, Moshe Idel, and others.[16] Indeed, since the late 1990s, a spate of studies has appeared on phenomena relating to contemporary Kabbalah, along with a series of anthropological and psychological works focusing on its social aspects.[17] This new trend, however, is still in its early days.

The correlation between the research status and popular status of Kabbalah confounds the notion sometimes found in academic circles that objectivity exists independently of sociocultural processes. In practice, the dissemination of kabbalistic research and kabbalistic books goes hand in hand.[18] As a result, a remarkable number of works, including radical ones that were never published in the past, such as the works of R. Abraham Abulafia and Sabbatian texts, are being published for the first time or made available online, both by researchers and by kabbalists.[19]

This phenomenon is not limited to Israel. In the West, too, there has been a resurgence of popular and scholarly interest in mystical and magical, including kabbalistic, phenomena.[20] (The interest relates to both Jewish and Christian Kabbalah. Christian Kabbalah has been part of kabbalistic literature at least since the Renaissance.)[21] Indeed, one of the characteristics of the new mysticism in general, and twentieth-century Kabbalah in particular, is globality. Over the past century, information technology and the population flow have helped create a "global village." As a result, the new mysticism is characterized by the dissolution of barriers between various regions and religions, which explains my wish to study twentieth-century Kabbalah in the global New Age context, as a phenomenon that belongs to the globalization process. Likewise, although the book focuses on Israel, the origin of most of the processes I will discuss, it frequently alludes to phenomena occurring outside Israel, and to the connection between those phenomena and Israeli processes.

Despite the research developments since the late 1990s, we still do not have an acceptable picture of twentieth-century Kabbalah as we have of earlier generations. Much of the existing research has focused on a few prominent mystics, such as Kook or R. Hillel Zeitlin, and their philosophies. And yet large sections of the corpus, written by major thinkers such as Kook himself, Ashlag, or the rebbe Qalonymus Qalman Shapira, have not been subjected to in-depth study. Likewise, current research tends to overlook "quantitative" phenomena, such as the dissemination of Kabbalah and its translation into popular tools, although this trend existed in earlier kabbalistic streams, such as the kabbalistic Mussar literature and the literature of the Hasidic world.

Over and above quantitative restrictions of this sort, the research is limited by biases stemming from various agendas that until recently were accepted without question. One example of such a bias is the tendency to deal with ideas rather than with social structures or practices—a tendency that precludes a more sociological or anthropological view of contemporary Kabbalah. With a few exceptions, such as Boaz Huss, most researchers of contemporary Kabbalah do not make use of contemporary cultural research tools and thereby miss the opportunity of situating twentieth-century Kabbalah in the broader context of Western culture. Another example of bias in Israel is the research focus on national issues, such as the Land of Israel or the redemption, at the expense of more personal issues, such as mystical experiences or psychological doctrines. (The connection that sometimes exists between Israeli mysticism and politics has given rise to popular and research attitudes that evaluate a given phenomena according to political preconceptions.)[22]

This short survey of the research situation regarding twentieth-century Kabbalah would not be complete without reference to the backlash unleashed by the revival of mysticism. Alongside an intensification of mystical discourse in recent generations, there has been, and still is (although decreasingly so), strong opposition to the destabilization of the modern narrative through the spread of mysticism. Various secular and even religious elites who have been bred on rationalism describe the new mysticism as dangerous, or at least "bizarre."[23] This antagonism has, to some extent, contributed to the dearth of research into contemporary Kabbalah, which has been labeled superficial and "popular," and possibly to reservations on the part of some readers. Before passing judgment, however, an in-depth study of this phenomenon, including its ideological and social aspects, is essential. It is with this in mind that I have written this book.

The above notwithstanding, I admit I am no "orthodox" postmodernist and believe implicitly in varying degrees of creative excellence. In this context, I would like to invoke the following beautiful Zen saying: "Although both flowers and weeds have Buddha nature, we love flowers, and we do not care for weeds. That, too, is Buddha nature." By extension, just as we are capable of recognizing the greatness of R. Yizḥaq Luria, R. Moshe Ḥayyim Luzzatto ("Ramḥal"), or R. Naḥman of Bratzlav, so are we capable of recognizing the greatness of Kook or Ashlag, or the insignificance of lesser personalities. Therefore, I propose a differentiation between qualitative phenomena (innovative and complex kabbalistic works) and quantitative phenomena (the popularization of Kabbalah). I have no sympathy with certain phenomena associated with the rise of contemporary mysticism, and since I do not intend to exhaust the topic, I will limit myself in certain cases (especially in relation to "popular Kabbalah") to a socioeconomic analysis of the phenomenon only.

OBJECTIVES AND STRUCTURE OF THE BOOK

The aim of this book is to present the main currents of twentieth-century Kabbalah by focusing on various leitmotifs that characterize it and differentiate it from the more classical forms of Kabbalah. As we shall see, these leitmotifs are connected by a series of historical and phenomenological links. As stated, this book does not attempt to exhaust the subject of Kabbalah, which, even as I am writing, is growing and expanding. (I have tried to refer in the preface and notes to some of the new research on topics that I have merely touched on in the present book.) The book aims at offering the reader a general overview, alongside a more detailed study of several key thinkers and processes. Its main purpose is to generate a theoretical, methodological, and substantive debate on the possibilities and problems of research into twentieth-century Kabbalah.

This book is not intended to be an anthropological field study of groups and practices. The main research tool used here is the same one used in the study of classical Kabbalah—namely, the study of texts. And yet, in researching contemporary Kabbalah as opposed to classical Kabbalah, direct observation and impressions also play a part. Although some insights in the book were triggered by a field perspective, these were incidental. I have, to some extent, availed myself of the fieldwork of other scholars, particularly Yoram Bilu. It is my hope that this book will help a new generation of researchers in the social sciences and humanities who wish to familiarize themselves with the world of contemporary Kabbalah.

Generally speaking, research into twentieth-century Kabbalah requires a slightly different approach than is entailed in research into classical Kabbalah. Most of the texts are clearly written and do not require reconstruction or interpretation by the researcher. Unlike earlier texts, we usually know the location and date of contemporary texts and the identity of their authors. The goal of the researcher into contemporary Kabbalah is twofold: to identify changes in twentieth-century Kabbalah vis-à-vis the longstanding and multilayered kabbalistic traditions, and to situate these changes in a broader ideological and social context, both on a regional and global plane.

The choice of the twentieth century as a research period is somewhat artificial, as is the choice of any historical periodization. Obviously, some of the processes I discuss in this book are mere continuations of trends that began in the nineteenth century, or are trends that have continued into this century, too. Nonetheless, the historicist character of modern awareness has engendered the notion of "twentieth-century man." In other words, twentieth-century culture perceives itself as having carved out a niche for itself. Therefore, the choice of the twentieth century as the temporal frame for this research was not guided merely by considerations of research expedience.

On a global level, the twentieth century can, in my opinion, be divided into the decline of modernism and the rise of postmodernism. It is hard to pinpoint the exact transition between these two periods. In any case, they are a useful research fiction more than empirical historical entities. (This is also true for periods such as "late antiquity" or "early modernism.")[24] The above notwithstanding, I propose, for the purposes of our discussion, that the end of the Second World War and the onset of the Cold War—approximately halfway through the century—be considered the start of the second part of the century. (It is harder to pinpoint the start of the first part of the century.)[25] The end of the Cold War ushered in the close of the century.

Of course, a complex relationship exists between modernism and postmodernism, and the question of whether the latter should be considered a period or simply a state of mind is the subject of much controversy. Moreover, much continuity between the periods exists in various spheres. The above notwithstanding, significant changes took place in the middle of the previous century relating to mysticism in general and to Kabbalah in particular. First, the decolonization process that took place after the Second World War enabled the development of a global spiritual movement that absorbed much from Far Eastern doctrines (as well as from Shamanic traditions, particularly from Latin America). The transfer of information from East to West in the 1950s occurred among elites, while the 1960s gave rise to a more popular movement—the counterculture—that challenged the prevailing hegemony of Western culture. Although this fascinating phenomenon has been widely researched, the process is still in full swing and has yet to be fully documented.[26] Exposure to the East also served to demarcate the two parts of the century in terms of twentieth-century Kabbalah. In the first half of the century, Kabbalah was influenced more by Western perceptions, while in the second half of the century, Eastern perceptions became more prominent.[27]

This distinction between the two halves of the century is especially relevant to the Jewish world in general and to Israel in particular. It was in the middle of the century that two events of monumental importance took place: the Holocaust and the establishment of the State of Israel. These dramatic events triggered demographic changes that, in turn, had a critical bearing on the status of Kabbalah. The destruction of the classical Jewish centers in Eastern Europe (in the wake of the Holocaust) and in Arab countries (following their reaction to the establishment of the State) was followed by the establishment of new centers—in Israel and the United States. New cultural structures also emerged in these centers, including new forms of mystical activity.

The currents and processes discussed in this book correspond in broad terms to the two halves of the century: Kook and Ashlag, whose doctrines will be discussed in detail, and other thinkers such as Zeitlin and Shapira, belong to the first half of the century. The corpus of this first period has obviously already been discussed at greater length than that of the second period. Thinkers such as the seventh rebbe of Habad (R. Menaḥem Mendel Shneurson), R. Yitzchak Ginsburgh, and R. Tzevi Yisra'el Tau clearly belong to the second half of the century. Because of the continuity between the two halves of the century, however, it is necessary to view the century from a broader, more comprehensive perspective. Most key thinkers of the early twentieth century discussed here, such as Kook, Ashlag, or the sixth rebbe of Habad (R. Yosef Yizḥaq Shneurson), had spiritual heirs who were active in the second half of the century.

The first chapter of this book provides a brief survey of the dissemination of Kabbalah in the twentieth century. Chapter 2 discusses the ideological motives and forces that fueled this process, with particular emphasis on the doctrines of two of the century's great kabbalists: Kook and Ashlag. Chapters 3 and 4 discuss these personalities and the circles they created. These chapters also take a look at the part played by the concept of power in their doctrines, and in the doctrines of other thinkers and groups. In my opinion, the concept of power is one of the links between contemporary Kabbalah and national and psychological trends of the twentieth century. The transformations this concept has undergone also help us evaluate with greater accuracy the relationship between contemporary Kabbalah and classical Kabbalah. Chapter 5 likewise traces the evolution of the key concepts of "sacred place" and "sacred leader" (or *Tzaddiq*), as well as the development of

Habad Hasidism and Bratzlav Hasidism in the twentieth century. Chapter 6 will continue the discussion on the expansion of the Habad and Bratzlav movements, clarifying the important issue of the interplay between the new mysticism and that major axis of the Jewish religion—Halakha. Chapter 7, the concluding chapter, discusses twentieth-century Kabbalah in the local context of Israeli society and in the global context of the Jewish world and the New Age movement, with a special focus on the social, psychological, and economic dimensions of the new mysticism. It closes with a review of the relationship between the new mysticism and postmodernism, and summarizes the innovations of twentieth-century Kabbalah versus those of classical Kabbalah.

The personality and heritage of Kook—one of the most profound and influential personalities in the world of twentieth-century Kabbalah—pervades this book. In addition, his intense involvement in the Zionist revival and the great influence of his heritage on the Israeli public, give him pride of place in a book that focuses on Israeli mysticism.

I

JEWISH MYSTICISM IN THE TWENTIETH CENTURY

MAJOR TRENDS

> Kabbalists, that is to say, experts in Kabbalah, are few and far between in our generation (you could count them on your fingers).
>
> —HILLEL ZEITLIN

In a lecture published in 1941 in his monumental work on the main currents in Jewish mysticism, Gershom Scholem described the status of contemporary Kabbalah as follows: "What it was at the beginning: the esoteric wisdom of small groups of men out of touch with life and without any influence on it."[1]

This description reflects Scholem's perception of Religious Judaism as being obsolete.[2] Based on this approach, Scholem and some of his students studied Jewish mysticism as a literary, philological-historical phenomenon rather than as a vital and dynamic phenomenon. However, as anyone involved in public life in the past few decades knows, Scholem's perception could not have been further from the truth.

In contemporary Israel, Kabbalah has a political dimension (for example, R.

Yizḥaq Kaduri and R. David Batzri), a socioeconomic dimension (for example, Philip Berg's Kabbalah Center), and sometimes even a quasi-military dimension (for example, kabbalist Yeshu'a Ben Shushan's participation in underground activities and R. Yitzchak Ginsburgh's support of similar activities). Therefore, before we even consider the issue of the dissemination of Kabbalah, we should discuss changes in its sphere of influence. These changes cannot be attributed solely to the growing influence of the religious world on the Israeli public, especially after the Six Days' War in 1967 and the displacement of the ruling Labor party by the right-wing Likud party in 1977. Over the last two decades of the twentieth century, we witnessed a more specific transformation in the status of mysticism, as not only Jewish mysticism but also non-Jewish and even nonreligious mysticism and magic penetrated broader sections of Israeli society.[3]

A few of the more salient examples of this growing interest in mysticism are the fascination of many young Israelis with Indian spirituality, leading to the proliferation of Indian themes in entertainment, literature, fashion, and advertising; frequent visits to Israel by masters from a large variety of mystical cults, often leading to the establishment of local followings;[4] television series such as *Cosmic Optimism* or *The Secret of Inner Happiness*, featuring Israeli stars with adopted Indian names (for example, Rafiq and Ujas); publishing houses (Astrolog, Or-'Am, etc.) that specialize in the translation and publication of mystical literature;[5] bookshops, such as Ha-'Idan Ha-Ḥadash in Tel Aviv or 'Olam Qatan in Jerusalem, that specialize in the distribution of Israeli or imported mystical literature; journals (especially the popular magazine *Ḥayyim Aḥerim*, or Alternative Living) devoted to mysticism, as well as articles in the general press;[6] festivals devoted to mysticism ("Shantipi" festivals, "rainbow gatherings"); and religious and secular bands (for example, Isbei Ha-Sadeh and Sheva') specializing in "spiritual" lyrics.[7]

The changing status of Kabbalah is not only a result of the changing status of mysticism in general but also a cause of it, since Kabbalah in its more or less popular forms is an integral part of the new Israeli spirituality. This trend has found concrete expression in a number of ways: the establishment of settlements, mainly in Judea, Samaria, and the Galilee, by students of Kabbalah (such as Bat 'Ayin by Ginsburgh's followers and Or Ha-Ganuz by the followers of the Ashlagian kabbalist R. Mordekhai Sheinberger); popular Kabbalah courses (precise data on the number of participants is lacking, but I estimate there to be tens of thousands); books popularizing Kabbalah (such as Yigal Arikha's *Practical Kabbalah*); the infiltration of kabbalistic themes into literature, art, pop songs, and movie scripts;[8] the existence of a pirate radio station devoted to Kabbalah (*Pnimiyut Ha-Torah*, or The Inner World of Torah, also under the auspices of Sheinberger) and radio programs of the "Ask the Kabbalist" kind; and the mass influx of pilgrims to the tombs of kabbalists, particularly to Meron in the Galilee and to the grave of the Baba Sali (R. Israel Abuḥatzeira) in Netivot, as well as the *hilulot* (celebrations marking the anniversary of the Tzaddiq's death) that take place there.[9]

Needless to say, this situation is not unique to Israel. All of the aforementioned phenomena exist—sometimes to an even greater extent—in various centers in the West. In the United States, for example, mysticism is flourishing because of the expansion of experiential Christian groups, such as the born-again Christians, in public life there. In Europe, by contrast, the decline of Christianity has been offset by the revival of more pagan trends.[10] Kabbalah plays a large part in the revival of mysticism, particularly within the virtual reality afforded by the Internet. Research into twentieth-century Kabbalah, research into the science of religions, or even sociological research are all very far from exhausting or even mapping out the full scope and significance of these phenomena.

In mapping the spread of Kabbalah in the twentieth century, I focus first on the qualitative dimension—namely, innovative, creative, and radical doctrines. I also, however, briefly discuss more quantitative issues, such as the mass dissemination, influence, and institutionalization of Kabbalah, which are significant from an external and sociological perspective. In addition, the mapping focuses on four main trends: the Hasidic world, the Lithuanian world (by which I mean the spiritual movement that originated in Lithuania before spreading to other centers), the Oriental-Sephardic world, and the Religious-Zionist world. Most of the trends presented here will be dealt with in greater depth in the course of the book. This introductory mapping, although far from exhaustive, is extremely important for obtaining an overall picture, before embarking on a more detailed description of each particular trend.

Hasidic Trends

On the qualitative plane, several trends emerged in the twentieth-century Hasidic world that produced outstanding and creative writers. In the mystical context, two groups deserve special mention: Toldot Aharon, originating in the group founded by R. Aaron Roth (author of *Shomer Emunim*) that exists to this day, albeit on a smaller scale, and Piasecszna Hasidism, which existed until 1943 under the leadership of R. Qalonymus Qalman Shapira.[11] Shapira established a fraternity dedicated to intensive mystical activity, known as the Bnei Maḥshava Tova, whose members perished with him in the Holocaust.[12] Today, some elitist groups still base their spiritual journey on his doctrine.[13] (R. Shlomo Carlebach, the "Dancing Rabbi," a pioneer of the kabbalistic orientation within the New Age movement was also influenced by Shapira.)[14]

The Izbicha-Radzin branch of Hasidism, originally founded by R. Mordekhai Yosef Leiner, author of *Mei Ha-Shiloaḥ*, in the nineteenth century and upheld through the twentieth century by rebbes of this dynasty espoused a more radical doctrine. Toward the end of the nineteenth century, this doctrine was spread through the works of R. Zadok Ha-Kohen of Lublin.[15] This brand of Hasidism has made a major comeback in recent decades. (Carlebach was one of its major proponents.)[16]

A further branch worth mentioning is that of the Bratzlav Hasidim, which, from its origins as a small and persecuted group, has become a significant social and cultural phenomenon, comprising mainly the newly religious.[17] This form of Hasidism comprises a large number of subgroups, including the main stream (known also as Ziqnei Bratzlav, or Bratzlav Elders) in the Mea Shearim neighborhood of Jerusalem, under the leadership of R. Ya'aqov Meir Schechter; R. Eli'ezer Shick's branch in Yavniel;[18] the followers of R. Yisro'el Odesser, known as Ba'al Ha-Peteq (the recipient of a disputed revelation from R. Naḥman of Bratzlav that supposedly took the form of a note containing the famous "mantra" "Na, Naḥ, Naḥma, Naḥman Me-Uman"), whose main proponent is R. Israel Isaac Bezançon; the followers of R. Shalom Arush of the Ḥut Shel Ḥessed Yeshiva in Jerusalem (with a branch in Rishon Le-Tziyon); the followers of Arush's teacher, R. Eli'ezer Berland, in the Shuvu Banim Yeshiva in the Old City;[19] and the followers of R. Gedaliah Qenig in Safed.[20] Sometimes, these groups are characterized by internecine tension.

From a quantitative perspective, the swift rehabilitation of the larger Hasidic courts (such as Belz, Ger, Tsanz, and Vizhnitz) after the Holocaust is noteworthy. This phenomenon, while on the whole failing to contribute to the pool of innovative thought, is highly significant from a sociopolitical perspective. Moreover, at least two of the classical courts that enjoyed great influence also generated a corpus of innovative thought that is extremely interesting from a research perspective: the prolific works of the two last Habad rebbes, R. Yosef Yizḥaq Shneurson and R. Menaḥem Mendel Shneurson, and the writings of the Satmar rebbe, R. Yo'el Teitelbaum (author of *Va-Yo'el Moshe*, inter alia).[21]

From a sociological angle, these two warring courts, Habad and Satmar, are radically different. Habad Hasidism spreads mainly through the recruitment of the newly religious. It uses advanced technology and effective organization to address the "world at large," thereby attracting a wide variety of sympathizers, both Jewish and gentile. (Sympathy for Habad Hasidism has been considerably eroded, however, by supporters of the "Messianic Faction," who upheld their beliefs even after the rebbe's demise.) Satmar Hasidism, by contrast, tends to be segregationist. Its growth can be attributed mainly to natural increase and to the political influence it wields within the ultraorthodox community as a result of its uncompromising fundamentalist stance.

Finally, this survey would not be complete without a reference to R. Hillel Zeitlin, a unique personality operating on the fringes of the Hasidic world. Zeitlin, who underwent a certain process of secularization before returning to the Hasidic world, was an extremely influential publicist and was largely responsible for the infiltration of kabbalistic ideas into pre-Holocaust literary and cultural discourse. The intense mystical content of his works, as well as his contact with other mystics of his time, such as R. Avraham Yizḥaq Ha-Kohen Kook, have been extensively dealt with in Jonatan Meir's work.[22]

Non-Hasidic Ultraorthodox Trends

An interesting phenomenon that emerged in the course of the twentieth century and peaked toward the end of the century was the convergence of Hasidic and non-Hasidic trends in the ultraorthodox world. The adoption of Hasidic patterns of leadership and thought by Lithuanian Jews who formerly opposed these patterns contributed to this process. For example, Lithuanian "Torah luminaries" such as R. Ya'akov Kanievsky (known as the Steipler) and his son R. Ḥayyim Kanievsky became rebbes of sorts, handing out blessings and remedies, and preserving a "dynastic" structure that originated in Hasidism. This process was facilitated by the adoption of the Hasidic model of total belief in the sages (*emunat ḥakhamim*) and their rulings (*da'at Torah*) by the rabbis' adherents, even on secular issues.[23] Moreover, the status of Kabbalah, which in the past had been the heritage of a select few, gained ground among the Lithuanian public.[24]

For example, although some notable ultraorthodox leaders, such as R. Avraham Yes'ayahu Karelitz (known as the Ḥazon Ish) and R. Eli'ezer Menachem Shach, paid little attention to Kabbalah or disregarded it altogether, others, such as Kanievsky, incorporated kabbalistic themes into their writings.[25] One of the important halakhic experts (*posqim*) of this world, R. Yo'el Kluft of Haifa, was known to explore esoterica—a proclivity that largely accounted for his influence. And the prolific output of the kabbalist R. Shlomo Elyashiv (known as the Ba'al Ha-Leshem, after his four-volume book *Leshem Shvo Ve-Aḥlama*) in the late nineteenth and early twentieth century was probably a factor in propelling R. Shalom Elyashiv, his grandson, the current leading authority on Torah law (*poseq hador*), to a position of prominence. (Ba'al Ha-Leshem's influence on Kook is discussed in Chapter 3.)

One final point worth mentioning is the infiltration of kabbalistic themes into the literature of the Mussar school, an ethical movement that dissociated itself from Kabbalah at its inception in the late nineteenth century.[26] In Lithuania in the early twentieth century, the *mashgiaḥ ha-ruḥani* (moral mentor) of Telz Yeshiva, R. Yosef Leib Bloch, introduced kabbalistic themes into his Mussar talks fairly openly.[27] Later, R. Yizḥaq Hutner also (albeit more covertly) introduced a strongly kabbalistic conceptual element into his talks, which later became the basis of the series *Paḥad Yizḥaq* (which began to appear in various forms during the 1950s and is still being published).

At the end of the twentieth century, the *mashgiaḥ mussari* (ethical mentor) of Ponevezh Yeshiva (the flagship school of the Lithuanian world), R. Ḥayyim Friedlander, actively disseminated the teachings of the great eighteenth-century kabbalist R. Moshe Ḥayyim Luzzatto ("Ramḥal"). Likewise, R. Shlomo Wolbe, who studied with Kluft and Hutner, laced his talks and books with kabbalistic motifs (despite assertions that "esoterics do not concern us").[28] A possible explanation for these developments is that while the Mussar movement originally minimized overt kabbalistic discourse, instead advocating psychological self-improvement, in the twentieth century many members of the Mussar movement used these themes to formulate complex psychological doctrines.

There are other ultraorthodox schools that have not been included in the typology proposed here. One important school that I will discuss in the course of this book is the kabbalistic circle founded by R. Yehuda Leib Ha-Levi Ashlag, author of *Ha-Sulam*, a multivolume commentary on the kabbalistic classic the *Zohar*, among many other works.[29] Although Ashlag's roots were Hasidic, he was not, in my opinion, a Hasidic thinker. (On the contrary, I shall show the influence of the anti-Hasidic R. Elijah, the Gaon of Vilna [Hagra] and his followers on Ashlag's thinking.) The Ashlag circle continued to exist qualitatively under the leadership of Ashlag's son R. Barukh Ashlag and his mystical circle, Bnei Barukh.[30] This school enjoyed a huge quantitative boost thanks to Berg's Kabbalah Center, which succeeded in recruiting top-tier celebrities, such as Madonna.[31] Finally, we must note the influence of R. Aryeh Kaplan, a prolific ultraorthodox writer and thinker from the United States, some of whose books focus on kabbalistic meditation.[32]

The Oriental-Sephardic World

The qualitative dimension of Sephardic kabbalistic works, which have enjoyed a revival in recent decades, has been almost completely overlooked by academic research. Until recently, scholarship, with the exception of sociological studies, has failed to assess the contribution of Sephardic Jewry to medieval and modern kabbalistic output.[33] (This "distribution of labor" reflects a certain research assumption that the Oriental-Sephardic world belongs to the quantitative rather than the qualitative dimension.)[34]

Although I will focus on the more ideological aspects of the Sephardic Kabbalah in the course of this book, it is first worth considering the quantitative aspect, which is more familiar and evident. This quantitative dimension is reflected in the emergence of quasi-Hasidic dynasties of kabbalists with magical powers (such as the Abuḥatzeira family); the widespread participation in mystical-magical events and rituals, such as the pilgrimage to Meron; and the proliferation of kabbalistic Yeshivas, which have become, inter alia, Yeshivas for the newly observant and successful publishing houses.[35] Among the heads of kabbalistic Yeshivas, the most influential is R. Ya'aqov Moshe Hillel, dean of the Ahavat Shalom Yeshiva, who wields significant political and economic power in addition to being a prolific and extremely erudite writer. The Shas movement—recently the subject of much research—has played an important role in the cultural and political empowerment of the Sephardic ultraorthodox world, and naturally also of Sephardic Kabbalah, largely thanks to the glorification of R. Yizḥaq Kaduri, known as *Zeqan Ha-Mequbalim* (the Eldest Kabbalist).[36] This process in turn has had consequences for the Shas leadership, so that even relatively "rational" *posqim* such as R. 'Ovadia Yosef have begun referring to doctrines of reincarnation and messianic aspirations, as anyone with even a fleeting acquaintance with the Israeli media can testify.[37]

Kaduri himself—like the Sephardic Kabbalah he represents—is identified in the public consciousness with magic, because of his distribution of amulets, or "blessed oil." Many Sephardic kabbalists, such as Kaduri and the "X-Ray Rabbi," R. Ya'aqov Yisra'el Ifergan, deal with "practical Kabbalah," providing magical answers to many personal, economic, and social problems (which the petitioners feel that the modern State of Israel has failed to resolve satisfactorily). A panegyric literature of sorts has grown up around these kabbalists, and the fact that they are wooed by politicians who are aware of their public influence has enhanced their image as miracle workers. (It is a known fact, for example, that Kaduri's support contributed greatly to Benjamin Netanyahu's marginal victory in the 1996 elections.)[38] Ironically, Hillel's comprehensive pamphlet condemning magic, *Faith and Folly*, was endorsed by none other than Kaduri.[39]

THE RELIGIOUS-ZIONIST WORLD

The history of Religious Zionism in the twentieth century reflects a growing transition—both quantitative and ideological—from rationalist perceptions to mystical patterns of leadership and thought. Undoubtedly, the main force behind this development was R. Avraham Yizḥaq Ha-Kohen Kook. Although Kook has been the subject of considerable research, his doctrine has generally been viewed in a philosophical context, so much so that knowledge of Kabbalah has not been considered a prerequisite for understanding his works.[40] Similarly, existing studies have not come close to exhausting the mystical elements in the writings of his students and followers, such as R. David Kohen, known as *Ha-Nazir* (the Nazarite), author of *Qol Ha-Nevu'a* and many other works, some of which are still in manuscript form, and R. Ya'aqov Moshe Ḥarlap, author of the multivolume *Mei Marom* and other works, some of which have recently been published and others of which are still in manuscript form.[41] As we shall see, the ongoing publication of the manuscripts of Kook and his followers is in itself an indication of the hold that the mystical dimension has on this circle, and of a hunger for the mystical dimension in the thought of Kook and his followers.

As is well known, members of the Kook circle wielded substantial political, social, and cultural influence from the 1950s on (predominantly among the *Ze'irei Ha-Mafdal*, or NRP [National Religious Party] Young Guard), particularly after the Six Days' War.[42] Recent decades have seen the rise of the third and even fourth generation of Kook's students, who have effectively assumed the leadership of a substantial portion of the National-Religious camp.[43] It is worth noting that members of this leadership (such as R. Tzevi Yisra'el Tau, R. Yehoshu'a Zuckerman, R. 'Oded Vilensky, R. Shlomo Aviner) achieved this status thanks to their dissemination of the works of Kook and his son, R. Tzevi Yehuda Ha-Kohen Kook ("Ratzia"), and not because of their familiarity with classical Halakha.[44] This phenomenon was part of a lengthy sociological transformation, including the introduction of "philosophical thought" programs into the classical Yeshiva curriculum. Thus, in several new Yeshivas (Ramat Gan, 'Otniel, premilitary academies, and the like), the study of Hasidic works, the writings of Kook, and other non-halakhic material has begun to significantly encroach upon the traditional study of the Talmud.

Finally, some Hasidic teachers, such as R. Yitzchak Ginsburgh, exerted a strong influence on radical Religious-Zionist circles, such as the "hilltop youth." The Religious-Zionist public's increased interest in mysticism is matched by a growing focus on magic. The Religious-Zionist public, particularly its Sephardic element, increasingly seeks blessings and amulets from kabbalists and miracle workers, such as, respectively, the former chief Rabbi Mordekhai Eliyahu and "The Prophet," Nir Ben-Artzi.[45] In the concluding chapter, I discuss the sociological implications of this metamorphosis against the broader context of the changes that have overtaken the Religious-Zionist public in recent decades.

Kabbalah outside Israel

So far, this brief survey has focused on mysticism in Israel—the book's main focus. Nevertheless, I believe it important to include some discussion of the mystical scene abroad, aspects of which will be discussed in the course of the book in various contexts (particularly in Chapter 6, in connection with the rise of neo-Hasidism). First and foremost are the works of Abraham Joshua Heschel, a thinker of Hasidic extraction who was instrumental in introducing kabbalistic and Hasidic discourse both into the Conservative Judaism movement in the United States and into Christian theology there. As Arthur Green suggests, his description of the mystical experience was based in part on his personal experience.[46] Heschel's writings on Hasidism, together with those of other thinkers such as Green, Martin Buber, Elie Wiesel, and Jacob Samuel Minkin, contributed to the incorporation of Hasidic stories into twentieth-century Western culture.[47]

Another influential actor in the kabbalistic scene abroad was Eli'ezer Mordekhai Théon, whose thought influenced Jewish and Christian circles in Europe and North Africa. Théon, who was associated with Madame Blavatsky's theosophist movement, was succeeded as leader of its kabbalistic branch by Pascal Temanlys, who set up the Argaman Center, still active in Israel today. This is not the place for an in-depth exploration of the history of twentieth-century Christian Kabbalah, from the theosophist movement and Aleister Crowley's Golden Dawn movement at the start of the century to the psychological interpretation of Kabbalah by Ze'ev ben Shim'on Ha-Levi (also known as Warren Kenton) at the end of the century. A more thorough discussion of this phenomenon, which is currently expanding (thanks mainly to the Internet), would no doubt distract readers from the main thrust of this book—Israeli, or at least Jewish, mysticism. It is my hope, however, that growing research interest in Christian Kabbalah in Israel and Europe will not neglect its recent history.[48]

Some kabbalists began their work abroad, later moving to Israel as part of the general demographic trend of aliya, especially in the second half of the century. Some of the leaders of the third generation of Kook's followers, such as Zuckerman or Tau, are of European extraction, as is R. Avraham Zagdon of Bratzlav. Others, such as Carlebach and Ginsburgh, emigrated from North America. This phenomenon is not merely of biographical interest. Rather, it reflects the flow of knowledge that contributed to the fusion of kabbalistic doctrines with Western perceptions—one of the salient features of twentieth-century Kabbalah.[49]

Among those kabbalists who immigrated to Israel, one outstanding personality is R. Yehuda Léon Ashkenazy, also known as Manitou.[50] Ashkenazy obtained his kabbalistic training in Morocco (then under French rule) during the Second World War. He subsequently taught many students in France and was largely responsible for the revival of Jewish study and ritual there after the war. In his Paris period, Ashkenazy had contacts with other outstanding French Jewish thinkers, such as Emanuel Levinas and André Neher, who were also influenced by Jewish mystical works.[51] In 1956, Ashkenazy met Ratzia, as well as other kabbalists such as R. Barukh and R. Mordekhai 'Attiya, thus triggering the association of

French Jewish intellectuals with the Kook circle—an association that continued with Ashkenazy's follower R. Shlomo Aviner. After the Six Days' War, Ashkenazy immigrated to Israel, where he became the revered spiritual leader of many French immigrants.

In discussing the relationship between the development of Kabbalah in Israel and abroad, we must not lose sight of the fact that kabbalistic discourse and activity in the United States enjoys a certain degree of autonomy. Thus, for example, some classical and new kabbalistic works are distributed in the United States only. In general, the term *Jewish world* is helpful, since a flow of information certainly exists between various Jewish centers (particularly since the emergence of the Internet). However, the existence of the Jewish world does not negate the unique features of each center, which should be studied in its local context, as we have done with Israeli Kabbalah.

In discussing Kabbalah outside the confines of the Jewish world, we cannot fail to mention the great interest that Kabbalah has elicited among top-ranking intellectuals in the West, including the postmodern philosopher Jacques Derrida, the author and researcher of semiotics Umberto Eco (in particular in his book *Foucault's Pendulum*), and the literary critic Harold Bloom.[52] This phenomenon proves, yet again, that the dissemination of Kabbalah should be perceived not as an expression of popular or superficial culture but rather as a true transformation of the literary and ideological structure of contemporary Western culture.[53]

2

THE DRIVE TO DISSEMINATE KABBALAH

A distinctive feature of twentieth-century Kabbalah was its dissemination through a number of different circles. This trend was already under way at the beginning of the century, as the proliferation of Kabbalah guides for beginners from that period testifies.[1] In attempting to elucidate this phenomenon, one must grant equal weight to "external" (sociological) factors and to "internal" (ideological) factors. The above notwithstanding, my main focus, as a researcher of Jewish thought, will be on ideological factors, although I will also discuss social factors in more detail in the ensuing chapters.

From an internal perspective, the dissemination of Kabbalah in the twentieth century can be attributed to an ideology that advocated it. This ideology was shared by all kabbalistic streams. Another factor contributing to the dissemination of Kabbalah was the emergence of new exegetical approaches to kabbalistic texts (such as the psychological and historiosophical approaches) that rendered Kabbalah more accessible to the masses.

In many cases, the premessianic or messianic consciousness ("The Footsteps [advent] of the Messiah" or "The Beginning of the Redemption") shared by many currents of Religious Judaism in the twentieth century intensified the trend toward the dissemination of Kabbalah. In many texts, the long-standing claim that the study of Kabbalah hastens the process of redemption was applied to our generation.[2] The events of the twentieth century, in particular the Holocaust and the establishment of the State of Israel, were perceived as "the birth pangs of the Messiah" (*Ḥevlei Mashiaḥ*) or as "the strokes of redemption" (*Pa'amei Ge'ula*). This interpretation intensified not only mystical discourse as such but also the call for its dissemination.

In classical Kabbalah, periods of seclusion and esotericism alternated with periods of dissemination and revelation.[3] Also, various kabbalistic streams, such as "prophetic" Kabbalah, favored the dissemination of Kabbalah, while more conservative streams, such as Naḥmanidean Kabbalah, opposed it. Frequently, trends toward disclosure and dissemination went hand in hand with a messianic ideology. Finally, the separation between these two approaches is not always clear-cut, as a dialectic tension between revelation and disclosure may be found in many texts (such as the Zohar).[4] Be that as it may, the twentieth century witnessed an enormous intensification of the trend toward dissemination with a concomitant marginalization of opposing voices (although those voices still exist, as we shall see at the end of this chapter).

The out-and-out victory of the pro-dissemination camp over the course of the century is even more conspicuous against the background of the decline of the study of Kabbalah in the nineteenth and early twentieth centuries. The growing secularization of the Jewish world in this period led to a significant reduction in the number of students of Kabbalah. (This phenomenon was more evident in the West than in the Middle East, although in the 1950s a kind of compulsory secularization of some of the communities who immigrated to Israel from Middle Eastern countries took place.) Large sections of the orthodox public were forced to adopt an apologetic stance vis-à-vis the study of Kabbalah, which contributed to its suppression.[5] In more conservative circles, too, the study of Kabbalah was struck from the curriculum in favor of the study of Hasidic discourse of a less explicitly kabbalistic nature and the texts produced by the new Mussar movement.[6] Therefore, what would become an almost axiomatic call for a more intensive and widespread study of Kabbalah in the late twentieth century was, in the early twentieth century, the legacy of a select few. In examining the dissemination that occurred during the twentieth century, I focus on the two major kabbalistic doctrines of the century: that of R. Avraham Yizḥaq Ha-Kohen Kook and that of R. Yehuda Leib Ha-Levi Ashlag.

R. Avraham Yizḥaq Ha-Kohen Kook

Kook, one of the most outstanding proponents of Religious Zionism and the first chief rabbi of Palestine, was one of the main advocates of the dissemination of Kabbalah in the twentieth century.[7] His belief in the necessity of dissemination tied in perfectly with his messianic perception of the return to the land and the accomplishments of the Zionist movement as signs of the beginning of redemption (*Atḥalta Di-Ge'ula*). His dialectic perception of the secularization that accompanied the return to the land as "a descent that precedes an ascent" enabled him to also view this secularization as an apt opportunity for disseminating Kabbalah.[8] Kook warned of the danger of letting the opportunity slip by: "In the present generation, purifying the heart and occupying the mind with lofty ideas drawn from the secrets of Torah has become a prerequisite for the survival of Judaism. In this way, the descent that triggered the use of such an exalted means, itself becomes the ascent."[9]

These and similar statements demonstrate the importance of the study of Kabbalah in Kook's national-messianic vision. The drive toward the dissemination of Kabbalah, in Kook's case, also had a practical outcome—a call to incorporate kabbalistic texts into the Yeshiva curriculum: "My main intention in my pamphlets, and in all I write, is simply to stir the hearts of Torah scholars, both old and young, to delve into the inner recesses of the Torah, be it in the field of Mussar . . . Kabbalah . . . Hasidism, or the writings of the Vilna Gaon [Elijah] and Ramḥal [R. Moshe Ḥayyim Luzzatto], and to study all books with the commentary of the Holy Zohar, The Book of Illumination [*Sefer Ha-Bahir*] and the Book of Creation [*Sefer Yetzira*]."[10] Given the priority the Jewish religion grants to Torah study, we should not underestimate the importance of a process of this kind. Kook saw it as an imperative of the times to deliberately override traditional reservations regarding the study and dissemination of Kabbalah, as indicated by his radical statement, "I invoke the verse 'There is a time to act for the Lord' in order to publicly discuss the Secrets of Creation [*Ma'ase Bereshit*], in the light of what my spirit has absorbed from the spirit of God that envelops those who fear Him and enter into His secret."[11]

In other words, the above verse (Psalm 119:126) provides a kind of moral justification for R. Kook's antinomian activity—in this case, overriding the traditional ban on public study of the Secrets of Creation (and Secrets of the Divine Chariot [*Ma'ase Merkava*]).[12] This daring move was inspired by the quasi-prophetic revelation of the Holy Spirit to him.[13]

Here, I focus particularly on the personal dimension of Kook's vision of the dissemination of Kabbalah—a dimension that has, in my opinion, been sadly neglected in previous studies in favor of the national dimension. Throughout the book I will attempt to show how the overlap of national and psychological dimensions is a hallmark of twentieth-century Kabbalah. This overlap is even more pronounced in the case of Kook. The combination of the personal (inspired by powerful mystical experiences) and the national is one of the reasons for the extensive distribution and influence of Kook's doctrine.[14]

My analysis in this book of the personal and intimate dimension of Kook's writings is based on the recent publication of writings by Kook and his followers that were formerly concealed or even censored.[15] These writings, in particular the collection known as *Shmona Qevatzim*, have generated a new wave of academic and Torah scholarship that, in my opinion, is merely in the initial stages.[16] One of the aims of censoring these writings in the past was to contain this personal, mystical dimension, which is now erupting in full force.[17]

I believe that the timing of this new phenomenon—the publication of formerly censored works and the subsequent renewed academic interest—is not fortuitous. Rather, it is part of the growing emphasis on personal experience that arose in the last decades of the twentieth century, fostered by the New Age movement.[18] Nor is it fortuitous that some of the writings are being published by postnational Yeshivas, such as the Ramat Gan Yeshiva, which lean toward the study of mystical texts.

A study of formerly censored texts shows that one of the major themes in Kook's works was the author himself. Indeed, Kook attests to this in a number of texts: "It is possible that, if I were writing for myself and about myself, rivers of far greater depth and truth would be revealed to me than any truth or novellae I could hope to discover through them (other forms of writing)." "I need to speak more about myself, I need to become much clearer about myself. By understanding myself, I shall come to understand everything—the world, life—until my understanding shall connect with the source of life itself." "Sometimes, a person can only lift himself up out of his lowliness through writing down his innermost thoughts, thereby rectifying the internal defects caused by materialistic propensities. 'Then said I: Lo, I am come with the roll of a book, which is prescribed for me' [Psalm 40:8], 'I delight to do Thy will, O my God, Yea, Thy law is in my inmost parts' [Psalm 40:9]."[19]

These statements support the hypothesis that even when Kook wrote about national issues, he was, to a large extent, also grappling with his personal, even mystical, experiences. This hypothesis is supported by his own contention that he was addressing not only the national, and even cosmic, dimension but also the personal and psychological dimension. In the following passage, for example, he describes the relationship between body and spirit: "Sometimes the spirit's contamination is absorbed into the body, and the spirit becomes transparent and pure. In its purity it is full of power, and in its power it refines and purifies the body, elevating it to an exceedingly high level. Examples of this can be found in the general and in the specific, in the universal and in the particular. This phenomenon is particularly evident in the 'footsteps of the Messiah' and its attendant events."[20] Note, in particular, the end of this quote, in which Kook posits that the premessianic period calls for a dual perspective—one that is both national and psychological. This is particularly relevant to the issue we are discussing here—the study of Kabbalah in our generation. For although Kook saw the dissemination of Kabbalah as an imperative of the times, the need to disseminate Kabbalah—a leitmotif of his writings—was clearly also a product of his personal experience.

The link between the national and personal was a direct consequence of Kook's perception of himself as a prophetic figure heralding the revival of prophecy at a national level.[21] In his opinion, the study of Jewish mysticism was a prerequisite to the revival of prophecy. For a figure of his stature, the personal could not be divorced from the national, since he himself, as well as other members of his circle, perceived the revival of prophecy as a key factor in the revival of the nation in its land.[22]

This point is illustrated by the following text, which deserves to be quoted in full:

> One who, after repeated attempts, feels that his spirit can only be at peace through studying the secrets of the Torah, should understand clearly that he was created for this purpose, and no motives in the world—be they material or spiritual—should deter him from seeking the source of life and true well being.[23] He should realize that in perfecting his own nature he is perfecting and redeeming not only himself but also the community at large and even the world. For each perfect soul always perfects the nature of the world as a whole, and true thoughts, when allowed to flow unobstructed in one area of life, are a source of blessing to all of life. And as the spiritual recesses of the soul expand through fulfillment of the soul's true nature, it [the soul] becomes the basis and source of many other souls and from it springs an abundance of life and a wellspring of blessing. The above, however, depends on the degree of one's humility.[24] Nor should such a person be troubled by the question that concerns all those with spiritual leanings, namely, if he devotes himself entirely to holy

> aspirations, when will he have time for his family, worldly matters, and other parts of the Torah that are of a more practical nature? When will he have time to develop Talmudic argumentation skills, and perform acts of kindness and practical deeds? For only when he is connected to his creative source, with those letters of the Torah that relate specifically to his soul,[25] only when he is linked up to his spiritual power and constantly striving to perfect himself, will all gates open up before him, and provide him with all his needs.[26]

In this passage, Kook equates studying Kabbalah with spiritual self-fulfillment for those who feel called to this study. Kook's argument is that only true self-fulfillment—namely, fulfillment of one's inner purpose or destiny—can lead to national and even cosmic rectification (*tiqqun*): "but also [perfecting] the community at large and even the world," "for each perfect soul always perfects the nature of the world as a whole." In this passage, Kook is effectively stating that the personal is inextricably linked up with the national.

The following text, published in the 1980s, highlights the personal element in Kook's doctrine:

> The pleasure and delight I feel when immersing myself freely in divine mysticism is not fortuitous, but rather an expression of my inner nature. This is my main objective. The role of any other talent I may possess—whether practical or intellectual—is secondary to my essence. I must be true to my inner self, not seek the approval of people, or a career. The more I know myself, the more I allow myself to be true to myself and stand on my own two feet in my spiritual awareness—which is composed of knowledge, awareness, emotion, and poetry—the more will the light of God enlighten me and my powers develop to be a blessing to myself and to the world.[27]

This text indicates that the previous text, albeit of a general nature, was also a product of Kook's personal experience. This experience bestowed on him the insight that through studying Kabbalah as a means to his own spiritual self-fulfillment, he would help promote the more general objective of rectifying the world. In order to fulfill this mission, however, it was sometimes necessary to contravene social conventions.[28] Kook's personal testimony of how he felt drawn to mysticism is paralleled in *Shmona Qevatzim*: "If I am more lax in the study of exoterics and Halakha, this is because of the spiritual pull Aggada and esoterics exert on me."[29] He also states, "It is not by chance that an inner force impels me toward the study of the esoteric."[30]

Through these texts, Kook shares with us his sense of spiritual purpose, the "inner spirit" that is his raison d'être. As mentioned above, Kook identified this inner spirit as the spirit of prophecy. This strong feeling of destiny was what channeled his personal beliefs into a public program. He saw himself as one who was entrusted with a mission that sometimes required him to defy convention.[31] This theory is borne out by a text that links Kook's passion for mysticism with his national goal, the popularization of kabbalistic literature:[32]

> It was not by chance that the Lord of all souls implanted in me a thirst for the esoteric, for all that is elevated and exalted; it is not by chance that He brought me to the Land of Israel, and graced me with a bold spirit and inner purity. . . . All these were granted to me to illuminate the world, by creating a literature imbued with the light of the secrets of Torah, a popular literature suited to all, overflowing with poetry and vitality, supported by common sense and sound criticism, for the greater glory of the People of God, and the eternal salvation that has begun to emerge in the Land of Israel.[33]

In one of his many poems (which were in themselves a reflection of the poetic urge to self-expression, an urge not evinced by most kabbalists over the generations), Kook gives clear expression to the hope that his internal, mystical world will generate a popular kabbalistic literature:

From the points of my thought
That gather into herds
I shall take letters and they
Shall become articles
And the articles shall become pamphlets
And the pamphlets books
Books that shall find their way
into each town . . .

And those who aspire to my goal
Shall increase daily
Then shall my quest be answered
That is deeper than the abyss

For the Chosen
will become herds
And from the darkness and the depth
Shall illumine all sides.[34]

This poem expresses Kook's longing that his doctrine, which had hitherto been espoused by elitist circles ("the Chosen") only, would turn into a mass movement of sorts ("the herds")—a longing that was, in fact, fulfilled.[35] The quasi-messianic nature of this aspiration is also manifest in the following quotation: "My soul shall emit bolts of lightning, and flashes of fire. *The entire world* shall see and wonder, consider and marvel, shall awaken as from slumber to the wonder of my light, and a new light shall shine forth over Zion."[36] These texts clearly indicate that the metamorphosis of Kook's doctrine into a mass movement (a major aspect of the dissemination of Kabbalah in the twentieth century) was, in fact, an integral feature of his personal program. Without a doubt, Kook's many followers see the fulfillment of his vision as proof of his prophetic status, and as legitimization of their infiltration of the leadership of the State of Israel, which they invest with a cosmic function.[37] It should be noted that the Kook circle today is much more than a mere ideological group, and comprises many institutions (Yeshivas, pre-military academies, girls' high schools), settlements, journals, and political factions and movements.

The fulfillment of his mission to translate his inner world into a popular program had not only a social function but a more immediate and therapeutic result: Kook's poetic-mystical writing was a form of release, a way of communicating with others his sense of loneliness (caused not only by his spiritual superiority but also by the desire to shake off all social constraints) and frustration.[38] His loneliness and frustration were intensified by the need to meet the demands of the real world and devote time to the study of Halakha, as the following statement testifies: "For a long time, my inner thoughts and feelings were buried in the recesses of my heart. They never emerged and were never expressed because of futile preoccupations, practical constraints and various scholarly pursuits. The suppression of the soul, however, is agony, and the spiritual pressure it causes forces me to express myself. 'I called out of my affliction unto God and He answered me' [Jonah 2:3]."[39]

Kook saw his personal redemption as synonymous with the redemption of Israel.[40] Therefore, his doctrine cannot be described merely as a messianic doctrine, and the dissemination of Kabbalah by him cannot be seen merely in this narrow context. The distinction between the personal and the national in his writings is extremely artificial, as he himself testifies: "The constant striving to find my essential self is also the key to finding the entire nation and the whole of humanity, in its broadest sense."[41]

The personal aspect of Kook's kabbalistic writings also determined their nontechnical and nonclassical aspects. The writings are not to be seen merely as a popular or updated translation of classical Kabbalah.[42] Kook wove kabbalistic themes into his personal experience. The result is dissimilar, both in style and content, to classical kabbalistic works, as we shall see at length in the next chapter. As Kook himself stated, kabbalistic concepts are delivered into the kabbalist's hands, rather than the other way around.[43] Kook's writings, then, constitute one of many examples of the uniquely individualistic and innovative flavor of twentieth-century Kabbalah.

Despite my focus on Kook's personal motives in disseminating Kabbalah, and on the personal tools he chose in order to do so, it would be a mistake to overlook his kabbalistic sources. I am referring not specifically to earlier texts but to a closer source. Kook was affiliated with the Vilna Gaon's kabbalistic tradition. One of the second generation of disciples of the Vilna Gaon, R. Yizḥaq Ḥaver, also believed that the dissemination of Kabbalah in our generation was the means for delivering Judaism from secularization: "For in recent generations . . . but for the revelation of the Torah's inner light, many would have fallen by the wayside."[44] Nevertheless, this program was realized mainly by Kook and some of his followers.

R. YEHUDA LEIB HA-LEVI ASHLAG

I am happy that I was born in this generation, when the science of truth may be publicized.

—ASHLAG

From this you will realize that the atrophy and darkness that characterize our generation on an unprecedented scale are because even the servants of God have ceased to study the secrets of the Torah. . . . The tremendous sorrow this state of affairs caused me prevents me from dwelling on this theme.

—ASHLAG

Ashlag, originally from Hasidic circles in Poland, immigrated to Palestine in 1921 after studying Kabbalah with an anonymous teacher.[45] In 1922 he took it upon himself to actively disseminate Kabbalah, especially through his translation of the Zohar into Hebrew and through his commentary on the works of R. Yizḥaq Luria, known as the Ari. His aim was to translate kabbalistic doctrine into more modern, psychological terms. Here, I shall focus less on this exegetical literature and more on Ashlag's articles, which clearly reflect his views, as well as on personal letters, which shed light on his more intimate feelings, as in the case of Kook's personal correspondence.[46]

Although Ashlag was aware of the innovate nature of his work, he claimed that he was merely expounding the original, "uncorrupted" meaning of the Lurianic texts (which, in his opinion, had not been properly understood).[47] In one letter, part of which was censored by the printers, Ashlag revealed some of the deeper reasons for his identification with Luria (he believed he was "impregnated" with Luria's soul).[48] Ashlag's view of himself as the expounder of the true meaning of mystical texts was bound up with his view of himself as a saint, or *Tzaddiq*, for, according to him, the hallmark of a Tzaddiq was an ability to elucidate the secrets of the Torah. (Ashlag's view of himself as a Tzaddiq is reminiscent of the way Kook viewed himself.)[49]

In addition to his strong identification with Luria, Ashlag imbued the dissemination of Kabbalah with an evolutionary motif.[50] According to him, Judaism evolved from a biblical language into a homiletic and halakhic language and finally into a kabbalistic language—the pinnacle of this linguistic evolution.[51] After the Zohar, however, the continuity was broken, until Luria came and repaired the breach.[52] Ashlag believed his mission was to explain the true meaning of the Ari's doctrine. The evolution of kabbalistic doctrine forced Ashlag to attempt to find innovative interpretations of the Kabbalah, as well as to elucidate Lurianic texts.[53] Like Kook, he felt that the time was ripe for rendering the Kabbalah accessible to all. He used the same argument as Kook to explain the spiritual heights attained by his generation or the proliferation of the Chosen.[54] Ashlag's prediction that "from this generation on, the words of the Zohar will be increasingly revealed" has, in a sense, been fulfilled.[55]

In order to justify the dissemination of Kabbalah, Ashlag drew on psychology—a field that was close to his heart. He saw Kabbalah as a remedy for the "bitterness" of the modern existential quest. He also believed that Kabbalah enhanced kindness and altruism.[56] The doctrine of altruism, which lies at the heart of Ashlag's teachings, explains why Ashlag considered Kabbalah to be the pinnacle of the Jewish religion. Kabbalah, he believed, encourages pure observance of the commandments without ulterior motives and fosters the desire to give.

The psychological dimension, however, also had political and national implications.[57] According to Ashlag, when the Jewish people emphasized "the external," they were simply empowering the nations of the world, who represented the external in the Creation. When the Jewish people emphasized "the internal," by contrast, they were empowering themselves and hastening the redemption, since the Jewish people represented the internal in the Creation. According to Ashlag, this equation explained anti-Semitism and even secularization. For when Jews forsake the internal, the nations of the world "consider the Jews superfluous, and the world has no desire for them, Heaven forefend. . . . So they perpetrate all the terrible destruction and slaughter that our generation has witnessed."[58]

He also openly linked neglect of Kabbalah and its dissemination to the greatest tragedy to befall the Jewish people in the twentieth century—the Holocaust:

> Of all the glory the Jews enjoyed in Poland and Lithuania, etc., all that is left is some scraps in our Holy Land. From now on, it is incumbent upon us, the few

> survivors, to rectify this serious wrong. From now on, each and every one of us . . . shall take it upon himself . . . to intensify the internality [*pnimiyut*] of the Torah, and give it its rightful due. . . . By so doing, each and every one of us shall merit to intensify our own internality. . . . This shall in turn impact upon the entire nation . . . and all the nations of the world shall recognize and acknowledge Israel's ascendancy over them.[59]

Here it should be noted that Ashlag's statements on the Holocaust are part of an entire range of responses to this horrendous event in twentieth-century Kabbalah, by personalities such as R. Qalonymus Qalman Shapira; some of Kook's successors; the sixth and seventh Lubavitcher rebbes; and R. Shalom Noaḥ Brezovsky, the rebbe of Slonim, whose writings currently enjoy some influence.[60] A study of these texts shows the impact the Holocaust had on the development of Kabbalah in the second half of the century. It would appear, however, that the Holocaust's main impact was not on a philosophical plane but rather in the damage it caused to the continuity of the kabbalistic tradition, because of the death of many kabbalists. Paradoxically and tragically, this disruption enhanced the innovative character of kabbalistic writing in the second half of the century.

Ashlag's followers continued his disseminatory activities, thereby fostering his image as the greatest kabbalist after Kook.[61] The circle established by Ashlag branched into different directions. His son, R. Barukh Ashlag, set up an elitist group that studied Kabbalah and the rituals of *kavvana* (devotion) intensively.[62] Michael Laitman, the current leader of this group, now known as Bnei Barukh, converted it into a mass movement of sorts and has gained considerable influence in Israel and abroad (mainly in Russia and Latin America).

Yehuda Leib Ashlag's disciple Yehuda Tzevi Brandwein inherited the leadership of the Kabbalah Center" in 1969 and continued the trend toward popular dissemination of the Kabbalah. The trend reached a peak under the leadership of Philip Berg, Brandwein's successor and a former sales representative. (Other disciples of Brandwein, such as his son Avraham, or R. Mordekhai Sheinberger in Jerusalem, continued disseminating Ashlag's doctrine in a more discreet manner.)[63] Berg turned the Kabbalah Center into an economic empire with dozens of branches throughout the world. This enormous enterprise has no qualms about charging inflated prices for "kabbalistic items" or recruiting celebrities, such as Madonna.[64] One of the hallmarks of the Ashlag circle is its legitimization of the study of Kabbalah without understanding it. Although this view has sources in classical Kabbalah, it was developed mainly by Ashlag and, especially, by members of the Kabbalah Center, who claim that mere ownership of kabbalistic books (purchased, naturally, from them) act as a remedy for the soul.[65]

Ashlag, like Kook, predicted the popularization of his doctrine, but through a reverse process. In a fascinating thesis, Ashlag claimed that in the past Kabbalah had been concealed for fear that it would be used for harmful purposes as well as beneficial ones.[66] Since abuse of Kabbalah was more likely in the spiritually challenging present, he argued, perhaps Kabbalah should remain concealed. "So far," Ashlag stated, "it has been necessary to confine the science of truth behind bastions and ramparts, so that nothing alien or foreign shall penetrate it, and so that . . . it shall not turn into a market commodity." He then answered that the spiritual decline of his generation led to the "spurning" of wisdom. It was therefore unlikely that Kabbalah would be used for destructive or profit-making purposes by "impious disciples," for they would not find any customers. Thus, paradoxically, it was the generation's spiritual decline that enabled the ban on studying or disseminating mysticism to be lifted. Ashlag clearly failed to predict that in the postmodern world, the desire for spirituality—or at least for the trappings of spirituality—would soar, and that Kabbalah would be improperly used in a way he considered impossible.[67]

Although Ashlag's attempt to disseminate Kabbalah, with all the problems inherent therein, triggered opposition during his lifetime (an opposition that intensified considerably over time), his works were enthusiastically endorsed by prominent rabbis, including Kook and even the Badatz (High Rabbinical Court) of the *Edah Ha-Ḥaredit* (ultraorthodox community).[68] As with Kook, we may wonder to what extent such endorsement was facilitated by his successors' censorship of his writings, aimed particularly at concealing his blatant sexual symbolism.[69]

As with Kook, Ashlag's urge to disclose his doctrine was offset by his awareness of the need to conceal it because of the controversy it elicited—a controversy he attributed to the evil force, or Other Side (*Sitra Aḥra*).[70] Indeed, in a letter relating to the controversy surrounding him, Ashlag wrote that R. Ḥayyim Vital, Luria's disciple, in his anxiety to save the Ari from "slander and libel," had "doctored" the Ari's writings.[71] Given his personal identification with the Ari, Ashlag evidently felt that the same could happen with his own doctrine.

Other Circles

Support for the dissemination of Kabbalah was not restricted to the two aforementioned circles. One can, for example, find a similar ideology in the writings of R. Hillel Zeitlin.[72] The trend toward the dissemination of Kabbalah also occurred to a large extent within Sephardic kabbalistic circles.[73] For example, R. Mordekhai 'Attiya, a senior staff member of the Nahar Shalom kabbalistic Yeshiva, wrote an article in 1962, attributing the duration of the Exile to neglect of Kabbalah and the end of the Exile (the redemption) to intensive study of Kabbalah.[74] In spirit,

'Attiya's approach resembles that of the Kook circle. It places special emphasis on the importance of studying Kabbalah in the Land of Israel, and on the link between immigration to Israel and the hastening of the redemption.[75]

'Attiya also saw a correlation between the low rate of immigration and neglect of Kabbalah. Although 'Attiya did not advocate the study of Kabbalah by the masses, he did believe that "a Torah scholar who failed to study Kabbalah was liable to be severely punished—as he was causing the exile of the Shekhina and of Israel." In other words, failure to study Kabbalah had theurgical implications—the disruption of the relationship between God and his Shekhina. It would appear that 'Attiya, like Ashlag, attributed the tragic events of the twentieth century (emphasized in his article) to this omission, since according to him disruption of the heavenly spheres brings about "death and harsh decrees."

Others, such as R. 'Ovadia Haddaya, head of the Bet El kabbalistic Yeshiva, also believed in the necessity of disseminating Kabbalah.[76] However, some key Sephardic figures opposed this trend. For example, R. Ya'aqov Moshe Hillel, one of the foremost contemporary Sephardic kabbalists, condemned "deluded people" who believe they can bring about the redemption through the uncontrolled dissemination of Kabbalah, as well as the tendency of the newly religious who have barely completed the *teshuva* (repentance) process to study Kabbalah.[77]

This short review would not be complete without reference to the ideology of disseminating "the essence of Torah" (*pnimiyut*) as advocated by various Hasidic movements such as Bratzlav and Habad.[78] In Habad Hasidism, the widespread dissemination of Kabbalah as a practical program began under the fifth rebbe (R. Shalom Baer Shneurson), who introduced the study of Kabbalah in the Tomkhei Tmimim Yeshiva that he established in 1897.[79] This program received significant momentum under the seventh rebbe (R. Menaḥem Mendel Shneurson), who used modern information technologies and various distribution agents to helped popularize Kabbalah.[80] Among those agents, one should especially mention R. Yitzchak Ginsburgh and R. 'Adin Steinsaltz.[81] Such teachers were active outside Habad circles, unlike the Habad *mashpi'im* (spiritual mentors), who taught mystical contemplation within the educational and social frameworks of Habad Hasidism itself.[82]

In the non-Hasidic sector of the ultraorthodox world, a transition took place from opposing the dissemination of Kabbalah to holding a more positive attitude toward it (see Chapter 1), although this attitude was usually less public than in other circles.

OPPOSITION TO THE DISSEMINATION OF KABBALAH

As I pointed out at the start of this chapter, the drive to disseminate Kabbalah was offset by opposition to the study of Kabbalah.[83] This phenomenon, together with opposition to kabbalistic discourse itself in many circles, delayed and hampered the dissemination of Kabbalah throughout the century. However, these voices faded toward the end of the century and were marginalized within religious Jewish discourse. Among those opposing Kabbalah itself in the twentieth century were, first and foremost, Hebrew University Professor Yesh'ayahu Leibowitz, who determined in his blunt manner that "all kabbalistic literature is idolatrous."[84] Several other thinkers, such as Eli'ezer Berkowitz, Eli'ezer Goldman, and David Hartman, were hostile to various degrees toward Kabbalah and chose, at least in their writings, to ignore the kabbalistic literature.[85] Finally, R. Yiḥya Kappaḥ of Yemen is well known for his scathing criticism of Kabbalah in the pamphlets *Milḥemet Hashem* (War of God) and *Da'at Elokim* (Knowledge of God), written in the first part of the century.[86] This criticism caused a schism within Yemenite Jewry, but it was largely put aside with the community's immigration to Israel.

In addition to those who were totally opposed to the study or dissemination of Kabbalah in any form or manner, members of many of the aforementioned circles were opposed to the *public* dissemination or study of Kabbalah. (The striking exception was the Ashlag circle. Note in this context the ruling of halakhists such as R. 'Ovadia Yosef, who called the Kabbalah Center "a desecration of God's name").[87] Similarly, although the study of Kabbalah penetrated the world of the Mussar movement, some members of the movement explicitly condemned the widespread study of mysticism. R. Eliyahu Dessler, for example, wrote in his book *Mikhtav Me-Eliyahu*: "The mind is able to entertain lofty thoughts that are beyond the perceptions of the heart—thoughts a person is unable to absorb into his heart, or put into practice in real life. This disparity between knowledge and action is extremely dangerous. . . . For this reason the science of Kabbalah is called esoteric . . . and is not accessible to everyone. For it is dangerous. . . . And what is the danger? . . . That lofty and abstract ideas are not properly absorbed into the heart."[88]

In this passage, Dessler, in the spirit of the Mussar movement, offers a psychological explanation for limiting the study of Kabbalah. According to him, the exalted nature of mystical knowledge can create a dangerous schism between mind and feeling, and consequently between feeling and action. Dessler takes this idea even further in his interpretation of the confession that is part of the Yom Kippur service: "for the sins we have sinned before Thee with knowledge," referring to a kind of knowledge "that surpasses one's [spiritual] level . . . (for example, studying Kabbalah before one has refined one's character, for excessive intellectual knowledge causes the heart to despise the inner substance of this knowledge)."[89] This text implies that it is wrong to study Kabbalah from an intellectual standpoint only, without attempts to refine one's character or internalize its message, since one will fail to appreciate its value and will eventually come to debase it.

Paradoxically, the most strident and consistent opposition to the dissemination of Kabbalah came from members of the Kook circle.[90] His son, R. Tzevi Yehuda Ha-Kohen Kook ("Ratzia"), attempted a hierarchical classification of kabbalistic knowledge and restricted the study of the most obviously kabbalistic works (such as *Tanya*, by the Hasidic thinker R. Shneur Zalman of Liadi, or *Nefesh Ha-Ḥayyim*, by R. Ḥayyim of Volozhin, the successor of R. Elijah of Vilna) to the most advanced students. Younger students were introduced to kabbalistic works in a gradual manner, through the works of Maharal of Prague, and some of Kook's works (but not his more obviously mystical writings, edited by R. David Kohen ["Ha-Nazir"]). This curricular practice continues to this day in the Merkaz Ha-Rav Yeshiva.[91]

Ratzia placed a cautious interpretation on his father's words concerning the inner drive to study Kabbalah. According to this interpretation, the study of Kabbalah was the prerogative only of one "who had a natural, internal yearning" and only "at special times when he felt a special urge." Even such a person was obliged to spend the rest of his time studying the exoterics of Torah. Ratzia further cautioned that "the study of esoterics must not be prompted by mere curiosity," and that "such study should not be embarked upon hastily, but rather with extreme circumspection."[92] Given these views, it is easy to understand the aforementioned curricular gradation.

Ratzia's disciple R. Tzevi Yisra'el Tau (one of the founders of the Har Ha-Mor Yeshiva, which broke away from the Merkaz Ha-Rav Yeshiva at the end of the twentieth century) is even more strongly opposed to the dissemination of Kabbalah, especially its more popular ecstatic and magical forms.[93] On the phenomenon of neo-Hasidism and neomysticism, Tau writes: "These people cannot 'relate' to, or 'connect' with, anything that does not provide them with immediate pleasure. They seek the sacred in singing and dancing, in the pouring out of the soul, thinking that this is the path to holiness. It's a sham! This is not holiness. . . . The study of Torah is the total opposite. . . . It is not through guitar and dancing that one attains holiness, but rather through persistent toil and struggle."[94] He likewise condemns popular magic: "We must strongly condemn the widespread phenomenon of 'remedies.' . . . This phenomenon encourages fantasies that are far removed from intellect and science. The world of science deals with medicine, and invests huge efforts in the study of medicine . . . all of which they tend to totally disregard! All they have are 'remedies.' . . . People prefer fiction to fact. . . . A society in which science is reduced to 'remedies' and 'talismans' will soon fall under the influence of 'quacks,' gravitate toward the 'trendy' arts of computation, amulets, and numerology, and fall into the hands of charlatans and so-called mystics, leading to the destruction of intellect and discernment, and ultimately of all the Torah represents."[95] The attitude of Kook's successors toward the dissemination of Kabbalah, particularly Tau's disdainful attitude toward the yearning for personal self-fulfillment (involving the infringement of social conventions), contrasts strongly with the attitude of Kook himself. This is but one of many examples of the disparity between Kook's doctrine and the way it developed in ensuing generations. In the next chapter, we will focus on another expression of this disparity—this time on the national plane.

3

THE CONCEPT OF POWER IN NATIONAL MYSTICISM

One of the features of twentieth-century Kabbalah was the rise of "national mysticism," generally accompanied by a fervent support of Zionism, in particular in its more nationalistic guises.[1] Although the doctrine of national mysticism predated R. Avraham Yizḥaq Ha-Kohen Kook (see, for example, the sixteenth-century writings of R. Judah Loew [known as Maharal] of Prague, which were widely acclaimed in the twentieth century, especially by the Kook circle), it gained considerable momentum in the course of the twentieth century.[2] In this chapter, I attempt to clarify the concept of national mysticism by focusing specifically on the place of "power" within it. This chapter is therefore devoted to a nationalistic interpretation of power, and the following chapter to its more psychological manifestations. The heightened interest in the psychological and nationalistic aspects of power should be viewed as two different, albeit related, expressions of the distinctive nature of twentieth-century Kabbalah.

Power is one of the keywords of political and psychological culture in the twentieth century.[3] Indeed, just as Karl Marx emphasized the economic factor, and Sigmund Freud the sexual factor, behind many sociocultural processes, so did Friedrich Nietzsche (in the nineteenth century) and Michel Foucault (in the twentieth century) identify the underlying power relationships that motivate contemporary people. In my previous book, I discussed the centrality of power in twentieth-century modernist and postmodernist, and even Zionist, discourse, and especially models of power in rabbinical literature and classical Kabbalah (up to the sixteenth century).[4] Although the centrality of power in contemporary national-mystical discourse derives from these early sources in classical Jewish literature, it derives equally from the modern and postmodern contexts of the twentieth century.

In my opinion, the focus on power is an important feature of twentieth-century Kabbalah and is part of the intensification of the national-political debate within it. The significance and implications of this concept in twentieth-century kabbalistic works clearly differ from those of earlier kabbalistic writing, reflecting the shifting focus of kabbalistic discourse from the intellectual-spiritual field to the emotional-practical field. This trend, which began in the sixteenth century, gathered momentum in the nineteenth and twentieth centuries. As a result, the concept of power in twentieth-century Kabbalah has less to do with divine, theurgical processes than with terrestrial, human processes. The events of the twentieth century, moreover, have prompted another turning point in kabbalistic discourse, underscoring its political and psychological dimensions. Power, therefore, can be viewed as a test case of how events of that century have affected the structure and ramifications of kabbalistic discourse.

On a broader level, the focus on power in twentieth-century Kabbalah should be examined in the context of the transition from classical to modern Jewish thought. In Jewish diasporic experience, a schism evolved between the belief in an omnipotent God who bestowed some of his power upon his Chosen People and the political and military reality of inferiority and impotence. This disparity between faith in an absolute power and a historical reality of powerlessness generated a "compensatory discourse" in which hidden forms of power of a magical or theurgical nature could be activated through Jewish ritual or through the Hebrew language. This discourse helped redress the Jewish people's sense of powerlessness through focusing on its privileged access to supernatural sources of power.[5] The kabbalistic doctrine played a key role in this process.

In the course of the twentieth century, the Zionist revolution enabled the Jewish people to once again experience military, political, and external power, as well as to realize some of their aspirations regarding the Latter Days. It is not surprising, therefore, that the question of power played an important part in Zionist thought.[6] The Zionist movement, however, was basically a secular movement. Disillusioned with hopes of divine intervention, it focused on terrestrial modes of behavior. It did not, therefore, link the political reality with the messianic, mystical, and religious hopes and concepts that had evolved over successive generations. The secular nature of Zionism was reflected in its recognition of the practical boundaries of power, and in the integration of the Zionist movement into the pacts and concessions of international politics.

Religious Judaism, in general, found another way to resolve this disparity. The ultraorthodox stream saw the realization of Zionism as a betrayal of the messianic dream. In its opposition to Zionism, the ultraorthodox camp invoked sources that idealized the diasporic experience of powerlessness. Ultraorthodox thinkers, such as the rebbe of Satmar, emphasized the "three oaths" mentioned in the Talmud, which proscribed any attempt to exercise power in the diasporic reality. By contrast, Religious Zionism saw the empowerment of the Jewish people as an affirmation—not a negation—of divine power. It was these interpretations that enabled cooperation between the Religious Zionists and the secular majority.[7] Religious-Zionist thought stood at a problematic and complex crossroads. It is not surprising that it spawned different currents with discrete views on the issue of power, as on other modern issues (such as secular studies or gender relations).

Among the various Religious-Zionist responses to Zionism, two stand out: the rationalist stream and the mystical stream. The rationalist stream within Religious Zionism emphasized "natural" perceptions of power and redemption (inspired by the Maimonidean doctrine), whereby earthly actions did not require mystical interpretations in order to acquire Jewish-religious validity or legitimacy.[8] The mystical stream within Religious Zionism, however, particularly the Kook circle, saw Zionist activity in distinctly messianic terms and argued that on an arcane level known only to mystical visionaries, even secular Zionism was an expression of the messianic vision. Until the 1970s, the Religious-Zionist political leadership comprised mainly adherents of the rationalist stream, who accepted the limits of power in the international arena. Yet the last decades of the century saw the rising power of adherents of the mystical stream, such as Ephraim Eitam, the former leader of the Religious-Zionist Party and a newly observant alumnus of the Merkaz Ha-Rav Yeshiva.[9]

In this chapter, I focus on the views of the mystical stream of the Religious-Zionist camp. I will begin by reviewing the evolution of the concept of power within the Kook circle—the main proponents of national mysticism in the twentieth century. First, we shall examine how Kook and his successors' perception of power reflected the trend toward the modernization of Kabbalah and away from the classical Kabbalah of previous centuries.[10] It should be noted that in the past four centuries in general, Ashkenazi Kabbalah (which was more obviously influenced by the modernization process) generated two main exegetical paradigms of Lurianic Kabbalah (which was dominant in Jewish mystical discourse from the sixteenth century on).

The first paradigm, which is more prevalent in Hasidic circles, focuses on the psychological problem of the illusion of a reality apart from God. In Hasidic discourse, this problem and its solution (the eradication of the separate reality) are situated at the individual, rather than the national, level.[11] Thus, the world of Hasidism revolves around the figure of the Tzaddiq, the chosen individual who shows the way to the revelation of God's all-encompassing presence.[12] In Hasidic doctrine, therefore, the concept of power is used mainly with reference to the personal power of the Tzaddiq and its magical dimensions.[13]

The second exegetical paradigm of Lurianic Kabbalah was elucidated by R. Moshe Ḥayyim Luzzatto ("Ramḥal") in the eighteenth century. Luzzatto explained the language of the Kabbalah as alluding to a problem that was political in essence. According to him, history created the illusion that power and control existed outside of God.[14] The messianic rectification (*tiqqun*) therefore was to reveal God's absolute power on the stage of history. Thus, the manifestation of divine power in the world was inextricably linked with the manifestation of the power of the Jewish people in human history. This exegetical paradigm was adopted by R. Elijah, the Gaon of Vilna (Hagra) and his disciples, some of whom immigrated to Eretz Israel in the nineteenth century.[15] The twentieth-century adherents of this school, such as R. Shlomo Elyashiv and R. Naftali Hertz, had ties with Kook.[16]

Although Kook viewed power from a national perspective based on the writings of Luzzatto and his successors, in his experience the personal dimension was inextricably tied up with the national one. Kook saw himself as a Tzaddiq, and his writings revolved around the concept of personal powers no less than around that of national power. In certain respects, Kook resembled the Hasidic Tzaddiq described above, with the difference, as he himself claimed, that he was "building a nation."[17] Moreover, he cautioned against adhering to Tzaddiqim since this could lead to adhering to their shortcomings, too. Instead, he proposed adhering to the nation's soul, which in his doctrine was entirely good.[18] In other words, while the Hasidic Tzaddiq used his power to build his own community, the Tzaddiq as defined by Kook and his circle used his power to restore the national "stature," which was an earthly reflection of the divine stature.[19] Be that as it may, the personal dimension in Kook's doctrine was fueled mainly by his own intense personal experiences rather than by a textual tradition, Hasidic or otherwise. I shall therefore move on from this historical background to focus on the experiences that were instrumental in shaping Kook's perception of power.

Power and Experience in the Works of Kook

Kook's perception of power is an excellent example of how modern concepts have influenced the development of kabbalistic doctrine.[20] Several researchers have postulated that Kook drew his ideas from the writings of Nietzsche, Henri-Louis Bergson, and Arthur Schopenhauer.[21] All of these nineteenth-century philosophers focused on the issue of power, and twentieth-century Western thinkers (particularly Foucault) were largely indebted to them.[22]

However, as part of his nationalist tendency, which as a rule rejected the Western influence on Jewish discourse, Kook created a clear distinction between the Western concept of power and his own concept of power, which was anchored in Kabbalah.[23] This perception revolved not only around the nation but also around the figure of the Tzaddiq. Kook saw the Western doctrine of power (as propounded by Nietzsche) as the power of the "blind serpent," or as a "lust for power" (as Nietzsche himself put it), devoid of any ethical content, unlike the ethical power of the Tzaddiqim, "who are graced with the power of the heart."[24] According to Kook, the devotional power of the Tzaddiq was able to affect the entire world. The influence of the mystical elite (that is, the Kook circle) on the world was, in his doctrine, hidden and internal.[25] The fact that the national collective drew its power from the actions of this elite explains Kook's emphasis on the power of the chosen individual. These individuals were described by R. Ya'aqov Moshe Ḥarlap, one of Kook's disciples, as "the spiritual elite, endowed with superior souls, who live on broader horizons . . . who incessantly glide and flow over a divine expanse of immense truth, who look upon the nation with a clear and direct vision."[26]

As part of his evolutionary historiosophy, Kook predicted that civilization would aspire to an awareness of the supremacy and power of "benevolence."[27] In such statements, Kook contrasted the desire for anarchical power, as described by Nietzsche and Schopenhauer, with the theurgical power of the Tzaddiq.

These misgivings regarding the concept of power (other than that wielded by the Tzaddiq) can be found also in Kook's more national deliberations that were censored and later collected by R. Tzevi Yehuda Ha-Kohen Kook ("Ratzia") in the book *Orot* (Lights). These misgivings clearly had political repercussions. Thus, for example, in the essay "War" (*Ha-Milḥama*), written in response to the First World War, Kook determined that the exclusion of Jews from world politics was not only the result of "coercion" but was "also willed."[28] He was in favor of putting off the establishment of a political entity until the time was ripe, thereby avoiding the wars and hostilities that inevitably accompanied the establishment of a state.[29] Despite this political emphasis, a study of the references to power in *Orot* shows that Kook's national and political discussions on power occur within the framework of his personal, mystical experiences. One example is Kook's description of a vision in which the ascending light of the Prophet Elijah was mirrored in the restoration of the Jewish people's power via the Zionist enterprise.[30]

Despite his reservations about military and political power, Kook generally viewed the national revival as a chance for the renewed expression of the nation's life forces, which, according to him, were divine forces. For him, the reinstatement of the Jewish nation's military and political power was a messianic portent.[31] Even the famous passage below on fitness training for Jewish youth—which Ratzia unsuccessfully tried to censor— emphasizes the correlation between national-military power and the Tzaddiq's devotional power: "Physical fitness, as practiced by Jewish youngsters in Eretz Israel in order to strengthen their bodies to be stalwart children of the nation, refines the spiritual power of the supreme Tzaddiqim who are immersed in the unification of the Sacred Names . . . and neither manifestation of light can exist without the other. . . . Therefore, the youngsters should practice sports in order to strengthen their body and spirit for the might of the nation as a whole."[32]

Kook saw power not only in the context of the power of the Chosen but also in the context of his own personal and intimate experiences. Thus, he ends a passage describing a vision of the redemption of souls via the tremendous force of the prayer of the Upright with the following words, which speak for themselves: "If I speak of lofty matters and fear travels through my bones, I shall not be scared, for God is with me, and what harm can the flesh do me?"[33]

Kook viewed the greatness of his soul as a means for remedying the souls of all Jews, as Y. L. Sussman, a student of Ḥarlap's, testifies: "I heard from my rabbi and teacher, the Tzaddiq [Ḥarlap], may he rest in peace, that Our Master, the Tzaddiq [Kook], may he rest in peace, practiced the rectification of souls, and would often speak of great people from the World of Truth, who had failed in some matter, and required rectification. Our Master [Kook] would point to them as if they were in the room. He would effect the rectification by revealing the inner kernel of sanctity encapsulated in that failure, and would thereby rectify them. I heard this explicitly from his Holy Mouth.[34] According to this description, which is supported by Kook's writings, Kook saw himself as capable of purifying the souls of "illustrious people."[35] Likewise, we can infer from this passage that the attempt to discover the positive aspects of the actions of the secular Zionists was the external expression of the internal, mystical attempt to purify souls in the manner described above.

Sussman's comment reveals the tension between Kook's sense of spiritual grandeur and power (his inner world) and his sense of fear caused by normative religious concepts. (Indeed, it was just such a fear that prompted his successors to censor these passages.)[36] This same tension can be discerned in his confession: "My soul feels powerful and expansive, I feel a glorious power within me, and I am filled with power and freedom. The cowardice that dons the guise of piety cannot deceive me."[37]

This statement indicates that Kook, like Nietzsche, perceived himself as possessing enormous powers that clashed with the mediocrity and constraints of his religious environment—constraints that frustrated and infuriated him.[38] Nevertheless, Kook also felt the need to strengthen his physical and volitional powers, and his call to strengthen these powers at the national level must be understood in the light of his personal confession.[39] His self-perception was endorsed by his successors, who considered Kook the leader of his generation.[40] We shall now focus on how the members of the Kook circle perceived the issue of power.

POWER, EXPERIENCE, AND WAR AS PERCEIVED BY KOOK'S DISCIPLES

Although Kook's perception of power embraced both the national and personal dimensions, among his successors these dimensions split into two separate camps. This schism had a direct impact on the editing of Kook's "canonical" works.[41] His son, Ratzia, chose to highlight the political-national dimension when editing the anthology *Orot*. He even claimed that this book, which he called "The Holy of Holies," was his father's most important work.[42] R. David Kohen ("Ha-Nazir"), by contrast, who accepted Kook as a teacher par excellence, highlighted the mystical-experiential dimension of Kook's doctrine when editing the collection *Orot Ha-Qodesh* (Lights of Holiness).[43]

The works of the second generation of the Kook circle reveal a similar pattern. Kohen, an active mystic who practiced ecstatic techniques and strove to achieve prophecy (which he described also in terms of power) focused on mystical passivity rather than on political-military activism.[44] He experienced the dialectic tension between passive self-abnegation and an all-consuming perception of himself as a Tzaddiq and quasi-prophet (similar to the way his mentor, Kook, perceived himself), as reflected in the following text: "I am magnificent, a divine power sweeps through me, a power of courage and strength, a power of the salvation of His right hand. Just by remembering this I ascend to sublime heights. Prophecy is not only the Song of Songs . . . but also the strength and boldness of the salvation of God's right hand. The man, the prophet, the Tzaddiq, desires, invokes, implores, and his word takes effect. The power of God is within me."[45]

In the writings of Ratzia, by contrast, kabbalistic theurgy is translated into markedly political and military terms, as the following passage testifies: "The tremendous courage and boldness of spirit of the members of our community, who convened on 5 Iyyar [May 15, 1948] in Independence Hall in Tel Aviv and announced to the entire world and its governments the existence of a State of Israel . . . , is the same noble and courageous spirit of our holy military heroes. . . . Both derive from the same source: He who girds Israel with strength. . . . This bold spirit . . . is the foundation and source of all miracles and wonders. The spirit of courage . . . that man discovers in himself to fight the forces that try to destroy him, is a miracle that comes from above, the product of sublime, inner, spiritual forces."[46] These two texts indicate how Ratzia and Kohen developed the two poles of Kook's writings—both of which, in turn, point to his two sources of inspiration—national mysticism and personal experience.[47] Until recently, for political reasons, Ratzia was considered by broad sectors of the Religious-Zionist public as the true representative of Kook's doctrine. Naturally, these sectors emphasized political and national issues over internal, experiential issues, which were Kohen's province. The more political interpretation of Kook's writings went hand in hand with the metamorphosis of the Kook circle from an elitist circle of Tzaddiqim into a sociocultural movement. Since the start of the twenty-first century, however, the publication of the personal writings of Kook and of Kohen have tied in with the emphasis on personal experience among the fourth generation of the Kook circle.[48]

The nationalist interpretation of Kook's doctrine of power overshadowed the universal premises of his doctrine, particularly his criticism of nationalism. This criticism is evident in texts that have only recently been printed. In one of them, Kook contrasts "national power . . . that is achieved only through an iron fist and ruthlessness" with "our national honor . . . that preserves the honor of the individual" (that is, does not invalidate the individual).[49] Elsewhere, Kook condemns nationalism, which, according to him, is "contaminated" by hatred of one's fellow man.[50]

POWER IN THE JEWISH UNDERGROUND

The Jewish Underground, which was set up in the 1980s by, among others, people who were influenced by Kook's doctrine, generated a fascinating ideological dispute over the relationship between the power of the State of Israel and the power of individuals who wished to remedy the State's shortcomings. Elsewhere, I have described in detail the background and components of the Jewish Underground, and we shall deal with yet another aspect of this affair in Chapter 6.[51] Here, however, I wish to restrict the discussion to the dispute over the concept of power among the successors of the Kook circle following the exposure of the Underground.

A short review of the occurrences leading up to the creation of the Jewish Underground is in order. A series of terror events, including the carnage in the Jewish settlement in Hebron in 1980 and the right-wing government's relatively moderate response because of political constraints, led to a feeling of helplessness and even impotence among many of the settlers in the West Bank. The establishment of the Jewish Underground was a reaction to this feeling. It perpetrated acts of reprisal, including the 1980 attacks against the mayors of West Bank cities, the attack on the Islamic College of Hebron in 1983, and the attempt to blow up Arab buses in 1984. Some members of the Underground—led by the kabbalist Yeshu'a Ben Shushan and the ideologue Yehuda 'Etzion, formerly a leader of the Gush Emunim activists—even planned a theurgical move: the destruction of the Al Aqsa Mosque and the Dome of the Rock on the Temple Mount (Al-Ḥaram Al-Sharif) in order to speed up the process of redemption.

The kabbalistic members of the Underground acted according to a radical, national interpretation of classical, theurgical perceptions based on Kabbalah.[52] According to this interpretation, Islam's control of the Temple Mount fed the husks (*qelipot*) that strengthened Palestinian control over the Land of Israel in general. In other words, control of the Temple Mount allowed the forces of evil (that is, Islam) to draw power from the Sacred Place. According to one testimony, endorsement of the plan to blow up the Temple Mount sanctuaries came mainly from some veteran Sephardic kabbalists in Jerusalem.[53] A telling expression of the theurgical nature of the Temple Mount operation—an *It'aruta Di-Le-Tata* (awakening from below), designed to hasten a response from above—can be found in the following testimony, which points to internal differences between the planners of the operation:[54]

> "Perhaps," mused [Yeshu'a] shortly after the end of his interrogation, "we should have gone up to the Temple Mount, laid the explosives, connected the wires and . . . left it at that, namely, reveal our intention (vis-à-vis God) but not put it into practice?!"
>
> 'Etzion was shocked: "Not set it off?!"
>
> Yeshu'a: "Yes, not set it off. . . . In short, do our bit as far as 'an awakening from below' is concerned, and leave the rest to fate!"[55]

Despite support for the Jewish Underground by certain rabbinical authorities and kabbalists, the official settler leadership, as well as many spiritual leaders of the National-Religious public, sharply condemned their actions. Members of the Merkaz Ha-Rav circles, who saw themselves as the successors of the Kook circle, based their opposition on a view that straddled secular and religious Zionism, as well as terrestrial reality—with its compromises and limitations—and divine will. Merkaz Ha-Rav rabbis identified the sublime will and power, as revealed through the redemptive process, with the will and spirit of the people dwelling in Zion. Therefore, they rejected individual initiatives that were not approved by the people's elected leadership.[56]

As R. Yehoshu'a Zuckerman wrote, "Even though everything is still in its raw and early stages, and our latent power has only just begun to be translated into the miraculous victories of our political, agricultural, and military enterprise, everything conspires to show that we are moving toward the physical and spiritual redemption of our people. Far be it from us, therefore, to break away from the path of this courageous and holy public. The redemption is arriving bit by bit through the same power that grants the State its power."[57]

The Merkaz Ha-Rav circle proposed "strengthening the power [or spirit] of the people" as a solution to the problems that were troubling members of the Underground.[58] One of the key arguments invoked by Merkaz Ha-Rav circles in this polemic was Kook's statement that "our State, the State of Israel," is "the foundation of God's throne in the world."[59] The use of this argument in the 1980s was anachronistic. Kook made this statement before the establishment of the State (albeit correctly guessing the name of the would-be State). Moreover, he emphasized in this passage that the emergent State would promote "the Unity of God and of His name"—a far cry from the secular State of Israel today.[60] Indeed, R. Yisra'el Ari'el, the former rabbi of Yamit (who was arrested for advising Israel Defense Forces soldiers not to participate in the city's evacuation in 1982), in a defense statement on behalf of the members of the Underground, drew a distinction between "State" and "government" and thereby challenged the application of Kook's ideas to the Israeli government (as opposed to the Israeli State).[61] 'Etzion likewise argued that the application of Kook's vision was flawed since it enabled the emergence of a secular regime in the State of Israel.[62]

Basing their argument on the assumption that the State's elected leadership was an authentic expression of the people's power, the Merkaz Ha-Rav rabbis distinguished between legitimate and illegitimate means for opposing what they believed was the government's poor decision. In this polemic, the concept of power played a key role. The rabbis condemned individual or Underground power initiatives in the Jewish-Arab struggle, thereby effectively endorsing the concentration of power in the government's hands. (According to sociologist Max Weber, the State is, by definition, a power monopoly.) In other words, the Merkaz Ha-Rav rabbis' polemic against the Jewish Underground focused on the relationship between representation and power. Given the equation between divine power and national power, the question then arose of who could be considered the faithful representatives of national power. This polemic was clearly echoed in the early twenty-first century debates on the correct forms of opposition to the "disengagement" from the Gaza Strip.

Some rabbis—particularly R. Shlomo Aviner—based their views on classical perceptions of power as signifying restraint and inaction. This view was formulated to explain the disparity between the omnipotence of God and the powerlessness of the Jewish people in the historical diasporic situation. Aviner adopted this view as a means of severing the link between power and action made by members of the Jewish Underground. On one issue—the rebuilding of the Temple on the Temple Mount—Aviner even seemed to adopt the ultraorthodox position of refraining from action in favor of divine intervention. His colleague Zuckerman attributed this position to the founding father of his school: "On the issue of the Temple Mount, Kook resembles the [ultraorthodox group] *Neturei Qarta*."[63]

The debate surrounding the correct interpretation of the corpus of Kook's writings had sociological implications, too. This debate may be summed up as "power in the text" versus "power over the text," or ideological perceptions of power in the texts versus social control over the interpretation and distribution of these texts.[64] In other words, the debate related not only to the way rabbis of the Kook circle perceived power but also to the question of who had power over Kook's textual heritage. The rabbinical elite of the Merkaz Ha-Rav Yeshiva wished to be considered the sole legitimate interpreters of Kook's writings and therefore tried to censor these texts.[65] It is not by accident that those members of the Jewish Underground who were Torah scholars belonged to a sub-elite that did not hold rabbinical positions of power.[66]

National Mysticism in Other Groups

This chapter would not be complete without placing the perception of power by the Kook circle in the larger context of the concept of power in twentieth-century Jewish national mysticism. Evidently, the Kook circle was not the only one in that century to highlight the military or national dimensions of power over its mystical manifestations. We have already discussed the belief shared by the Kook circle and various Sephardic kabbalists that the dissemination of Kabbalah was part of the process of redemption in Eretz Israel.[67] Both camps also shared a nationalist interpretation of the concept of power, as well as other expressions of national mysticism.

The kabbalistic-nationalist doctrine of R. 'Ovadia Haddaya, who served as dean of the Old Sephardic kabbalist Bet El Yeshiva, is based, along with his opposition to renouncing territories occupied in the Six Days' War, on an extremely racist attitude toward other nations.[68] The concept of power plays an important part in Haddaya's writings. Given the similarities between Haddaya's doctrine and that of the Kook circle, it is not surprising that Haddaya was in contact with Kook.[69]

The most conspicuous example of the "nationalization" of the concept of power can be found in Habad Hasidism. The Habad leadership style has been inundated over the past few decades with military and power symbols and slogans, such as "God's army," the "Mitzva Tank," the tune "Didan Notzaḥ" (We Shall Be Victorious), R. Menaḥem Mendel Shneurson waving his fist, and so on.[70] Note that this militaristic style was criticized by ultraorthodox circles, such as Satmar Hasidim, who reject Judaism's reinstatement in political history through force.[71] Habad's position on this issue reflects a shift in emphasis from contemplation to action. This process, which began in the late nineteenth century with the fifth rebbe, R. Shalom Baer Shneurson, and continued even more intensively in the early twentieth century with the sixth rebbe, R. Yosef Yizḥaq Shneurson, was accompanied by a messianic activism (as reflected in R. Yosef Yizḥaq's statement "Repentance now equals redemption now") and gained even greater momentum under the leadership of the seventh rebbe, R. Menaḥem Mendel.[72] In general, the Habad position evolved from a stalwart resistance to Zionism on the part of R. Shalom Baer (based in part on the classical source of the "Three Oaths" that rejected Jewish power in the Diaspora) to an increasing identification with nationalist elements within the Zionist movement.[73]

This identification found expression in the extremely hawkish stance of the seventh rebbe, R. Menaḥem Mendel. Under his leadership, Habad Hasidism combined support of a militaristic policy with respect for R. Shalom Baer's anti-Zionist stance that shunned Zionist symbols, such as Independence Day.[74] In general, the history of Habad Hasidism in the twentieth century reveals a tendency to emphasize action over study.[75] This action is clearly of a messianic nature and emphasizes the more political dimensions of power. Thus, Habad shares the Kook circle's national and political perceptions of power, despite differences in the symbolic sphere. Again, if we compare the concept of the power of the Tzaddiq in Kook's doctrine to that of the Habad doctrine, we see that it follows a similar pattern to that described above. While in more classical Hasidic models the power of the Tzaddiq was largely confined to the community, the messianic consciousness of the seventh rebbe had national, and even international, repercussions.[76]

R. Yitzchak Ginsburgh's writings and talks represent a further step in the progression from increased interest in power, as evinced by contemporary Habad Hasidism, to active involvement, as evinced by radical Religious-Zionist circles. Ginsburgh, a newly observant Jew, was born in Missouri and studied Kabbalah after first completing his scientific education. Over the last decades of the twentieth century, he attracted a large community of admirers, including many of the settler youth.[77] Yet in his home in Kfar Habad, and among Habad Hasidim in general, Ginsburgh is considered a marginal and even eccentric figure (in part because of his intensive preoccupation with kabbalistic contemplation). However, through a judicious use of modern technology (which was popular with Habad Hasidism throughout the twentieth century) and the Internet, Ginsburgh has expanded his support base dramatically. His followers included, at various periods, authors and poets (Ilan Nov, Yonadav Qaploun), academics (Daniel Shalit), and radical political activists (members of the ʻOd Yosef Ḥai Yeshiva in Shechem [Nablus], and Motti Qarpel of the Jewish Leadership Movement), among others.[78]

The operational-political stratum of Ginsburgh's activities found expression in the alternative settlement of Bat ʻAyin, set up by his followers in the Gush ʻEtzion area in the occupied territories. At the start of the twenty-first century, a nucleus from this settlement perpetrated attacks against Palestinian citizens in retaliation for the Second Intifada. Ginsburgh's radical views on the Israeli-Arab conflict had already become apparent during the First Intifada, when his disciples took action against Palestinian citizens.[79] Later, his views even led—exceptionally—to his administrative detention (a measure usually adopted against Arabs). His support of the distinction between Jewish and gentile blood, and of the deportation of and harsh military actions against Palestinians, lost him some sympathizers, including some newly observant Jews, but gained him many supporters from among the "new generation" of settlers and the "hilltop youth." The repercussions of Ginsburgh's doctrine of national power peaked with the publication of an essay in the book *Kuntras Barukh Ha-Gever* that provided a religious-kabbalistic justification for Barukh Goldstein's shooting spree in the Cave of the Patriarchs (Meʻarat Ha-Makhpela) in Hebron in 1994.[80] Clearly, his support for individual acts of power links up with earlier debates surrounding the Jewish Underground.[81]

In his theoretical doctrine, Ginsburgh emphasizes the relationship between the term *power*, the theosophist term *essence* (of the sphere or of divinity), and the psychological term *selfhood* (in the sense of connecting with the self), thereby adding a political and national dimension to the psychological dimension of the classical Habad translation of kabbalistic theosophy. In his book on the Hebrew alphabet, he points to power, alongside vitality and light, as one of the three basic terms for understanding the significance of language.[82] For Ginsburgh, the concept of power is a key element of the psychological, poetical, and kabbalistic constructs that together create a radical, nationalist-kabbalistic doctrine.[83] It should be noted that one of the sources of Ginsburgh's doctrine of power is the psychological debate on the concept of strength (*taqifut*) in the book *Mei Ha-Shiloaḥ* by the Izbicha rebbe, R. Mordekhai Yosef Leiner.[84] This doctrine clearly has national overtones, as the following passage indicates: "Due to man's fear, it is best he desist and refrain from action, as is the case here, when they swore they would not force the end. 'And they traveled from Ḥarada [anxiety] and encamped [halted] in Maqhelot' [Numbers 33:25]. When God wishes to gather in the exiles, he shall instill strength [*taqifut*] into their hearts so that they will not fear. May this take place speedily in our days."[85]

When Ginsburgh first began teaching, he focused largely on this book. Evidently, the Izbicha rebbe, through his disciple R. Zadok Ha-Kohen from Lublin (on whose writings Ginsburgh's disciple 'Oded Ki Tov focused), also served as an important source for Kook on a variety of topics, including national mysticism, psychology, and antinomianism.[86]

National Mysticism in the Late Twentieth Century

Finally, the debate on the concept of power in national mysticism must be placed in the larger context of the rise of national mysticism in the twentieth century, in particular toward the end of the century. As well as the debate on power, it is worth bearing in mind the focus on historiosophical-national discourse in twentieth-century Kabbalah that interprets world history through the redemption of the Jews. An excellent example is R. Tzevi Ryback, a newly observant Jew of Russian origins, who wrote a comprehensive historiosophical work titled *'Al Qetz Ha-Tiqqun*, based on millenarian forecasts.[87] According to Ryback, the current exile supposedly ended in 1988 with the collapse of the Soviet Empire (*Golem*), while the year 2000 (or, more precisely, Rosh Ha-Shana 2000, exactly a year before the outbreak of the Second Intifada) marked the end of the Ishmaelite, or Arab, dominion, and the revelation of the Shekhina's "power of retribution" against Israel's enemies.[88] He wrote that the Ishmaelites drew strength from the Mixed Multitude (*'Erev Rav*) within the Jewish people, such as the "band of heretics" known as the Peace Now movement.[89] Like other kabbalists in the twentieth century, Ryback saw the dissemination of Kabbalah—as well as the return to Judaism—as a catalyst for redemption.[90] His book is based on the premise that events in this world are merely a reflection of events that have already taken place in the heavenly world. According to Ryback, the study of Kabbalah connects these two worlds, and thereby makes it possible to forecast the future.[91]

Another example of the evolution of a historiosophical-nationalist discourse is that of the philosophy of R. Yehuda Léon Ashkenazy ("Manitou"), who, although affiliated with the Kook circle, formed his own independent doctrine.[92] One of Ashkenazy's interesting innovations is his historiosophical analysis of the long-standing division into Ashkenazim and Sephardim, which he interprets as one element in an overall divine process that includes the forging of a Jewish identity in the Diaspora and the ingathering of exiles in the era of redemption. According to him, the Sephardim belong to the Second Temple Exile of Judah while the Ashkenazim can be traced back to the Babylonian Exile during the First Temple Period. Ashkenazy uses this basic typology in order to explain many processes in Jewish history. For example, he perceives the aliya of Ashkenazim ("Babylonians") as a clear sign of the redemption. The following quotation is important from a political perspective: "Although the Ashkenazim created the political context of the State . . . the feeling is that the people who dwell in Zion are Sephardim. . . . Ashkenazi nationalism is first channeled through political categories and only then becomes popular, while with the Sephardim it is the opposite. Their nationalism is internal, and it is only afterward that they subordinate themselves to the framework of a political State."[93] This diminution of the role of the Israeli political framework is reminiscent of some members of the Kook circle. According to this text, the Sephardim (the children of Judah) embrace a popular form of nationalism, which is more internal than the political form of nationalism adopted by the Ashkenazim. Note that in his criticism of the democratic framework, Ashkenazy is far more moderate than Ryback, for whom the political leadership is tantamount to "a gentile regime."[94]

4

PSYCHOLOGICAL NOTIONS OF POWER

The twentieth century is the age of the Ego.
—Chögyam Trungpa

The Ashlag Circle

In the previous chapter, I focused principally on the national perception of power. In this chapter, I will focus on the psychological perception of power, particularly within R. Yehuda Ha-Levi Leib Ashlag's circle—a subject I touched upon in Chapter 1. Although power is less pivotal for this circle than for R. Avraham Yizḥaq Ha-Kohen Kook's circle, I will show how it still serves as a key concept in the kabbalistic doctrine advocated by Ashlag and his disciples. Ashlag assigned importance to the political dimension of power, but he tended to overlook the national dimension of power that was so significant for members of the Kook circle, as well as other kabbalists, such as R. Tzevi Ryback.[1] Naturally, the national dimension was played down by Ashlag's successors (such as Philip Berg), all of whom aspired to the international distribution of Ashlag's Kabbalah and the recruitment of media personalities from the non-Jewish world.[2] Thus, while a psychological and a national dimension existed in the doctrines of both the Kook and Ashlag circles, in the Kook circle the national dimension predominated, while in the Ashlag circle, the psychological dimension predominated and was cultivated in successive generations.[3] This difference explains why Kook's doctrine, on the whole, appealed mainly to Jews and Israelis, while Ashlag's doctrine had more universal appeal and was widely acclaimed abroad, mainly in the Americas but also, more recently, in England and Russia.[4]

Indeed, the emphasis on the psychological is the main innovation of Ashlag's doctrine.[5] It was he who continued and even developed the psychological interpretation of the Kabbalah that existed within Hasidic currents. Ashlag's interpretation of Lurianic Kabbalah revolves around the problem of egocentrism versus altruism, or "the desire to receive" as opposed to "the desire to give," as he himself put it.[6] Ashlag associated these desires with the two basic forces of creation—namely, the divine force (the desire to give) and the human force (the desire to receive).[7] As a rule, the concept of power in Ashlag's thinking relates to the psyche, as borne out by his statement in a letter that true worship and rectification (*tiqqun*) consist in discovering these psychological forces.[8] This statement testifies to the distinctly psychological focus in Ashlag's doctrine of power. Furthermore, Ashlag's view of the Tzaddiq was also governed by his philosophy of altruism. The Tzaddiq, with whom he personally identified (see Chapter 2), was a "giver" (*mashpi'a*) par excellence.[9]

While the theurgy of the Kook circle was national, that of the Ashlag circle was manifestly psychological. In keeping with his Hasidic origins, Ashlag emphasized the pleasure that man can give God, which is the highest form of giving. It is through this form of giving that man resembles his Creator.[10] Therefore, in worshipping God, man must focus solely on the deity's theurgical needs and divest himself of any egoistical considerations. In this respect, Ashlag simply took the classical kabbalistic idea of "worship as a divine need" to its logical conclusion and turned it into the cornerstone of a fascinating psychological doctrine. This definition of worship attaches great weight to interpersonal relations. According to Ashlag, interpersonal commandments took precedence over commandments between man and God because, by giving altruistically to others, one could attain the spiritual level of giving altruistically to God.[11]

In order to give altruistically to God, one must have first received from Him. However, by shunning a "free" gift, the recipient becomes a "new vessel" that takes solely in order to give.[12] Ideally, man should take from God only in order to satisfy God's own need to bestow his goodness. (In practice, God's greatest gift to man is giving him the possibility of "paying Him back.")[13] Thus, the "screen" that—according to this doctrine—initially blocks the divine light actually purifies the recipient and elevates him to the intermediate level of "taking in order to give."[14] This purification process also has a physical dimension. By observing the commandments solely in order to please God, one purifies the body's physical drives.[15]

Another psychological aspect of the concept of power is the idea of "overcoming all obstacles" in order to worship God in a manner that "transcends reason." This idea, also taken from Hasidism, is especially dominant in the teachings of Ashlag's son, R. Barukh Ashlag, who defines power as the transcendence of normal, rational, and psychological processes. This idea is closely connected to Ashlag's basic premise of giving and taking. While normal, "rational" behavior is egocentric and based on taking, behavior that transcends reason opens the doors to giving.[16]

How does man attain this level of transcending reason? According to R. Barukh, one may achieve superhuman powers by accepting the authority of the Tzaddiq, the personification of the desire to give, who is graced with these powers. Therefore, accepting the authority of the Torah sages is equivalent to "divine worship that transcends reason."[17] This theme ties in with the somewhat cultish structure of the Bnei Barukh group, but it is also part of the general tenor of the elder Ashlag's philosophy on the destruction of the ego.[18]

Transcending reason and destroying the ego can occur only when man ceases to rely on his own strengths. The first and most important stage in the transition from being a taker to being a giver is renouncing the ego in favor of a state of passive reception of the divine power. In his letters, Ashlag set forth detailed psychological guidelines as to how to effect this switch, which supplement the more abstract discussions of his other works. In these guidelines, Ashlag advocates self-reliance before taking action (based on the maxim, "If I am not for myself who will be for me?") and self-abnegation after taking action ("I did not perform this commandment through my own power and might, but rather through the power of God . . . and was compelled to act in this way.")[19]

In a similar vein, Ashlag asserts in another letter that "there is no happier state than when man despairs of his own strength . . . and as long as the urge to worship God comes from himself, his prayer is not complete."[20] Nonetheless, Ashlag continues, man despairs of his own strength only after he has experienced the limits of his own strength; only then does he feel the need to transcend them.[21] Ashlag takes this idea even further by arguing that the Jewish claim to Eretz Israel is contingent on this process.[22] This would seem to indicate that Ashlag subordinates national considerations to psychological ones. A contemporary political application of this idea is Michael Laitman's appeal to discard normal political considerations on the issue of the occupied territories and seize Eretz Israel by means of "a faith that transcends reason."[23]

Ashlag's psychological guidelines apparently had a substantial influence on R. Yitzchak Ginsburgh's psychological doctrine. Ginsburgh (who, according to one testimony I heard, studied with the Bnei Barukh group in his early career) took the process of destroying the ego to the extreme in a short but powerful booklet entitled *A Chapter in Divine Worship*, which he considers one of his most important works. This book is based on two premises: first, that "doing good does not come from oneself. . . . Rather, the good act . . . derives from the power of the Shekhina that resides in each Jew"; and second, that "he who does evil should not be shocked at all at what he has done . . . since the animal soul, which is the essence of the average man . . . is capable of any evil."[24] In other words, goodness derives from God, while evil derives from man (except for the Tzaddiq, in the narrowest sense). The closer man gets to that which is good, the more passive he becomes, until "every movement of soul or limb expresses the existence of the Holy-One-Blessed-Be-He."[25]

Both Ginsburgh's and Ashlag's doctrines have their roots in Hasidism, and this is one of the reasons why Ginsburgh, in his writings, does not need to allude to Ashlag's influence on this (and other) matters.[26] The relationship between Ginsburgh and Ashlag is one of many examples of the complex interplay between various twentieth-century kabbalists. Such interplay substantiates the logic of regarding twentieth-century Kabbalah as one discrete entity, despite the differences between the various blocs.

An interesting parallel to Ashlag's psychological concepts can be found in the teachings of R. Qalonymus Qalman Shapira, the rebbe of Piaseczna. In his book *Esh Qodesh* he writes that "man's worship and piety derives from the Holy-One-Blessed-Be-He, for it is He who gives him the will and power, the brain and heart to worship. And through the understanding that God gives man, he realizes that his worship of God does not come from him but rather that everything is from God, and that he himself has no part in it. Such a man sees his defects as his own, since truly they are his own, and he is the source of them."[27] Although this statement has a source in earlier Hasidic writings, it is also an expression of the intensification of the "passive model" of power in twentieth-century Kabbalah.

The importance of the concept of the abnegation of the ego in Ashlag's doctrine is counterbalanced by his emphasis on the individual and his journey in life. Thus, Ashlag is purported to have said that man is not shown the "clarification" (*birur*) or "rectification" (*tiqqun*) that he is required to accomplish, since he has to find this out for himself.[28] Moreover, while R. Barukh's rendering emphasizes transcending reason, other sources emphasize the importance of the intellect: "Our main preoccupation is with the intellect and its aspirations."[29] One should also bear in mind that R. Barukh, in a letter, clarified that his father's guidelines were meant to help people to be independent and "stand on their own two feet." Naturally, this is not so much a contradiction as a dialectic complexity.[30]

The delicate balance between individualism and obedience to the Tzaddiq is clearly elucidated in an essay that also has political implications. In it, Ashlag claims that the nations of the world lost their power because they oppressed individuals and minorities. According to him, it was appropriate for "the masses" to "submit" to the chosen individual, since "lofty ideas" emanated from these individuals, not from political leaders.[31] This assertion was doubtless the source of R. Barukh's statement, cited in his father's name, concerning the duty to obey and submit to the Tzaddiq (again, a title Ashlag claimed for himself).[32]

This complex interplay between the individual and the collective is taken further in one of Ashlag's most political works, "Essay on Peace." His premise is that an individual's worth is a function of the degree to which he serves the community, and that the freedom of the collective and of the individual are inseparable, as long as each individual fulfills his function without detracting from that of others.[33] This quasi-socialist doctrine is a direct offshoot of the general focus on altruism in Ashlag's Kabbalah. Ashlag bases this doctrine on the surprising and paradoxical statement that man's natural egoistical desire to receive is a function of God's solitary uniqueness.[34] Consequently, even in egoism there is a germ of truth, and as such, egoism is engaged in a constant struggle with kindness and altruism. Even revolutionaries who brought destruction to the world represented a truth of sorts—but a truth that was not rooted in kindness and altruism. Ashlag is almost certainly alluding here to the Russian Revolution and perhaps even to Nazism. Ashlag further states that since, in our generation, the struggle between truth and kindness has turned into a global struggle, it is impossible to attain peace on a national level.[35]

In his essay, Ashlag identifies a solution to the problem. He suggests that the destruction caused by truthful (egocentric) people triggers a transition to a higher developmental level—namely, the desire to give.[36] Egoism is a derivative of God's uniqueness—a uniqueness that focuses entirely on giving—and therefore true resemblance to God is ultimately achieved through giving. The giver is one of the Chosen, whose soul is "part of the Divinity above," and world peace will come about when the masses approach the level of the Chosen (that of altruistic giving).[37] From the above it is clear that Ashlag's political program is effectively an offshoot of his doctrine of the Tzaddiq, in particular, and of his more universal psychological doctrine, in general. In this respect (the correlation between the psychological and the political) Ashlag's doctrine resembles that of Kook, except that the emphasis here is far more universal than national.

The theme of evolution, as a historical process, plays a large part in Ashlag's doctrine, as it does in Kook's. According to this doctrine, egoism is a derivative of God's uniqueness and should not be destroyed, since at a higher level it (like other forces) will reveal the glory of God.[38] Evil, therefore, is perceived merely as a transitional stage in the evolutionary process. The problem with "world reformers" is that they wish to destroy parts of reality, and they often do so in a way that actually is an expression of egotism rather than altruism. The destruction sown by revolution is part of the "path of suffering" that triggers the world's painful and unwitting development. Had the masses followed the altruism of the Tzaddiq or the path of the Torah, the divine plan would have been implemented sooner and less painfully.[39] Elsewhere in his writings, Ashlag relates this process to the key axiom of his doctrine: selfishness isolates man from God and is the source of all suffering. Consequently, the way to abolish wars and suffering is to convert the desire to receive into the desire to give (the Tzaddiq's legacy).[40] Michael Laitman (the current leader of the Bnei Barukh sect), in his book *An Interview with the Future*, applied this idea to a contemporary phenomenon—"the suffering" of the State of Israel.[41]

To sum up, the way Ashlag and his successors perceived power was primarily psychological, with mild political undertones. Although the interplay between these two themes is extremely reminiscent of Kook's doctrine, the emphases are quite different, since the Kook circle's orientation was primarily political. But the Ashlag circle's psychological orientation was more universal, which explains its worldwide appeal and the global dissemination of Ashlag's doctrine today.

A common denominator of both circles was their reluctance to engage in magic. Although Kook exorcised dybbuks and rectified souls (*tiqqun neshamot*), generally he and members of his circle refrained from practicing magic.[42] Although Ashlag mentions magical "practices" involving the use of holy names, he warns the Tzaddiq to use his magical powers in exceptional circumstances only, since the exercise of magical powers by the Tzaddiq endowed the *Sitra Aḥra* (evil force) with similar powers.[43] Here, as elsewhere, the prohibition was disregarded by some of his successors, such as Philip Berg and his disciples, who sell "holy water" and "purify the energy" of New York businesses. In this respect, some of the successor movements of the Ashlag circle resemble other popular twentieth-century kabbalistic movements, which focused to a great extent on the exercise of magical powers.

Another common denominator of the Ashlag and Kook circles is the elitist model whereby the national and cosmic redemption stem from the "internal" activities of the Chosen, particularly the study of Kabbalah.[44] Clearly, there is a strong correlation in these circles between "power" and the dissemination of Kabbalah. I discuss this elitist trend in greater detail in Chapter 6, in my discussion on the place of the Tzaddiq in twentieth-century Kabbalah. Nevertheless, it is worth noting here that the emphasis on the power of the Chosen is shared also by less traditional currents of twentieth-century Kabbalah. An example is Leonora Leet's work, which links Kabbalah to New Age doctrines such as the teachings of Gurdjieff or Carlos Castaneda. In her book, Leet, in keeping with the New Age discourse, attaches considerable significance to the powers of "the master."[45]

Power and Psychology in Other Currents of Thought

Although we have far from exhausted the role of power in twentieth-century Kabbalah, I would like to summarize this discussion on the psychological dimension of power by placing it in a broader context—the intensification of psychological discourse in twentieth-century Kabbalah as a whole.[46] Contemporary kabbalistic authors, such as Ginsburgh and R. Pinḥas Raḥlin, have focused on the psychological dimension. Ginsburgh wrote an entire book on kabbalistic psychology, in which he discusses at length the differences between the kabbalistic approach to the psyche and the Western psychological approach, as well as the differences between various kabbalistic and Hasidic doctrines. He begins the book with a description of Kabbalah as the key "to personal psychological redemption," thereby psychologizing the Hasidic concept of "personal redemption."[47] Elsewhere he writes, "It is impossible to understand anything about Kabbalah and Hasidism unless it is linked to the psyche."[48] This statement, too, is a cogent expression of the psychologization of Kabbalah at the turn of the century.

Most of Raḥlin's works (which are widely distributed) focus on techniques of psychological contemplation, relaxation, and guided imagery, based on the doctrine of the Sefirot. Raḥlin is particularly interested in the psychology of the "repentance" process (*Ḥazara bi-Teshuva*) and in a kabbalistic explanation of the psychological difficulties that accompany this process.[49]

R. Ya'akov Meir Schechter, erstwhile president of the World Committee of Bratzlav Hasidim and leader of the conservative stream of this movement, shares this interest in psychology. According to him, "any expression of man, his thoughts, ideas, and actions and all the commandments he performs, are the fruits of his efforts. However, his essence is his good traits. A man with bad traits cannot be considered a man at all."[50] This argument, with its somewhat anomian overtones (see Chapter 6), places self-improvement above Torah observance and is designed to justify Schechter's call for a "focus on ethics," since improving one's character is the key to the theurgical perfection of the higher worlds.[51]

The infiltration of Kabbalah into the discourse of the Mussar movement has led members of the contemporary Mussar movement to engage in an in-depth psychological debate based on the principles of kabbalistic Mussar literature. Thus, for example, R. Shlomo Wolbe devotes a considerable portion of his book *'Alei Shur* to "personal work," based on self-knowledge. Self-knowledge, according to Wolbe, can be attained through constructing a personal "mandala" of sorts—that is, a circle in which man's attributes are arranged such that "the best attribute is above, and the worst below."[52] The attributes are then rearranged into a new mandala based on the work *Sha'arei Qedusha* by R. Ḥayyim Vital, the Ari's disciple, who divided human attributes into the "four elements." Wolbe recommends keeping a diary in order to keep track of the main "forces" operating on the psyche.[53] He then advises subjecting one's actions to a detailed scrutiny so as to expose the hidden motives of the psyche, which are "so hidden that they are beyond the reach of language."[54] Wolbe explains that he is advocating not an antinomian process of basing "personal work on the psyche" but rather an anomian process of directing one's psychic energy toward self-contemplation: "A person with spiritual goals will not be satisfied with 'simply' observing the commandments. Anything he can do to improve his character and behavior—even in the tiniest respect—is praiseworthy."[55] Although the concept of painstaking self-analysis exists both in classical Mussar works and in the new Mussar literature, it was Wolbe who, like his mentor, R. Yeruḥam Leibowitz of Mir, stressed the importance of psychological forces, and who, unlike Leibowitz, placed this emphasis within a kabbalistic context of sorts.[56]

5

SACRED SPACE AND SACRED PERSONS

There are people who stand in for whole communities.
—THÉON

Predictably, the historic event of the Jews' return to Eretz Israel lent impetus to the discourse on sacred space in twentieth-century Kabbalah, as in other areas of contemporary Jewish discourse.[1] This impetus, however, did not underscore the importance of Eretz Israel only, although naturally statements on the merit of the Holy Land figured prominently in it. As we will see, sacred space was frequently subordinated to the sacred person (the Tzaddiq), who played a central role in twentieth-century Kabbalah.[2] In other words, kabbalistic discourse in the twentieth century internalized the concept of sacred space and replaced it with that of sacred person.[3] Surprisingly, this process occurred not only among kabbalists outside Eretz Israel but also within circles that were identified with Zionism, such as the Kook circle.

In classical Kabbalah, two fundamental models of sacred space exist—geographical space and internal (experiential) space.[4] To some extent, both models already exist in Talmudic literature, which gives equal weight to both. For example, the redactors of the Babylonian Talmud, at the end of the tractate of *Ketubot*, deliberately included statements such as "He who dwells in Eretz Israel is considered blameless" and "He who take four steps in Eretz Israel is guaranteed the Afterlife."[5] Yet they also referred to the three famous oaths and stipulated that "He who goes from Babylon to Eretz Israel transgresses a positive commandment" and "He who dwells in Babylon is considered as dwelling in Eretz Israel." Evidently, there is a cultural reluctance to come down in favor of either approach—that which sees Eretz Israel as sacred space and that which considers any spiritual center, even abroad, as sacred space (that is, as possessing the quality of Eretz Israel).[6]

Generally speaking, the central, theosophical-theurgical stream of Kabbalah adopted the first approach, while the more mystical, "prophetic" and "ecstatic" stream adopted the second.[7] In order to understand this, we must bear in mind that throughout the generations, the key purveyors of mainstream Kabbalah were generally halakhic figures (hence the widespread acceptance of kabbalistic doctrine in the Jewish world). As such, they generally favored a *concrete* interpretation of sacred values—albeit believing that they mirrored processes in the spiritual world. This latter belief resulted in the theurgical conclusion that an action affecting entities in the lower world could also influence similar entities in the upper world. Consequently, the theosophical-theurgical stream generally rejected an allegorical interpretation of the commandments or of sacred persons and space. Kabbalists of this ilk did not interpret the physical land of Eretz Israel in a spiritual or metaphorical sense, both because of the many commandments that are associated with the land and because they perceived Eretz Israel as an extension of the divine presence (the "upper land") or of one of the *Sefirot* (emanations of divine power). It is not surprising, therefore, that Naḥmanides, a central figure of this kabbalistic stream, consolidated Eretz Israel's halakhic status by determining that conquering and settling the land were positive commandments.[8]

By contrast, for the "ecstatic" kabbalists, such as R. Abraham Abulafia, Eretz Israel symbolized an internal state rather than an actual place. Abulafia's follower R. Yizḥaq of Acre (who himself, as his name testifies, lived in Eretz Israel) wrote the following:

> The difference between *Ḥutz La-Aretz* [outside Eretz Israel] and Eretz Israel does not lie in the land of earth and dust, but rather in the souls/people [*nefashot*] who dwell therein. The land is a physical entity that is populated by souls. If

> these souls are the descendants of Jacob, then naturally they dwell in Eretz Israel—even if they live abroad—for the Shekhina encompasses them, and this is the true Eretz Israel. However, if the souls who dwell in the land are not the descendants of Jacob, the son of Isaac, the son of Abraham, that is, of the patriarch Israel, than those souls dwell in Ḥutz La-Aretz, even if they dwell [physically] in Eretz Israel or in Jerusalem. The Shekhina does not encompass them, nor does the spirit of prophecy grace them, and therefore they are truly in Ḥutz La-Aretz.[9]

In this text, R. Yizḥaq of Acre completely rejects the literal interpretation of Eretz Israel as a "physical space" but transfers the concept of "Eretz Israel" onto persons (as guardians of the soul). According to this interpretation, a Jew can dwell in Eretz Israel in the spiritual sense even if he lives abroad in the geographical sense. Conversely, a gentile who dwells in Eretz Israel in the physical sense dwells abroad in the spiritual sense. Abulafia's Kabbalah had a strong influence on Hasidic thought, via the Mussar literature of the Safedian kabbalists, who absorbed the mystical values of prophetic Kabbalah. No wonder, therefore, that Hasidic thinkers also usually considered Eretz Israel a mystical concept rather than a concrete place.[10]

SACRED SPACE IN THE WRITINGS OF THE KOOK CIRCLE

As a rule, twentieth-century kabbalistic discourse on sacred space can be divided into the two aforementioned models. Kook and his circle took the concrete concept of sacred space to new, unprecedented heights.[11] For example, R. Ya'aqov Moshe Ḥarlap, a close disciple of Kook's, identified Eretz Israel with the godhead itself, as the following passage testifies: "In days to come, Eretz Israel shall be revealed in its aspect of Infinity [*Ein Sof*], and shall soar higher and higher. . . . Although this refers to the future, even now, in spiritual terms, it is expanding infinitely."[12] He also stated, "Eretz Israel is the essence of life and higher wisdom; therefore the air of Eretz Israel makes people wise. However, the essence of life that exists within the sacred land and within the soil itself has yet to be revealed, in the Latter Days."[13]

Here, the concrete land not only corresponds to one of the Sefirot but is indistinguishable from the attribute of infinity, or the godhead.[14] Ḥarlap's concept of the soil of the land as possessing divine life stands in direct contradiction to R. Yizḥaq of Acre's denial of the value of "the land of earth and dust" as such. In this respect, Ḥarlap went even further than Kook. Whereas Kook applied the attributes of divinity to the Jewish people in the context of his "national mysticism," Ḥarlap did so to the land itself.[15]

As we have seen, Kook and some of his disciples, such as Ḥarlap and R. David Kohen ("Ha-Nazir"), aspired to prophecy, and even believed they were prophets. For them the collective return to the Land of Israel heralded the return of prophecy, for which the study of Kabbalah was a prerequisite.[16] For the Kook circle, the renewal of prophecy and the return to the land enabled an overall change of focus within the Jewish religion from a "diasporic Torah" to an "Eretz Israeli Torah."[17] This transition had antinomian features, including, possibly, changes in Halakha.[18]

However, as stated at the beginning of this chapter, the assertion that the works of the Kook circle were governed by a literal perception of the land must be qualified. A study of previously censored texts shows a more complex perception of the significance of sacred space. In one of these texts, Kook wrote,

> Moses's [spiritual] level was superior to that of Eretz Israel as a special sacred land that repels the secular attributes of other nations. However, it was equal to the [spiritual level] of Eretz Israel in its higher sense, [as a land] that absorbs the secular and sanctifies it. This sanctification of all that is secular in the world, and the expansion of the sanctity of Eretz Israel throughout the world through the incorporation of the spiritual essence of the nations within Eretz Israel, was Moses's sole intention in all the prayers he offered up, until he succeeded in implanting the wealth of all these [spiritual] attributes in Eretz Israel. However, due to the [spiritual] decline of the world, these attributes were concealed: "Until her triumph go forth at brightness, and her salvations as a torch that burneth" [Isaiah 62:1].[19]

In this passage, Kook combines two traditions in the rabbinical literature, which state that redemption is expressed (1) through Eretz Israel's expansion throughout the world, and (2) through the assimilation of synagogues and study-houses abroad into Eretz Israel. According to Kook, the land exists on a lower and higher level. At its lower level, the land is inferior to the spiritual leader and is separate from the rest of the world. However, at its higher level, Eretz Israel has the power to reach out to the world rather than repel it, since it is able to contain the secular within it and sanctify it.[20] This being so, the assimilation of the sacred into the land and the expansion of the land throughout the world are synonymous. While, at the lower level, the land is separate from the rest of the world, at the higher level, it embraces and contains the entire world within it.[21]

This process depends on the power of the spiritual leader, who is superior to the land at its lower level, since he reveals the land at its higher level. As elsewhere in the *Shmona Qevatzim*, classical kabbalistic symbolism affords us a better understanding of the text. According to this symbolism, the leader here corresponds to the *Tzaddiq Yesod 'Olam* (the Tzaddiq who is the foundation of the universe) or the

Sefira of foundation (*Yesod*) that is above the Sefira of kingdom (*Malkhut*), which corresponds to the land in its lower sense. It is within the Sefira of kingdom, however, that the Tzaddiq reveals the light of the land in its higher sense—namely, the Sefira of wisdom (*Ḥokhma*).[22] Although there is some blurring here of the distinction between Eretz Israel and the rest of the world in its normal sense, this is in fact a by-product of the vision of the land's expansion, in the final analysis in a literal sense as well. For our purposes, what is important here is that the sacred space is considered inferior to the sacred man, or Tzaddiq.

A closer reading of the text suggests that Kook is describing his personal experience as a spiritual leader. He identifies the leader with the land in its higher sense and describes Moses's mystical effort to sanctify the secular and incorporate all the attributes of the world into Eretz Israel. This is substantiated by another passage stating that "excessive fear of the secular causes great Tzaddiqim to fall from their level. Their greatness lies in strengthening themselves to raise all secular actions, dealings, and thoughts to a higher level of sanctity."[23]

Here, Kook clarifies that the task of sanctifying the secular is assigned not to Moses alone but to all "great Tzaddiqim."[24] Indeed, from Kook's experiential description of the way the Tzaddiq sanctifies thoughts and actions it is clear that he is referring to himself and his circle. Thus, the text cited above is as much about Kook as it is about Eretz Israel. And this is not the only place where Kook identifies with Moses. In another passage, Kook ends a discussion on the national issue with the following statement: "If we are unable to give full expression to all the passion that lies behind this lofty aspiration, we shall have to make do with a stammering rendition of something of our great aspiration."[25] The "stammering rendition" is doubtless another allusion to Moses, who was "slow of speech, and of a slow tongue." Once again, a cross-reading of the texts sheds light on the way Kook perceived his status. A passage that apparently speaks of the elevated status of the land (a reading of the text almost certainly endorsed by contemporary representatives of the Kook circle) actually reflects Kook's extremely high self-esteem, a characteristic shared by other outstanding Jewish mystics in the course of history, such as Abulafia and R. Naḥman of Bratzlav.[26]

SACRED SPACE IN OTHER CIRCLES

In Habad Hasidism, too, the sacred person has come to replace sacred space. As stated in Chapter 3, Habad Hasidism traditionally favored contemplation over action.[27] Therefore, Habad spearheaded ultraorthodox opposition to Zionism. However, over the twentieth century, Habad underwent a fascinating transition to activism, in which Eretz Israel played an important role. Evidently, Habad Hasidism's encounter with the Eretz Israeli reality, and its intervention in this reality, significantly contributed to its transition to activism and to the growing place occupied by Eretz Israel in Hasidic thought.

It is worth studying one of the interesting paradoxes in contemporary Habad thought in the context of the general models described above. As is known, R. Menaḥem Mendel Shneurson, the seventh rebbe of Habad, refrained from visiting Eretz Israel, and even claimed that American Jews had a messianic mission specifically in the Diaspora, in accordance with the classical Habad motto "Make Eretz Israel here."[28] This view represented a certain continuation of the stance of the fifth rebbe, R. Shalom Baer Shneurson, who opposed immigration to and settlement in the land.[29] The Habad Hasidim even applied the architecture of the sacred space to the home of the seventh rebbe in New York (known as *Beit Ḥayenu*, or "The House of Our Life"), designating his room "The Holy of Holies" and his waiting room "The Sanctuary." On the face of it, this is a clear reflection of the classical Hasidic perception of sacred space as something spiritual (and therefore not fixed) rather than physical.[30] In this case, the home of the sacred man, the Tzaddiq, becomes the sacred place (as we shall see in the case of Bratzlav Hasidism). However, a study of the messianic literature that evolved during R. Menaḥem Mendel's incumbency, in particular toward the end of his life, shows a far more complex picture. The view of sacred space as a spiritual entity goes hand in hand with a concrete perception of the land. By way of introduction, one should note that one of the interesting ramifications of the classical concrete model of sacred space can be found in the book *Emeq Ha-Melekh*, written by the Kabbalist R. Naftali Bakhrakh in the seventeenth century. Yehuda Liebes, in his article on Bakhrakh, cites the following passage from Bakhrakh's book:

> And behold, given that Adam [due to his sin] ceded authority to the seventy princes of the nations and awarded them lands above and below, and contaminated the external atmosphere, surely it is fitting that we rectify this—we, his children, the Jews, the holy people, as it says "For thou art a sacred people unto the Lord your God" [Deuteronomy 7:6; 14:2]. And the way to rectify this is through study of the Torah and the performance of commandments in our Diaspora, so that we make room for the Throne of His glory everywhere, and allow the Shekhina to shine forth in every place. Also, through the secrets of prayer we remedy the "synagogue" [the miniature Temple] thereby channeling sacred inspiration . . . toward the Holy of Holies in Jerusalem, which retains its sanctity even though it is in ruins. . . . In this manner the external atmosphere is purified . . . and shall attain complete purification in the messianic era. This is why the Sages say that in the future, synagogues and study houses will be set up in Eretz Israel[31]—namely, they will have the sanctity of Eretz Israel. This is

> [also] why the Midrash says that Eretz Israel will encompass the entire world . . . until Our Maker takes pity on us . . . through the Messiah, Son of David, to inherit the entire world by conquest en masse [*kibush rabim*].[32]

According to Bakhrakh, Jews are obliged to rectify other nations through Torah and prayer precisely because these nations are governed by external forces. Although the "physical" conquest of the world (in accordance with the rabbinical statement that Eretz Israel will spread throughout the world) is relegated to the messianic era, the diasporic Jews also have a premessianic task—that of purifying the "atmosphere" of the countries they inhabit, through study and prayer.[33]

Habad literature has a similar construct, although it bases the function of diasporic Jews on a more literal perception of the sanctity of the land and the diffusion of this sanctity in the messianic era.[34] R. Menaḥem Mendel's booklet "A Minor Temple—Our Rebbe's House in Babylon" elucidates the theme, which is liberally quoted and elaborated in Habad's contemporary messianic literature.[35] The pamphlet specifies that the rebbe's house is akin to a "minor temple" that accommodates the Shekhina in the Diaspora. This is because the Shekhina dwells among the Jewish people, and the prince of the generation (the rebbe) encompasses all Jews. Converting the rebbe's house into an Eretz Israel of sorts hastens the realization of the vision "Eretz Israel shall spread to all lands."

Thus, the dissemination of sanctity, according to Habad, begins at 770 Eastern Parkway, and the Messiah will begin his journey to Jerusalem from the rebbe's house.[36] The expansion of Eretz Israel to New York is what enables the connection between the rebbe's house and the Third Temple that will descend from heaven. As we saw with Bakhrakh, this perception of the expansion of the physical land paradoxically legitimizes diasporic life. Contemporary Habad, however, is in the grips of an acute form of messianism, which in the very near future (*be-qarov MaMaSh*, an acronym of the rebbe's name, Menaḥem Mendel Shneurson) awaits the effective (*be-fo'al MaMaSh*) implementation of this expansion.[37]

This view is somewhat reminiscent of Kook's view—namely, that the spiritual leader (Tzaddiq) is the one who sets in motion the expansion of Eretz Israel throughout the world. Thus, the elevation of the Tzaddiq above the land (in its narrow sense) is synonymous with the elevation of the status of the concrete land through the vision of its expansion in the Latter Days. The surprising similarity between the two views (of Kook and of the Habad rebbe) is due to their common structural logic, which combines the classical kabbalistic perception of sacred space as a spiritual quantity with the renewed emphasis on the concrete status of Eretz Israel following the return to the land.

R. Yitzchak Ginsburgh's approach is an excellent example of the growing emphasis on the concrete aspect of sacred space in the Habad doctrine. As we saw in Chapter 3, Ginsburgh had ties in the 1980s with radical settler circles. According to his followers, Ginsburgh himself admitted that people such as Motti Qarpel, Noam Livnat, Yisra'el Ari'el, and others influenced his doctrine. In this sense, Ginsburgh set up a kind of subgroup, based on feedback between the master (himself) and his disciples. In his prolific writings, Ginsburgh provides a contemporary interpretation of classical Habad's pantheistic doctrine in order to explain Habad's emphasis on the concrete land and Habad's transition to political activism.[38] According to these texts, our generation has been assigned the spiritual task of precipitating the divine presence in the physical world, through political and physical action (as opposed to mere contemplation).[39] This task requires religious worship of another kind, which explains why Ginsburgh, like Kook, raises the possibility of a return to prophecy and places a growing emphasis on the body. (In the following chapter, we will see how, for both these thinkers, the revival of religious life in Eretz Israel borders on the abrogation of traditional Halakha.)

Based on Ginsburgh's paradoxical hypothesis, Shlomo Fischer has shown how the very fact that the divine presence is not obviously revealed to man in the physical land indicates that even higher, mysterious levels of divinity—belonging to the realm of *'ayin*, or seeming nothingness—exist within it. This emphasis on merging with the physicality of the land led Ginsburgh to encourage a return to organic farming in Bat 'Ayin, the settlement he founded.[40] Ginsburgh's thesis on the revelation of divinity in the physical land is extremely reminiscent of Ḥarlap's statements on the same theme.

Although Ginsburgh greatly admired Kook's doctrine, in his classes he criticized Kook's view that the nation transcended the Tzaddiq. But their views may actually have been more similar than would appear at first sight. In any case, the ties between Ginsburgh and broad sections of the settler movement were not fortuitous. Both Kook and Ginsburgh link the doctrine of the Tzaddiq to the glorification of the concrete land, yet both give precedence to the doctrine of the Tzaddiq. In Ginsburgh's case, however, political activity on behalf of Eretz Israel is closely bound up with the agenda of posthumously reinstating the presence of the seventh rebbe. Thus, Ginsburgh's discourse is based on the Habad view that links Eretz Israel with messianic expectations surrounding the seventh rebbe.

Like members of other Habad circles, Ginsburgh believes that the rebbe did not die but merely "disappeared," and that by "saving" Eretz Israel from "Arab hands" one could "revive" the rebbe and restore him to the physical world.[41] The connection between these two objectives is clear. For the rebbe to return to the physical world, the land must be redeemed in preparation for the manifestation of the divine presence in the material world.

The assumption behind this process is that the rebbe is not only the Messiah but also the manifestation of divinity in the material world. This is the purport of Ginsburgh's pamphlet "Tzaddiq Yesod 'Olam," written in response to the condemnation of Habad by ultraorthodox groups following radical messianic claims of this kind voiced by the seventh rebbe.[42] In this pamphlet, Ginsburgh describes how the Tzaddiq—"the heart of all Jews"—is the link between the Jewish people and God. As such, argues Ginsburgh, praise of the Tzaddiq supersedes praise of God. The pamphlet specifies the divine attributes of the Tzaddiq whose physical body is the repository of the divine presence, as we will "see with our own eyes" in the messianic era.[43]

Despite this adulation of the rebbe, Ginsburgh describes paradoxical processes based on a kind of logical extension of the persona of the Tzaddiq and even the Messiah. For example, he explains the demise of the seventh rebbe as the withdrawal of his presence in order to make room for the manifestation of the messianic dimension that lies within every person. According to him, at one of the last Hasidic gatherings (*hitva'aduyot*) on the festival of Hosha'na Rabba in 1991, the rebbe offered participants the possibility of assuming the title of rebbe.[44] Elsewhere, Ginsburgh adds that through the dissemination of Kabbalah, everyone has the power to become a rebbe.[45] Thus, the motifs of power and the urge to disseminate Kabbalah—the two recurrent themes of twentieth-century Kabbalah—actually help contribute to the expansion of the Tzaddiq. This expansion, however, does not imply democratization: Ginsburgh's vision, which closely resembles that of some members of the Kook circle, is to build a "circle of souls" that will form a "single collectivity" (*knishta ḥada*), which, through repentance, will bring about the redemption.[46]

In addition to the messianic discourse of Habad in our generation, which has been emphasized by existing research, there is a growing emphasis on the Tzaddiq in twentieth-century Habad discourse.[47] Although the founder of Habad, R. Shneur Zalman of Liadi ("the Alter Rebbe"), played down the figure of the Tzaddiq (unlike foundational Hasidic texts, such as R.Ya'aqov Yosef of Polony's *Toledot Ya'aqov Yosef*), under the sixth and seventh rebbes there was a sudden increase in the scope and radicalism of discourse on the Tzaddiq. On a more popular level, this was reflected in the widespread distribution of "wonder tales" about the last rebbe, unlike earlier generations of Habad.[48] We can demonstrate the radicalism of the doctrine of the Tzaddiq under the last two rebbes through material that was collected and analyzed by Shelly Goldberg. Thus, for example, in one text the sixth rebbe (R. Yosef Yizḥaq Shneurson) claims that his father, R. Shalom Baer, interceded with God only for those who subordinated their "thoughts, opinions, wishes, and actions to the holy Rebbe."[49] In other words, R.Shalom Baer was urging his followers to submit to the rebbe, who continued to act even after his death. In another text, the seventh rebbe (R. Menaḥem Mendel) described his predecessor as "the supreme and omnipotent master" and "the epitome of goodness"—expressions that are usually reserved for God Himself.[50]

Bratzlav Hasidism, unlike Habad and also the Kook circle, adopted a more spiritual perception of sacred space, although one might have expected the opposite, given Naḥman's assertion that Eretz Israel was "Eretz Israel in its simple sense, with houses and apartments."[51] Naḥman entertained a basically spiritual perception of Eretz Israel, as borne out by the fact that he decided to leave the country as soon as he arrived on his famous visit.[52] Modern Bratzlav Hasidim consider Uman in the Ukraine their sacred space, and each year prior to Rosh Ha-Shana, Bratzlav Hasidim leave Eretz Israel for Uman. At the end of the twentieth century, the Sephardic halakhist R. 'Ovadia Yosef condemned this phenomenon in the context of the internal struggle within Shas (following Aryeh Der'i's visit to Uman in an attempt to acquire the image of a spiritual leader) on the ground that Halakha forbids one to leave Eretz Israel.[53]

Bratzlav Hasidim are aware of this paradox of "a pilgrimage abroad," and there is much controversy on this issue, even among themselves.[54] The pamphlet *Even Shtiya* (Foundation Stone) was therefore published in defense of this custom, which has been upheld by the Elders of Bratzlav throughout the generations.[55] In this pamphlet, the main argument is based on Naḥman's assertion in *Liqutei Moharan*, a collection of discourses, that Eretz Israel's sanctity is derived "from his Rosh Ha-Shana."[56] Rosh Ha-Shana, therefore, was not only a sacred period but also "the personification of R. Naḥman," as his close disciple R. Nathan of Nemirov put it.[57] Naḥman even reportedly promised that, if necessary, he would drag all those who came to Uman on Rosh Ha-Shana out of Hell by their sidelocks.[58] Within this construct, geographical sanctity is a derivative of temporal sanctity, which in turn is a derivative of the attributes of the "true Tzaddiq."[59]

Evidently, this trend is a continuation of the classical Hasidic tradition, in which sacred values are identified with the person of the Tzaddiq. Likewise, it is a continuation of the Hasidic tradition in which sacred space is identified with internal, or spiritual, states. Although the sacred place here has a concrete dimension (it is a specific tomb in Uman), it derives its power from the presence of the true Tzaddiq, in this case Naḥman, who, according to Bratzlav Hasidim, did not die but continues to act in the world.[60] Indeed, many pilgrims to Uman have testified that they felt the presence of Naḥman at his grave.[61] The contemporary Bratzlav perception is modeled on Naḥman's own perception, as testified by the fact that he left Eretz Israel almost immediately upon his arrival, since his journey was more spiritual than physical.

Despite the differences between the way Bratzlav Hasidism, the Kook circle and Habad perceive sacred space, they share a common denominator: in all three cases, the spiritual leader is the source of the sanctity of the land in its deepest sense. It is clear, however, that in the Hasidic circles, the doctrine of Tzaddiq occupies a more pivotal place than in the Kook circle, which gives precedence to national mysticism over the status of the Tzaddiq. The relationship between sacred person and sacred space is part of a larger debate that exists within the study of religions but has not, in my opinion, been sufficiently internalized in Jewish studies.[62]

Bratzlav Hasidism has managed to create a sense of continuity, despite the vicissitudes that it, like Habad and religious Jewry in general, has undergone following the return to Eretz Israel. Possibly one of the reasons for this continuity is the fact that this particular Hasidic sect has remained loyal to its founder, Naḥman, rather than set up a contemporary spiritual leadership. Indeed, according to Bratzlav Hasidim, Naḥman's presence continues to be felt in this world (as in the case of R. Yisro'el Odesser ["Ba'al Ha-Peteq"] and his followers' conviction that Naḥman handed him a note in person).

I would now like to briefly discuss one of the radical offshoots of Bratzlav Hasidism—R. Avraham Zagdon's doctrine. (See more on him in Chapter 6.) Zagdon is a prolific but controversial author, who was ostracized by most Bratzlav Hasidim but managed to garner a small, loyal following in Jerusalem, including some Religious-Zionist youth. In his kabbalistic model, Ḥutz La-Aretz (the domain outside Eretz Israel) is identified with "plurality"— namely, an obsessive preoccupation with the finer points of Halakha: "As we delve deeper and deeper into plurality and study more laws and derivative laws, we move further and further away [from the Source]. . . . We remain constantly in Ḥutz La-Aretz, in the realm of plurality, and all our Torah and reality is an expression of Ḥutz La-Aretz."[63] Yet he identifies Eretz Israel with "unity," which is synonymous with the Tzaddiq.[64]

In Chapter 6 I discuss the antinomian sensibility implicit in statements of this kind. Here, however, I would like to emphasize the total identification between the Tzaddiq (in this case, Zagdon) and sacred space.[65] In his opinion, other forms of Hasidism (including Bratzlav Hasidism) perceive only the "externality" of the concept of Tzaddiq, while he, Zagdon, represents the "internality" of the concept of Tzaddiq.[66] Zagdon's self-perception as the true Tzaddiq does not contradict his loyalty to Naḥman: like other contemporary Bratzlav leaders, Zagdon sees himself as Naḥman's spiritual heir. Even the initials of his name, A. Z., testify to his affiliation with the founder of Bratzlav, whom he identifies with the "attribute of AZ" (literally "then").[67] Zagdon further claims that while Naḥman's *Liqutei*

Moharan focuses on the externality of the Tzaddiq (that is, the *Athalta Di-Ge'ula*, or the beginning of the redemption), he, Zagdon, reveals the inner spirit of the book (that is, the total redemption, alluded to by the word AZ).[68] Thus, in Zagdon's case, not only the concept of Eretz Israel but also that of the redemption itself was totally subsumed by the issue of the status of the Tzaddiq, not as an abstract concept but as a person of flesh and blood.[69]

To sum up, the renewed encounter with Eretz Israel brought about a transformation in most currents of Religious Judaism in the twentieth century, leading some, especially the Kook circle, to emphasize the concrete aspect of sacred space.[70] As on the issue of power, the writings of Kook are open to several interpretations, including more spiritual and mystical ones. Be that as it may, successive generations of the Kook circle chose to highlight national elements, in particular the literal perception of Eretz Israel. Predictably, the writings of many Sephardic kabbalists in the twentieth century also strongly emphasize the concrete status of the land.[71]

The general picture provided by the above texts, however, is one in which sacred space is subordinated to the sacred person (the Tzaddiq). As a rule, in twentieth-century Kabbalah, in particular those currents that are associated with the New Age movement, the concept of sacred space has given way to more individualistic values. This is part of a more general trend to discard collective and traditional religious values, as we will see in Chapter 6 when discussing the attitude toward Halakha. This transition from sacred space to sacred person resembles a similar process that took place after the destruction of the Second Temple.[72] However, the contemporary process was accompanied, paradoxically, by the return to Eretz Israel and the discovery that the concrete Eretz Israel was unable to fulfill the religious aspirations associated with the mythical land.[73]

This discussion would not be complete without reference to the radical denial of the concrete Eretz Israel by Satmar Hasidim. As David Zorotzkin has shown, the Satmar Hasidim believe that the building of "Eretz Israel below" by the Zionists causes the destruction of "Eretz Israel above."[74] Therefore, according to the doctrine of the Satmar rebbe, R. Yo'el Teitelbaum, the return to the land not only fails to hasten the redemption but even hinders it. In other words, the realization of the vision of the return to the land in the political-secular context is an enormous obstacle to the true realization of the religious vision. As Zorotzkin points out, R.Teitelbaum has a similar attitude to the revival of the Hebrew language, which explains why Satmar Hasidic circles are opposed to the use of Hebrew as a secular language (note that this opposition is gradually becoming eroded, and that even the most ultraorthodox circles currently speak a hybrid of Yiddish and Hebrew).[75]

In the last decades of the twentieth century, the status and significance of Eretz Israel was high on the agenda of Israeli society in general, and of religious society in particular. Although I do not wish to address political issues here, it would be naive to discuss the issue of the sanctity of Eretz Israel without considering the political context—a context that has intensified the debate on the issue of sacred space in both religious and academic discourse. It should be remembered that this issue is an ancient one that has never been unequivocally resolved. In this context, it is worth citing Kook on the issue of Uganda: "It is a bad sign for the party if it thinks its members have a monopoly on wisdom and righteousness, and all else is vanity and conceit." He directed this statement at both parties in the controversy.[76]

In a similar vein, Kook spoke of the relationship between the religious, national, and liberal camps:

> It is not enough to recognize the positive side of each force. . . . Rather, one should go further, until one recognizes also the positive aspects of the negative side of each force, all in the right measure. And one should know that, for the sake of the special force toward which one is drawn, one must be influenced to some extent also by its negative aspect. This negative aspect tempers the force one is drawn to, enabling one to see it in its true proportion and saving one from the danger of hyperbole and exaggeration.[77]

The following passage, recently discovered in the Kook archives, develops a similar theme:

> Due to man's inability to comprehend the overarching aspect of divergent opinions, and the unifying thread that unites them, each generation and group reverts to the channel of its own spiritual outlook and believes that there can be no progress until the other outlook, which does not tally with its outlook, vanishes from the world. And no one has sufficient imagination to realize that the whole world does not share the same outlook, but only part of it [the world]. It follows that each part is necessary, and that together they make up the whole building. The contradictions do not come from the positive side of the outlooks, but from their negative sides, which stem from the sin of pride that says, "I alone shall rule" [1 Kings, 1, 5], which each outlook has adopted at various times and by different circles.[78]

SACRED SPACE IN THE LATE TWENTIETH CENTURY

The declining status of concrete sacred space in twentieth-century Kabbalah is, in my opinion, due also to larger processes, such as globalization, which is increasingly eroding the status of local space in favor of a global communications culture.[79] Philip Wexler already linked the new mysticism to the decline of physical space in contemporary society, which is based on "networking."[80] Twentieth-century Kabbalah, in turn, has created "supranational" sacred sites that have largely replaced the holy sites in Israel. Earlier, I discussed two examples of sites of this kind: the tomb of R. Naḥman of Bratzlav in Uman and the home of the Habad rebbe R. Menaḥem Mendel in New York.[81]

In this chapter, we discussed the dominance of the doctrine of the Tzaddiq throughout twentieth-century Kabbalah—not only in Hasidic circles (although non-kabbalistic circles, such as that represented by Rabbi J. B. Soloveitchik, have criticized this doctrine).[82] This trend fits in with similar processes in other mystical traditions, such as Sufism and Buddhism. The mystical literature of these sects in the twentieth century emphasizes the role and power of "the master" (the "guru" in eastern traditions). Reshad Feild, for example, one of the foremost writers within Western neo-Sufism, claims that the personal tie with the spiritual master, which is based on total obedience, is the key to spiritual experience.[83] In Buddhism, too, an entire literary corpus has grown up glorifying the spiritual master and claiming that the connection with him is essential for tantric practice.[84] As Chögyam Trungpa, one of the greatest Tibetan masters in the West, wrote:

> From the tantric point of view, the guru is a dictator—in the benevolent sense—who minds every step of your life experience and who also demands faith and trust. . . . The guru is regarded as a Buddha in the flesh, a Buddha in a human body. . . . That is why when you are accepted into the tantric tradition you take certain abhishekas or empowerments from the guru. . . . The guru's role is that of a warrior chief who puts you through all kinds of trials. . . . You have to be made to face certain challenges. . . . And when you commit yourself into a more involved situation like tantric discipline, the guru's word is regarded as absolute supertruth, not just ordinary old truth, but vajra truth, truth with power behind it. . . . Once we tread on the path of tantric practice, we switch from the bodhisattva's world of kindness and gentleness and democracy to the realm of the benevolent dictator. . . . If you disobey the guru's message on the level of form [body], speech, or mind, you are struck, you go straight to vajra [tantric] hell.[85]

Although this argument is a continuation of classical trends, it chooses to emphasize one particular element—the master-disciple relationship.[86] In Western culture, too, the magician or shaman has become a new cultural hero, as testified by the popular books and films that focus on figures of this kind.[87] Castaneda's best sellers, which describe his apprenticeship with a tribal shaman, have contributed significantly to this trend.

The ascendancy of the chosen individual in the late twentieth century exposes a structural contradiction in contemporary Western society. On the one hand, the democratic ethos calls for equality and therefore rejects hierarchical systems based on the adoration of powerful individuals. Moreover, the accumulation of power by charismatic leaders could challenge the concentration of power in the state's hands. We see this happening in the Israeli context, where "rational" systems of political conduct are being threatened by the practice of seeking blessings from kabbalists or consulting with Torah personalities over political decisions. It follows that religious circles and people who have adopted the democratic ethos, such as R. Soloveitchik, are critical of the institution of Tzaddiq.

On the other hand, capitalism encourages competitive private enterprise and therefore sanctifies the successful and charismatic individual, as demonstrated by the growing adulation of movie and media stars.[88] In this sense, the New Age movement serves the goals of late capitalism, which is based on symbolic production. The figure of the Tzaddiq, shaman, or guru has become, in this context, yet another symbol of power and glamour at the individual level, alongside the business or media superstar. Yet twentieth-century psychological culture, by successfully exposing the psychological and sexual weaknesses of the individual, has undermined the trend toward the adulation of both religious and secular "saints."[89] Accordingly, the mystics of the twentieth century, such as Kook and Kohen, were far more open about their own psychological weaknesses and difficulties than were most classical kabbalists, who were unwilling to expose themselves (with a few exceptions, such as Naḥman of Bratzlav).[90] A more extreme expression of the exposure of the chosen individual's weaknesses is the great publicity that has been given in recent decades to scandals, mainly of a sexual nature, involving spiritual masters from the East and their Western protégés.[91] This is true, also, of certain figures in twentieth-century neo-Kabbalah.

6

CIRCUMVENTION AND VIOLATION OF HALAKHA

One of the main issues in the study of Jewish mysticism is its attitude toward Halakha and the observance of the commandments—or the relationship between kabbalistic literature and halakhic literature.[1] A related issue is the link between a halakhic way of life (a system of daily rituals and customs) and kabbalistic behavior (mystical rituals, customs, and techniques). Do these two systems complement each other, contradict each other, or simply coexist?

One of the more salient manifestations of the changing face of Kabbalah in the twentieth century is its attitude toward Halakha. Throughout the history of Jewish mysticism, there have always been currents (such as Sabbatianism or Frankism) that played down the importance of mitzva-observance or even sanctioned the violation of Halakha. However, mainstream Kabbalah typically adhered to Halakha, and many outstanding kabbalists (including Ra'abad, Naḥmanides, R. Yosef Karo, and R. Elijah, the Gaon of Vilna) were also renowned exegetes of Halakha.[2] The link between Kabbalah and Halakha has a literary basis: many kabbalistic works focus on the rationales for the commandments in an attempt to reinforce ritual worship through the radical claim that the observance of commandments has a beneficial effect on the higher worlds.[3] The kabbalists' commitment to Halakha is striking when contrasted with philosophical approaches.[4] Currents such as Sabbatianism, which sanctioned "the righteous sin" and the violation of Halakha for the sake of spiritual growth, or R. Abraham Abulafia's prophetic Kabbalah, which "circumvented Halakha," were marginalized.[5] Even the Hasidic movement, which in its infancy encompassed trends that sanctioned the circumvention and violation of Halakha (and not necessarily through the influence of Sabbatianism), finally joined forces with the world of Halakha, and even produced its own halakhic works, such as *Shulḥan 'Arukh Ha-Rav* by the first rebbe of Habad or *Avnei Nezer* (on the laws of the Sabbath) by R. Abraham of Sochatshov.[6]

In the late nineteenth and twentieth centuries, by contrast, the influence of anomian thinkers (who circumvented or disregarded Halakha) and antinomian thinkers (who sanctioned the violation of Halakha under certain circumstances) rose sharply. Whereas in the early part of twentieth century, these thinkers veiled their anomian or antinomian ideas in allusions (which did not prevent them from being censored by their spiritual heirs), by the end of the century their successors began to express these ideas more openly and assertively, as anomian and antinomian trends emerged. As I argue in the following text, a characteristic of the modern and postmodern influence on the world of Kabbalah is a certain schism between Halakha and Kabbalah. While in the early twentieth century, this schism was almost certainly due to the influence of modernist movements, such as Zionism, in the late century it was due to the influence of New Age movements and other postmodernist trends.

Circumvention of Halakha (Anomianism)

In the world of mysticism, anomian trends are those that, while not actually contravening Halakha, focus on areas other than the performance of mitzvot and study of Halakha and use techniques that are extraneous to the world of Halakha. For example, "ecstatic" kabbalists, such as Abulafia and his spiritual heirs, practiced rhythmic breathing, seclusion, and combinations of letters—practices that are hardly touched upon in the rabbinical-halakhic literature. (By contrast, mainstream kabbalists—that is, those affiliated with theosophist-theurgical Kabbalah —focused on the meaning of the commandments and prayers.) Although these trends did not directly challenge Halakha, the funneling of spiritual energy into extra-halakhic channels undermined the status of the Talmudic-halakhic approach, both in theory and in practice. Thus, a more personal spiritual world evolved that was less committed to the social and somewhat standardized behavior patterns predicated by halakhists.[7]

ANOMIANISM IN KOOK'S WRITINGS

Before discussing antinomian tendencies in R. Avraham Yizḥaq Ha-Kohen Kook's works, I will review more moderate anomian tendencies in his mystical practices. One of the main mystical techniques practiced by Kook was that of *yiḥudim*. Kook's concept of yiḥudim was slightly different than that of classical Kabbalah, which involves meditating on the inherent unity between two apparently different aspects of God's name, usually for theurgical purposes but also for rectification (*tiqqun*) of the soul.[8]

Orot Ha-Qodesh, the most mystical of the classical but censored works of Kook, contains several important passages on yiḥudim, as does the uncensored *Shmona Qevatzim*, published in the late century. We shall begin with the following: "There are certain kinds of Tzaddiqim who can bring about the rectification of the entire world and the sincere repentance of all Jews. . . . Such Tzaddiqim exist in the pre-messianic period ['*Iqvata Di-Meshiḥa*]. . . . The way to prepare for this is through the practice of yiḥudim."[9] In this text, Kook implies that he is a Tzaddiq capable of rectifying the nation and, indeed, the entire world (attesting, again, to the fact that Kook perceived the Tzaddiq as a national, rather than as a communal, figure). It was incumbent on the Tzaddiq to prepare himself for the monumental task of rectifying the world by practicing the anomian technique of yiḥudim.

The passage in *Orot Ha-Qodesh* goes on to describe Kook's personal interpretation of this technique.[10] For him, yiḥudim is a technique whereby the Tzaddiq "reconciles" his own warring forces, thereby bringing unity in the world. Accordingly, the theurgical action here is not directed at higher worlds, but rather at the inner world of the Tzaddiq, who is entrusted with the task of rectifying the world. Here, as in the Hasidic texts cited later in the chapter, we see how this concept of the Tzaddiq has supplanted classical Torah (and kabbalistic) paradigms.

Our reading of the text is corroborated by another text on the same subject, in which Kook outlines a spiritual journey beginning with the development of an aesthetic sense and positive character traits, observance of the commandments, study of the Torah, and study of the interiority of the Torah, and ending with the practice of the yiḥudim "that surpass them all in their magnificent preparation for the revelation of the spiritual light in its full plentitude, that shall revive the spirit of each individual and implant a soul into the entire nation."[11] In this sequence, the yiḥudim take precedence over all traditional values, including the interiority of the Torah. It is interesting to note how, at the end of this text, Kook places the individual before the nation—something we might not have expected from such a national thinker. However, as we have had occasion to see, this contradiction is more apparent than real, since in Kook's thinking, the individual dimension (the inner harmony of the Tzaddiq) is inextricably bound up with the national dimension (the rectification of the entire nation by the Tzaddiq). From these texts it is clear that the practice of the yiḥudim represents an anomian, and sometimes even antinomian, tendency (for example, according higher priority to the yiḥudim than to the commandments).[12]

Kook's anomian tendencies did not exist in a vacuum but rather were shaped by modern events, as Kook himself testifies in the following text: "What is the current situation of the world? Just because no one, especially no Talmudist, wishes to examine the current situation of the world, should I for that reason refrain? No! I am not beholden to the masses, I shall walk my own path."[13] Clearly, Kook believed that his spiritual choices were linked to contemporary events. However, the sequence of the text implies that it was his (unconventional) choice of spiritual path that opened him up to contemporary developments, although the opposite may have been true (that is, his openness to modern, individualistic, trends may have generated his interest in the personal and anomian phenomena).

For a complete understanding of the anomian dimension in Kook's doctrine, it is necessary to introduce a sociological distinction made by the Kook circle between "Eretz Israeli Torah" and "diasporic Torah."[14] This distinction was used by the circle to legitimize a study technique and even a spiritual identity based on faith and ideas rather than on Halakha. Again we see how the return to Eretz Israel molded a new religious agenda. The social significance of this agenda is reflected in the fact that from R. Tzevi Yehuda Ha-Kohen Kook ("Ratzia") on, the leadership of the Kook circle was entrusted to teachers of "faith" rather than to halakhic authorities.

Anomianism in Twentieth-Century Hasidic Thought

Researchers have already argued that the Hasidic movement, which began in the eighteenth century, in a certain sense continued the anomian path of Abulafia and the prophetic Kabbalists.[15] The Hasidim's spiritual path emphasized extra-halakhic values, such as seclusion, joy, devotion to the Tzaddiq, and ecstasy, while rejecting more traditional halakhic values, such as the centrality of the study of Halakha or strict adherence to prayer schedules. Sometimes, this anomian tendency verged on antinomianism, as the polemical anti-Hasidic literature testifies. Nevertheless, the mitigation of the conflict between the Hasidim and Mitnagdim (who found new common enemies, such as the Enlightenment movement [*Mask-*

ilim]) cooled the Hasidic movement's revolutionary fervor and returned it to the fold of the halakhic establishment (though there were exceptions, as we shall see in connection with *Mei Ha-Shiloaḥ*).[16] Even the Mussar movement, which is considered the antithesis of Hasidism (they have been compared to the emblem on the Russian flag of two eagles facing in opposite directions), finally admitted that there was a need for a synthesis between Mussar and Hasidism.[17]

Anomian (and even antinomian) trends in the Hasidic movement intensified in the twentieth century. This phenomenon should be studied not as part of the history of Hasidism alone but rather as part of the broader context of the history of twentieth-century Kabbalah, alongside similar trends in other circles. This new Hasidic anomianism can be traced back to the early century, in the doctrine of R. Qalonymus Qalman Shapira, the rebbe of Piaseczna, who emphasized nonhalakhic techniques borrowed from Western hypnosis, and other writers who were influenced by him.[18] Shapira's works were widely acclaimed at the end of the century, thanks mainly to R. Shlomo Carlebach. The works of R. Hillel Zeitlin, too, who propagated Hasidic ideas in the pre-Holocaust period, were based on extra-halakhic principles. Similarly, in Habad, the development of extra-halakhic practices (such as special operations) in the twentieth century can be traced back to R. Yosef Yizḥaq Shneurson in the early century.

I would now like to focus on several cases of anomianism in the late twentieth century—a time when extra-halakhic discourse came out into the open. I wish to commence with the so-called neo-Hasidic circles operating in Israel and abroad that wished to revive the spiritual essence of Judaism by intensifying its mystical dimension. Some of these circles moved away from orthodoxy, thereby contributing to the infiltration of Kabbalah into the nonorthodox movements in the United States. An outstanding figure of the neo-Hasidic movement is R. Zalman Shalomi-Schachter, a former Habad Hasid, who became one of the leaders of the Jewish Renewal Movement, which branched off from the nonorthodox movements in the United States.[19] An offshoot of the Jewish Renewal Movement was the *Ḥavura* (spiritual fellowship) movement in the United States. (A. Y. Green, an important scholar of Hasidism, is among the leaders of this movement.)[20] Other branches of the Jewish Renewal Movement operated on the fringes of orthodoxy.

Foremost among these branches was the movement that evolved around R. Shlomo Carlebach in the United States. Carlebach, also originally a Habad Hasid, was ostracized by Habad because of his antinomian tendencies (he sanctioned women's singing in prayer services). Most of Carlebach's teachings were transmitted orally in the form of lectures and classes, and he had many followers, some of whom set up the settlement of Mevo Modi'in. This circle was characterized by its unorthodox attitude on gender issues. For example, some of Carlebach's female followers, such as Mimi Feigelson in Jerusalem and Sarah Rabinowitz in New York, became spiritual teachers in their own right.[21] This represented a sharp departure from classical Kabbalah's attitude toward spiritual instruction by women.

The second neo-Hasidic group emerged in Israel around Ohad Ezraḥi, a newly observant Jew and a former disciple of R. Yitzchak Ginsburgh, who set up a spiritual community called Ha-Maqom, which has since dissolved. The anomian practices of this community led to his excommunication by the rabbinical establishment in Israel.[22]

I will now discuss the antinomian features of these groups, with an emphasis on two features in particular. The first feature is their focus on mystical techniques and ecstasy, sometimes even as an alternative to halakhic Judaism (for example, the Carlebach Minyanim have largely replaced halakhic prayer with ecstatic prayer, even if the liturgy has not been changed). The second feature is their readiness to absorb non-Jewish traditions as a source of mystical inspiration, giving rise to phenomena such as "Torah Yoga" and "Jewish meditation," which have generally become an integral part of the prayer ceremony. Spiritual eclecticism in general is a prominent feature of the New Age movement.[23]

R. Zalman Schachter has close ties with shamans among the native North Americans and with Buddhist masters, such as Chögyam Trungpa.[24] Carlebach had ties with the Indian master Swami Satchidananda. (He even claimed that had R.Menaḥem Mendel Shneurson of Habad's attended the Woodstock Festival together with Satchidananda, a great tiqqun would have resulted.) Ezraḥi, for his part, masterminded the idea of the Ashram Yeshiva, and the community he eventually set up was based mainly on Far Eastern techniques.[25] By contrast, his former mentor, R. Yitzchak Ginsburgh, condemns Torah Yoga and other Far Eastern imports (such as tai chi) on his Internet site as being the emanations of "the forces of darkness."[26]

Another interesting example of the adoption of New Age practices is the writing of R. Ya'aqov Avraham Ozolbo, an influential figure in Bratzlav circles in France and Israel, and author of the popular guide *Dibur La-Avarim*, published by Bratzlav Hasidic circles. In his book, Ozolbo uses the texts of R. Naḥman of Bratzlav to develop a sophisticated method of body-soul communication, with explicit references to similar techniques used by alternative healers. By presenting this technique as indispensable for divine worship, the author invests it with an anomian element: "The dialogue with the body begins where any commandment ends, in the space before any other commandment takes its place." Having paid lip service to the halakhic framework, the author dispenses with the issue of the commandments for the remainder of the book. The technique itself consists basically of focusing on one's inner world ("personal redemption," as the author puts it) and barely differs from various imagery techniques practiced in New Age circles.[27]

The next example I wish to discuss is Ginsburgh's doctrine, which may, on the face of it, seem a surprising choice. Ostensibly, Ginsburgh's doctrine, with its emphasis on observing the commandments, appears to be nomian.[28] However, a closer study of some of his teachings (for example, his emphasis on the interiority of the Torah as the key to spiritual life at the expense of Halakha) reveals certain nuances that are situated somewhere between anomianism and antinomianism.

In his book on the spiritual leader, Ginsburgh claims that the written laws (the Mosaic Code) are merely "residues" of Moses (the archetypical spiritual leader), while the rebbe represents "the essence of Moses." He sees Moses (and therefore the rebbe) not as the lawgiver but rather as existing above the law. Since Moses (the rebbe) receives power directly from God, the law is merely a continuation (or extension) of Moses's spiritual essence. The natural corollary of this argument is that faith in Moses—and therefore in the rebbe as the essence of Moses revealed in each generation—is above faith in God. Consequently, Moses (and the rebbe) has the power to enact emergency dispensations (a spiritual level known as "the Messiah within Moses").[29]

Ginsburgh qualifies this conclusion (which is why, in my opinion, he is situated on the seam between anomianism and antinomianism) with the rider that an emergency dispensation need "not necessarily" contradict the Torah.[30] Nevertheless, he emphasizes that "the rebbe" of each generation has no need of halakhic backing or precedents to justify his actions: "He is sure of himself, and has no need for precedents. He is the embodiment of Moses himself. . . . More than anyone else, the 'rebbe' is able to recognize the exceptional needs of the generation."[31] In another text (which he also qualifies), Ginsburgh goes even further in suggesting that there is a need for a new Torah to be revealed by God himself (through the Tzaddiq, who is a kind of personification of God).[32] To my mind, these ideas, though they have some backing in classical Hasidism, are clearly the product of a modern, antitraditionalist consciousness in which religious life is regulated by current exigencies rather than by the cumulative halakhic practices of previous generations.

Although similar concepts exist elsewhere in Ginsburgh's writings, I have focused on the preceding passage as illustrating an important point: that among numerous contemporary teachers, who draw their inspiration from classical Hasidic doctrine, the centrality of the spiritual leader (the Tzaddiq) has replaced the centrality of Halakha.[33] The growing importance attached to the Tzaddiq is itself a hallmark of twentieth-century Kabbalah. The emergence of a new world of religious practice around the figure of the Tzaddiq began already in classical

Hasidism, which created an entire system of rituals around the figure of the rebbe—the *tisch* (festive gathering around the rebbe), *yeḥidus* (personal interview with the rebbe), *shirayim* (consumption of food from the rebbe's table), *qvitel* (written petition to the rebbe), and so on. The further intensification of this rebbe-centric phenomenon in our time is particularly evident in Habad Hasidism, in which participation in the rebbe's "operations" plays a major role in religious life. This phenomenon gained momentum toward the end of the century, culminating in the emergence of messianic celebrations of R. Menaḥem Mendel (the song *Didan Notzaḥ* [Victory Is Ours], the declaration *Yeḥi Ha-Melekh* ["long live the king"]), and rituals performed by members of contemporary Habad's messianic faction aimed at revitalizing the "absent" rebbe.[34] No wonder that certain halakhists, such as the Lithuanian leader R. Eli'ezer Menaḥem Shach, condemned these activities as contravening Halakha.[35]

This change of focus in religious worship from Halakha to spiritual leader is particularly evident in a small kabbalistic-messianic movement founded by Avraham Zagdon. Students of his Yeshiva study Bratzlav Hasidic texts, especially the works of Zagdon himself, in the belief that these works, even more than the Talmud, bring about the rectification (tiqqun) of the soul. This movement is characterized by the creation and widespread advertising of symbols bearing the letters "AZ," the initials of Zagdon's name. This practice, with its messianic undertones, brings to mind the "Na Naḥ Naḥma Naḥman me-Uman" mantra, allegedly transmitted to R. Yisro'el Odesser by Naḥman (although this latter practice originates from the more classical Hasidic tradition of reciting "the names of Tzaddiqim"). An extraterrestrial visiting Israel and encountering the proliferation of graffiti and street performances broadcasting these phrases could be excused for thinking that they are major tenets of the Jewish religion.[36] Be that as it may, Zagdon's doctrine and activities verge on the antinomian rather than merely the anomian, as I will show.

Finally, anomian thought has even infiltrated contemporary Mussar literature (which has generally been significantly influenced by kabalistic discourse), as witnessed by a growing emphasis on the individual's inner world and criticism of routine observance of the commandments. For example, R. Shlomo Wolbe, one of the foremost personalities of the later Mussar movement, wrote, "When a person stands in judgment before his Creator, it is as if no-one else exists apart from him. . . . If he is questioned about the commandments he has performed . . . what caused him to perform them, and he says the *Tzitzit* [ritual fringes] his mother clothed him in when he was young . . . and the *Tefillin* [phylacteries] that his father bought him . . . where then is his self?"[37] This text is not merely a call for personal responsibility but a scathing criticism of orthodox society, which performs religious rituals by rote and leaves no place for individualism (the supreme value, according to Wolbe). This criticism is endorsed by the following text that specifically addresses the Yeshiva world: "There is a great problem with Yeshiva students who live in dorms for many years, constantly surrounded by others, so that they are never alone. Such students can easily lose their individuality. . . . How sad it is to see our beloved Torah students without an iota of individuality, people without history. The entire course of their lives has been mapped out by others. May God preserve us from this kind of existence."[38]

VIOLATION OF HALAKHA (ANTINOMIANISM)

The view that religious law can be violated for higher spiritual purposes (antinomianism) has many precedents in the Jewish religion and can be found in the rabbinical literature, in various kabbalistic texts (such as the fourteenth-century *Sefer Ha-Qanah*), and in the Sabbatian and Frankist movements. These antinomian tendencies range from relatively mild phenomena to more radical trends.[39]

As stated, antinomian trends have usually been marginalized or ostracized and were never part of mainstream Judaism, which emphasizes the observance of the commandments. Even the Hasidic revolution, despite its spiritual audacity, did not normally transgress the bounds of Halakha. Toward the end of the nineteenth century, antinomian discourse in the Hasidic movement intensified, especially around R. Menaḥem Mendel of Kotzk. This fascinating and controversial rabbi was rumored to have desecrated the Sabbath, although there is no way of ascertaining the source of these rumors.[40] He clearly bequeathed his antinomian doctrine to his disciple R. Mordekhai Leiner, the rebbe of Izbicha and author of *Mei Ha-Shiloaḥ* (who later split off from his teacher to set up his own dynasty).[41] Leiner, in turn, bequeathed this doctrine to his successors, such as his grandson R. Gershon Ḥanokh Leiner of Radzyn (the author of *Sod Yesharim*) and his prolific student R. Zadok Ha-Kohen of Lublin, who adapted it to their own purposes.[42]

Leiner and his successors exerted considerable influence on various twentieth-century figures whose doctrines sometimes verged on the antinomian, including Kook, Carlebach, Ginsburgh, and Mordekhai Gafni, among others.[43] If we focus our study of twentieth-century Kabbalah not only on new and radical works but also the repercussions of these works, we can see that *Mei Ha-Shiloaḥ* has become a centerpiece of the many popular Torah classes that have sprung up for the public since the end of the century.[44]

Mei Ha-Shiloaḥ, which was written in the nineteenth century, does not technically fall within the purview of this book. Nevertheless, given its great impact on current thinking, a brief review of its fascinating and complex antinomian doctrine is in order.[45] In it, Leiner posits the legitimacy of a religious act that is guided by inner intuition even if it contravenes Halakha. However, only a certain caliber of religious person who is sincerely guided by God's will (rather than by halakhic precedents) "depending on the period and time" is permitted to undertake such an act.[46] Leiner goes on to describe another type of religious person who is also capable of connecting with his inner voice, but only through a complex and painful process of "doubt" and "elucidation." Leiner suggests a series of innovative techniques designed to help such a person clarify the will of God other than that revealed through Halakha.[47] It should be noted that Leiner's mystical doctrine, as well as that of his successors, includes a national dimension, and that the clarification of God's will includes considerations of national import.[48]

Antinomianism in the Writings of Kook

I will now discuss the more latent features of antinomianism in early twentieth-century mystical thought, beginning with a review of the antinomian thought in the doctrine of a kabbalist who plays a major role in this book: R. Avraham Yizḥaq Ha-Kohen Kook. Of all twentieth-century thinkers with an antinomian proclivity, Kook was the most prominent.[49] Although he posited several justifications for violating Halakha, we will focus on only two of these: prophecy and singularity (*segula*).

The relationship between prophecy and antinomianism in Kook's thinking is something of an enigma. The starting point for attempting to decipher it is a text that was published in stages—first in a censored version (in *Orot Ha-Qodesh*), then in its complete version in a book published by Aviezer Ravitzky, then in an intermediate version in the anthology *Ḥadarav*, and finally in its original place in *Shmona Qevatzim*:[50]

> I listen and hear from the depth of my soul, from the bottom of my heart, the voice of my Master calling. And I tremble in great fear; have I descended so far as to become a false prophet, to say that God has sent me, while the word of God has not been revealed to me? And I hear the voice of my soul ringing out, the seeds of prophecy sprouting, the sons of prophets awakening, the spirit of prophecy roaming the land, seeking an outlet, seeking out mighty men filled with courage and sanctity, who know how to marshal their words and speak the truth, and recount how the word of the Lord was revealed unto them. They shall not lie or flatter, but shall speak the truth. And the spirit of truth that is more precious than gold shall elevate the people, and Israel shall stand on its feet, shall begin to feel its singularity from days of old and will know that falsehood has not prevailed, that falsehood has not clothed itself in majesty.

The most striking feature of this passage is Kook's prophetic consciousness. Equally striking, however, is the conundrum of why Kook should have questioned his own integrity ("have I descended so far as to become a false prophet?").[51] I believe the answer lies in Kook's discomfiture with his legitimization of the violation of Halakha.[52]

The parallel that Kook draws between prophecy and antinomianism comes to light in an analysis of the sequence of various texts. The publication of *Shmona Qevatzim* has enabled us to date the various texts and thereby cross-reference mystical and halakhic texts and his correspondence with his disciples. Prior to the publication of *Shmona Qevatzim* we only had the edited versions of his texts, the original dates of which were either lost or obscured, so that we were unable to construct a systematic picture of the development of Kook's thought and how this was related to external developments.

The aforementioned passage on prophecy was written in 1913. Sometime during the three preceding years, Kook wrote a passage on the relationship between Halakha and prophecy, which was first published in its censored version (in *'Arphilei Tohar*), but which I shall now quote in full (from *Shmona Qevatzim*): "It is necessary, sometimes, to violate the Torah, and when there is no one to lead the way, this occurs through a breach. In any case, it is always better that such a thing occur by accident, as it says, 'it is better to err accidentally than deliberately.' Only when prophecy exists among the Jews can this be rectified through an emergency dispensation, which takes place in a permissible manner and through an open commandment. However, when the light of prophecy is blocked, this rectification can only come about through a long-term breach that saddens the heart from an external perspective, but gladdens it from an internal perspective."[53] This radical text states that when "prophecy exists among the Jews" (a situation Kook yearned for), it will be possible to change Halakha openly. However, in the absence of prophecy (in his generation), only a "long-term breach" (a reference to the secular public) can bring about such a change, and this "breach" "gladdens [the heart] from an internal perspective."

Three years later (1916) Kook published a long halakhic responsum on whether it was permissible to sacrifice oneself to save others, with a systematic debate on what constituted an "emergency dispensation" and "migdar milta'" (that is, a decree arising from exceptional circumstances).[54] In the course of this debate, Kook distinguishes, halakhically, between a false prophet who violates commandments as a matter of course and a true prophet who does so under "exceptional circumstances" only. The fine line between a true prophet and a false one is further illustrated in the following quote: "Even a reputable prophet, who has always received the word of God as a true prophecy, needs boundaries to prevent him from erring on the side of false prophecy. . . . The prophet himself must weigh his prophecy on the scales of the Torah."[55]

Shortly after, in 1918, Kook's close disciple R. Ya'aqov Moshe Ḥarlap wrote a letter to Kook describing a vision he had at the Western Wall. In this vision, Ḥarlap received the following divine message: "You must write to the rabbi who is now abroad, with whom you are spiritually so close, that he should pray for you, and raise you to the level of Divine Inspiration (*Ruaḥ Ha-Qodesh*), just as he himself strives to attain higher levels."[56] The fact that Kook was qualified to raise Ḥarlap to the level of the Holy Spirit implies that Kook attained, or strove to attain, a level higher than that of the Holy Spirit.[57] The message continues: "Had you been together now, you would already have risen on high, for you are both affected by the external [i.e., negative] forces, especially you, to a degree that is impossible to measure. Had you, however, been together, you would have been able to totally banish these external forces, and would have risen to a high level, and raised all of being with you . . . etc. etc. etc. It is the task of you and your rabbi to rectify the entire world. Would that at least two people like you could be found in the world, etc." The profusion of "etceteras" in the text implies that Ḥarlap is willing to hint at his mentor's quasi-messianic consciousness only.[58] Ḥarlap's description of Kook's prophetic consciousness is corroborated by Dov Schwartz, who brings evidence that R. David Kohen ("Ha-Nazir"), another close disciple of Kook's, also aspired to prophecy and practiced techniques that led in that direction. This indicates that Kook was not the only one preoccupied with prophecy and that this concern was shared by members of his circle.

It is my belief that by juxtaposing the aforementioned texts, which were written over a period of a few years, we will arrive at an answer to the riddle of why Kook feared he might be a false prophet. In the first text, Kook considered the return of prophecy as legitimizing far-reaching changes in Halakha.[59] Contemporary testimonies by Kook and Ḥarlap show that Kook was referring not only to national aspirations (as the censored version implies) but to personal ones, too. Although, for the time being, he had to make do with the sense of "inner joy" at the "breach" perpetrated by secular Jews, his true aspiration was to effect lasting changes in Halakha "in a permissible manner" through the renewal of prophecy.[60] The fact that these antinomian prophetic trends were adopted by some members of the Kook circle testifies to their intensity.

And yet, Kook was afraid of crossing the boundary between true prophecy and false prophecy, according to the halakhic criteria he himself established shortly thereafter (a false prophet being someone who revoked commandments as a matter of course rather than as an emergency measure). He may have feared that his sanctioning of "long-term breaches" coupled with his desire to introduce temporary changes in Halakha (through an emergency dispensation) brought him dangerously close to the definition of a false prophet.

This interpretation is substantiated by other texts in which Kook clarifies that a prophetic violation of Halakha is permitted only as "an emergency dispensation," but that, in the Latter Days, "the Holy-One-Blessed-Be-He shall reveal the supreme glory and splendor of the Torah to the entire nation, until prophetic regulations will be perceived as ordinary Torah regulations, i.e., prophetic regulations will become Torah regulations."[61] This text demonstrates that Kook's utopian vision of introducing isolated changes to Halakha on an emergency basis had evolved into a vision of a broader replacement of Halakha through a prophetic revelation directly from God.

Despite these antinomian aspirations, Kook's formal halakhic position remained relatively conservative, especially in the 1920s and 1930s, when (in his capacity as chief rabbi of Palestine) he backtracked somewhat on his earlier vision.[62] This conservatism was exploited by his disciples to inculcate "hypernomianism"—stricter than usual adherence to the minutiae of Halakha—into the Religious-Zionist public, especially with reference to the laws of modesty.[63] Friction even arose between the Kook circle and the more classical Religious-Zionist institutions, such as Bnei Aqiva, the Yeshiva high schools, and Hesder Yeshivot, on related issues such as the mingling of the sexes, Torah studies as opposed to secular studies, army service, and the like.

Now that we have clarified the source of Kook's self-doubt, let us attempt to understand the correlation between prophecy and antinomianism through a typology of the prophetic experiences that prevailed in the Kook circle. As we saw in Chapter 2, the renewal of prophecy played a key role in Kook's vision of revival. For him, this vision was not simply an abstract or vague aspiration but, as the quasi-prophetic visions described in his manuscripts testify, an existential and empirical one.[64] Although most of these testimonies were either censored or obscured, one of them survived intact—the vision of the Prophet Elijah radiating the light of the Zionist revival—and was printed verbatim in *Orot*. This passage indicates that Kook perceived the Zionist revival not only in national-pragmatic terms but also, and even principally, in personal-prophetic terms.

Kook's prophetic consciousness revolved mainly around sight, as the prevalence of terms such as *vision*, *light*, *sight*, and *gazing* in his writings indicates. The sense of hearing, however, also played a prominent part in his prophetic consciousness. In a passage cited by Avinoam Rosenak, Kook claims he heard the voice of God in the sounds of the universe (even in the ringing of the telephone). In a parallel text, Kook equates hearing the word of God in sounds of the universe with the Holy Spirit (*Ruaḥ Ha-Qodesh*).[65] Interestingly, Kook's self-questioning regarding his integrity as a prophet occurred in the context of "hearing" the word of God. By contrast, when he describes his visionary experiences, he writes with extreme self-confidence.

In order to understand this phenomenon, we shall resort to the concepts of "primary" and "secondary" representational systems, as posited by hypnotic literature. Evidently, Kook's primary representational system was based on sight (the acronym of his name, Rei'ah, means "sight," and many of his books have the word *light* as part of their titles). This explains why his self-doubt occurred in the context of an auditory experience. Moreover, based on other parallels in Jewish and global mysticism, hearing is not as clear as seeing and therefore lends itself more to doubt.[66]

This model of representational systems may shed some light on the tensions that existed not only within Kook himself but also within the Kook circle. Academic research has already discussed the tensions between Kook and Kohen. No wonder, then, that Kohen preferred hearing to vision, as reflected in his techniques and experiences.[67] Kook, however, was a man of vision and "silence," as Kohen testified in his diary in a passage that has not yet been sufficiently analyzed:[68]

> Perhaps the turning point of my spiritual essence and life has arrived . . . the descents and ascents are equally balanced, like a scale, and in a personal manner. Through "hearing" the Holy Spirit [I advance] to the extent that it becomes a divine oracle. Logic is a ladder and conduit to prophecy. Understanding [*Binah*] is based on the voice of abstract logic and a higher spirit. . . . Not so the doctrine of the Rav [Kook]. His doctrine is based on the "light" of sanctity, an immanent light that is the source of wisdom [*Ḥokhma*], not understanding. . . . This is why the Rav has difficulty classifying his opinions systematically, for that is the task of understanding that is devoid of any visible light.[69]

In this passage, Kohen describes the difference between his doctrine (as reflected in his editing of Kook's works) and Kook's. While Kohen attempted to attain prophecy through hearing and logic, associated with the Sefira of understanding, Kook attained prophecy through vision and inspiration (light), associated with the Sefira of wisdom.[70] Thus, Kohen ascribes the difference between his approach and that of Kook (Kohen evidently feared he might lose his independence by surrendering to his rabbi's doctrine) to the different primary representational systems that guided them on their journey toward prophecy.[71]

This ties in with our main theme—the antinomian perspective in Kook's writings. Clearly, Kook's antinomianism was connected to his self-perception as the chosen Tzaddiq to whom, in a certain sense, the laws of ordinary mortals did not apply. This prophetic consciousness was not peculiar to Kook but was shared by several members of his circle, hence Kook's use of both the singular and plural forms. For example, he refers to "the great man" (whose greatness is eroded by the minutiae of Halakha) and "the bearer of a great soul" (who understands the purpose of the commandments at their highest level) who instruct the individual in his chosen path. At the same time, he refers to "the masters of higher vision," the Tzaddiqim (who need to study and pray only occasionally), or uses the hybrid phrase "those with a clear vision and great Tzaddiqim" (who suffer when dealing with the minutiae of Halakha).[72]

The hypothesis that even when Kook writes in the plural he is referring to himself is, to my mind, erroneous, since it fails to explain his frequent and explicit use of the singular (as in, for example, the text beginning "My soul" [that cannot be concealed, even in the fulfillment of Torah and God-fearingness]). More probably, Kook, alongside his intensive focus on his own needs, nature, and aspirations, was, through his use of the plural, referring to a prophetic elite that was not bound by ordinary norms.[73] As we saw in Chapter 3, this elite was responsible for rectifying the generation and was capable of predicting the historical process leading to the redemption.

The following passage ties in with the nature of the prophetic experience enjoyed by different members of the Kook circle: "The masters of higher vision" (who have attained spiritual freedom) "cannot be enslaved by any servitude, since all servitude is of flesh and blood. . . . Even recognition of God's sovereignty by the masses is servitude of flesh and blood, since God's sovereignty has lost its glory, and has been diminished by the darkness that flesh and blood have cast over its light." (Note the symbolism of light in the text.) In other words, since the "masters of higher vision" can see the light that has been diminished (or materialized, in another version) by the masses, they are allowed antinomian freedom. (The visual aspect of this process is clear.) Taking the overtly kabbalistic symbolism of this text even further, Kook appears to be saying that ordinary recognition of God's sovereignty, which parallels the Sefira of kingdom (*Malkhut*), restricts the freedom of the much higher Sefira of understanding (*Binah*), which can be attained by the masters of higher vision, who are actually situated even higher than understanding, in the visual domain of the Sefira of wisdom.[74]

As we have seen, in addition to granting antinomian freedom to members of the secret prophetic elite, Kook was also sympathetic toward overt antinomian breaches of Halakha by secular Jews. Again, although on the face of it Kook appears to be speaking in national terms, his attitude toward secularism is also tied up with his personal experiences and self-perception. Kook's liberal position on this issue is reflected in a letter to R. Ya'aqov David Wilowski ("Ridbaz"), who attacked him for his sympathy toward secular circles.[75]

This letter is effectively a defense of Kook's famous apologetics of secular Zionism.[76] He begins the letter by stating that although he would like to express "simple ideas," his ideas are in fact taken from the Kabbalah, since "one who is capable of delving into the inner secrets of the Torah is filled with the compassionate light of the compassionate Torah." He then goes on to explain his sympathy toward secular Jews by distinguishing between "singularity" and "choice":[77]

> There are two main elements that together build the sanctity of Israel and its connection with the divinity. The first is the element of "singularity" [segula], that is, the natural sanctity in the soul of Jews bequeathed by their forefathers. . . . This singularity is the intrinsic, sacred power implanted in the soul by the will of God, like any phenomenon in the real world that is immutable. . . . The second is the element of choice, which depends on good deeds and the study of Torah. The element of singularity is much larger—immeasurably larger—and holier than the element of choice. It is, however, an incontrovertible fact that this intrinsic singularity is revealed nowadays only inasmuch as the element of choice permits. Therefore, good deeds, faith, and the study of the Torah are of paramount importance. The Holy-One-Blessed-Be-He, who shows compassion in each generation, fashions the souls that are to appear in the world so that sometimes the element of choice predominates, and the element of singularity is in a hidden, unrecognized state, and sometimes the element of singularity predominates, and the element of choice is concealed. . . . In the premessianic period ['Iqvata Di-Meshiḥa] the element of singularity predominates. . . . In our generation, there are numerous souls who, despite being deficient in the element of choice and therefore guilty of bad deeds and bad opinions (Heavens forefend!), are nevertheless illuminated by the light of singularity, and therefore love the Jewish people and Eretz Israel. . . . Anyone who wishes to bring them back to the fold but lacks the deep understanding and perception that enables one to differentiate between the sacred element of singularity and the contaminated element of choice . . . could himself become contaminated, Heavens forbid. . . . Indeed, the Holy-One-Blessed-Be-He has implanted in such a person's heart the desire to shun and execrate such people [the secular Zionists], so that he should not be harmed by them.
>
> But those who are constantly engaged in inner contemplation, and are immersed in the light of the holy Torah and awe of God . . . , are familiar with the nature of intrinsic singularity, and are able, through "adherence of thought" to separate the husk [choice] from the kernel [singularity]. It is therefore incumbent upon these Torah scholars to bring these sinners—those who posses this intrinsic singularity—back to the fold. . . . As the Holy-One-Blessed-Be-He well knows, I do not attempt to bring back all sinners, but only those who, in my opinion, possess a large degree of intrinsic singularity. There are many ways of

determining this, and many more books need to be written on this subject in order to clarify even a fraction of this momentous topic.[78]

Although this text appears to address issues that are of importance to the Jewish people as a whole, such as generational differences and the need to bring secular Zionists back to the fold, it has a subtext, too.[79] This subtext states that the masters of higher vision (who practice "inner contemplation") are able to separate the "kernel" from the "husk," through "adherence of thought" (*dveiqut ha-maḥshava*—a mystical term) and through their insight into the psyche of secular Jews.[80] Kook adds the caveat that the whole issue is extremely complex and requires clarification. There is also a further personal dimension in the subtext, namely that the tendency to accept or shun "sinners" is God-given, like "singularity" (segula) itself, and is, therefore, a reflection of one's nature. Thus, in this passage, Kook once again demonstrates his basic premise—that understanding one's own psyche enables one to understand the psyche of others, and that it is such an understanding that enables one to rectify their souls. Kook is careful to add, however, that he does not attempt to bring "all sinners" back to Judaism—only those who show potential. This passage, therefore, does not contradict the sharp criticism that he, as a seasoned halakhist, leveled at the religious behavior of the pioneers.

A recently published text shows that Kook saw himself as one whose soul was endowed with a powerful degree of singularity. This explains not only his desire to bring the secular back to the fold but also his actions and self-perception:

> Who can know me? Who knows the passion of my heart that truly burns with the fire of a higher love for God? "My soul yearneth, my heart and my flesh sing for joy unto the living God" [Psalms 84:3]. Who can understand that I am unable to find interest in anything limited, due to the force of my yearning for the eternal delight of the Infinite, that "I am love-sick"? [Song of Songs 5:8]. Not only do others not know me, I do not know myself. How much must I fight with myself, in order to retain my belief in my own greatness, and to retain my belief in the greatness of my soul—a greatness that is not the result of action but rather is intrinsic and anchored in its singularity? All study and commandments are but a small reflection of its true worth.[81]

Kook is beset by conflict on two levels: between the inner man and his environment, which failed to recognize his singularity and superiority, and between his sense of superiority and his own inability to recognize his singularity.[82] The doctrine of singularity and choice almost certainly originated in Kook's own psyche, and in the conflict between his actions and his singularity, which is reflected in (and transcends) these actions. Kook's belief in the greatness of some secular Jews was a corollary of his belief in his own greatness. Therefore, he saw himself as one of the Chosen who was capable of influencing individuals with superior souls who had shaken free of normative religiosity.[83] Kook's justification of his sympathy for the secular, which he based on the distinction between "choice" (action) and "singularity" (essence), was a consequence of a process of self-analysis.

Kook's belief in his own singularity had substantial repercussions on his religious behavior. In the aforementioned passage, in which he claims that Tzaddiqim need study and pray only "occasionally," he describes these Tzaddiqim as "superior souls" who radiate a "sublime, singular light." "All the beautiful sanctity that irradiates them from outside," he continues, is only "a reflection of the reflection of light that is stored inside them."

In other words, the principle of singularity and choice served not only to defend certain secular Jews but also to justify the antinomian trends of the Chosen, such as Kook himself. The Chosen must act according to the dictates of their souls, and not according to external norms—which are simply a reflection of the soul's hidden powers. Although Kook scrupulously observed Halakha in his private life, it would appear that a certain tension existed between his halakhic scruples and his secret aspirations.[84]

In recently published texts, Kook links the concept of singularity to that of prophecy—both of which lead in antinomian directions. According to him, singular behavior is the recognition that everything that happens to one contributes to the fulfillment of one's destiny. This is reminiscent of the antinomian doctrine of the author of *Mei Ha-Shiloaḥ*, who retroactively justified even sin as a manifestation of man's profound religious intuition. It likewise ties in with Kook's perception of himself as a man with a mission—that is, as a "singular" (Chosen) person. Kook intimates that the commandments are merely the concrete expression of singularity. Therefore, even though Torah observance may have waned over the generations, singularity increased.[85] This is the basis of Kook's defense of secular Jews.

The tension that, according to Kook, existed between prophetic renewal and normative Halakha was echoed also by his contemporary, R. Hillel Zeitlin. Zeitlin saw all commandments as "the need of the hour" guiding man to the Torah's "original [higher] meaning" which is revealed through prophecy, among other means.[86] Thus, the tension between prophecy and Halakha was part of a general trend in twentieth-century Jewish mysticism.

As a fitting conclusion to this debate on Kook's antinomianism, let us consider a passage from his poetic works, which at times reflect his spirit more accurately than his philosophical works:[87]

> Expanses, expanses, expanses of God my soul desires. Imprison me not in any cage, either physical or spiritual. My soul roams over the Heavenly expanses, unrestrained by the boundaries of the heart, of deeds, ethics, logic, and manners. It roams above all of these, it soars above everything that has a name, above all pleasure, allure, and beauty, above all that is lofty and noble. "For I am love-sick" [Song of Songs 2:5].[88]

ANTINOMIAN TRENDS IN THE JEWISH UNDERGROUND

We have already discussed the controversy that raged within the Kook circle in the 1980s in connection with the Jewish Underground. Succeeding generations of the Kook circle were equally divided on the issue of antinomianism. In most cases Kook's underlying antinomianism was obscured or censored by his followers.

While rabbinical leaders who opposed the Underground accused its members of "transgressing the bounds of Halakha," sympathizers of the Underground defended their actions on halakhic grounds (in articles published in various journals, such as *Teḥumin* and *Tzipiya*). Others defended the Underground on antinomian grounds, too, some of them based on Kook's writings. Yehuda 'Etzion, for example, gave full vent to his opposition to the rabbinical establishment and to his quest for prophetic, extra-halakhic sources of inspiration, claiming that the halakhic norms stipulated by the rabbinical establishment were rooted in "diasporic Torah." In his essay on Kook titled "From the Flag of Jerusalem to the Redemption Movement," 'Etzion claimed that Kook wished to establish a Sanhedrin of sorts.[89] Furthermore, according to 'Etzion, Kook was responding to a divine order "which he heard with his inner ear" instructing man "to define his role within the Revival in general, and to devote himself to the holy mission of its implementation."

However, in 'Etzion's opinion, this prophetic consciousness was not confined to Kook only: "We shall seize all these [perceptions] from the Rav in fear and trembling." 'Etzion also claimed that in Kook's doctrine, a prophetic calling was a source of authority: "Biblical prophecies are coming true. . . . 'And I heard the voice of the Lord' (Isaiah 6:8). . . . Hearing the voice of the Lord is possible only when it is as clear as daylight, that the calling is essential. . . . This is the experience of a spiritual awakening and holy mission that we are about to embark on with trembling and awe, but also with resolve and courage." Consequently, in referring to the reinstatement of the Sanhedrin at the end of the article, 'Etzion writes that he "draws [the source of his authority] from the future" (and not from a halakhic precedent) and that "the source of our authority . . . is the holy mission itself."[90]

'Etzion's analysis of Kook's acute prophetic consciousness, and how this tied in with his wish to revive the Sanhedrin and with his antinomian thinking, is correct. 'Etzion's prophetic consciousness of a redemptive mission that invested him with a different authority to that of the "diasporic" rabbis was inspired by Kook. 'Etzion, however, evidently uneasy with his interpretation of Kook's doctrine, added the following caveat:

> I implore you, my readers, not to attribute words to me that I never said. I am not referring here to a direct prophetic revelation, but rather to a holy mission. In this context, speech and writing are mere reflections and interpretations of the holy mission, not prophecies in themselves. Even the attribute of divine inspiration—which we refer to here—is not a real prophecy but rather a 'step toward prophecy,' that is, an infrastructure for prophecy.[91]

In other words, the Underground activities initiated by 'Etzion were a "step toward prophecy" or "an infrastructure for prophecy," rather than the expression of "a direct prophetic revelation." Despite 'Etzion's caveat, however, his writings call to mind a true prophetic consciousness with an antinomian potential.[92] The late Yehuda Ḥazani—a member of the Gush Emunim leadership who defended the Underground[93]—also based his defense on Kook's writings, specifically a paragraph that appeared in a censored version of *'Arphilei Tohar*. The uncensored version of this text states that "it is necessary, sometimes, to violate the Torah," and that in the absence of prophecy, "this rectification can only come about through a long-term breach that saddens the heart from an external perspective, but gladdens it from an internal perspective."

The opponents of the Underground were forced to contend with these kinds of interpretations of Kook's doctrine. Rabbis such as Avraham Shapira and Ya'akov Ari'el turned the Underground episode into a lever for consolidating rabbinical authority against the mystical visions of people such as Yeshu'a Ben Shushan.[94] Merkaz Ha-Rav rabbis saw Ben Shushan's kabbalistic arguments as undermining the primacy of Halakha in establishing norms. One such rabbi, R. Tzevi Tau, described members of the Underground as kabbalistic theurgists: "This is a messianic cult, which wishes to bring about the redemption to the People of Israel with weapons in their hands. They entertain patently idolatrous thoughts as to how to pressurize the King of the Universe into redeeming Israel following the explosion of the mosques. These ideas have been concocted by superficial, trivial-minded students of Kabbalah, who are impelled by their curiosity to delve into sacred matters, and who, with their petty-mindedness, wreak destruction and havoc."[95]

This criticism of the members of the Underground was accompanied by calls to restrict the study of Kabbalah (partly as a reaction to the growing dissemination of

Kabbalah): "R. Tzevi Yehuda, *zatz"al* [of blessed memory], disqualified anyone who was too young, too immature, insufficiently pious, or unfamiliar with the Shas [Talmudic learning] and the *posqim* [legal codes] from studying Kabbalah, lest this impede his sound personal development" (R. Yehoshu'a Zuckerman). "Without guidance . . . not only may they [students of Kabbalah] not succeed, they may also suffer spiritual failure, as we have seen in our times, those who stumbled and caused others to stumble (a hint to the wise is enough)" (R. Avraham Shapira).[96]

Antinomian Trends in Hasidism

In this section, I would like to focus particularly on antinomian elements in the doctrine of R. Avraham Zagdon, a messianic figure on the margins of Bratzlav Hasidism in the late twentieth century. While earlier in the chapter we referred to his antinomian leanings in general, I wish to focus here on specific antinomian allusions in his books. We shall begin with the following quotation:

> The dispute over this issue throughout the generations, including our own, is not new. Ramḥal [R. Moshe Ḥayyim Luzzatto] propounded the same doctrine, as did our rabbi [R. Naḥman of Bratzlav] and all the true Tzaddiqim, and each time a dispute ensues as a result. . . . We can understand the roots of this dispute. The Torah comprises only 600,000 letters, no more. But the source of the Torah—the hidden Torah which is at the root of everything, the esoteric Torah . . . —lies in the secret of the space between these 600,000 letters of the Torah. Before there were letters, there was the space between the letters. . . . The letters themselves represent Torah today, and that is why we have experts in *Ḥoshen Mishpat* [the legal portion of the Code of Law], experts in other specialties of the Torah, experts in Kabbalah, *Pshat* [the plain sense], etc. However, they fail to see the space between the letters.[97]

In this passage, Zagdon compares his dispute with the Hasidic establishment to the polemic that arose around Luzzatto's suspected Sabbatianism. He claims to reveal the higher Torah (the Torah of redemption, as he refers to it elsewhere)—that is, the space between the letters—while others see only the letters themselves.[98] These ideas represent an anomian, if not antinomian, departure from the normative Torah-halakhic system.

Similar themes occur in another of Zagdon's books, *Or Ha-Ganuz*, where he writes, "Therefore Habakkuk came and stressed one principle! 'The righteous man shall live by his faith.' The word 'lives' is to be taken literally, as it says, 'if he merits, it becomes an elixir of life,' et cetera. Every aspect and essence of the Torah . . . all boil down to one thing: Recognition of God and His Torah. However, the Torah itself is surely not the end—but rather the means for recognizing God's unity."[99] In this text, Zagdon explicitly states that the Torah is only a means to the end, which is the Tzaddiq's faith and recognition of God. According to him, only the Torah of the Tzaddiq is an "elixir of life," while study of the minutiae of Halakha is "a deadly poison." The expression "et cetera" implies that these ideas represent merely a fraction of Zagdon's antinomian doctrine. Elsewhere, Zagdon states that Torah without the Tzaddiq is like a body without a soul. As we saw in Chapter 5, the Tzaddiq alluded to here is none other than Zagdon himself—the bearer of "a new Torah."[100]

In another of his works, Zagdon alludes to his self-perception as a Tzaddiq who has come to replace the Torah. He states that "there is no obvious sanctity or purity in him [the Tzaddiq]," since the Torah he reveals has the quality of Shabbat, in which everything is latent and inert. He has no need to reveal all "aspects of sanctity," since he is perfect in himself and requires no external manifestation of his perfection. This is because Tzaddiq has the quality of "hayitiv"—of fusion with the divinity. Therefore, the Tzaddiq is a silent figure who symbolizes the space between the letters rather than the text itself.[101] Despite the radicalism of this doctrine, from a structural perspective these views mirror the views of the Kook circle, with its emphasis on the Tzaddiq's silent inner life.

Antinomianism evolved in other Hasidic circles, too. Ohad Ezraḥi, who we referred to above in an anomian context, was excommunicated by leading rabbinical figures because of his sanctioning of premarital sex and experimentation with drugs. In practice, this kind of behavior is prevalent among National-Religious youth with a "spiritual" orientation.[102] The "hilltop youth" populating many illegal outposts in Judea and Samaria typically behave in an antinomian manner. These circles combine political radicalism (which challenges the settlers' organized leadership) with a "return to nature," a spiritual quest and violation of Halakha. The following statement, from a member of the hilltop youth, testifies to the mood in these circles: "There, on the hilltops, there is freedom, Mother, a life of truth, a life in which we worship God. Not the miserable God of the rabbis, of Father, and of the Yeshiva high school, but a living God."[103]

Antinomianism and Mysticism in the Late Twentieth Century

Historically speaking, the rise of anomian and antinomian trends in twentieth-century Jewish mysticism is related to a basic structural feature of contemporary Kabbalistic discourse: its lack of emphasis on the commandments and their reasons. Up to the twentieth century, mainstream classical Kabbalah was theurgical in its claim that one of the main reasons for the commandments was their effect on God. In recent generations, however, the theurgical element has declined, as borne out by the fact that the twentieth century did not produce any comprehensive kabbalistic work on the reasons for the commandments.[104] Moreover, statements (such as those in *Nefesh Ha-Ḥayyim* by R. Ḥayyim of Volozhin, R. Elijah of Vilna's foremost disciple) to the effect that prayer must be totally channeled toward theurgical, rather than personal, aspirations can hardly be found in twentieth-century Jewish mysticism.[105] We may conclude, therefore, that twentieth-century Kabbalah reflects the anthropocentric and individualistic nature of modern culture, which emphasizes man's rather than God's "needs."

The rise of anomian and antinomian trends in twentieth-century Kabbalah testifies to the overall erosion of Halakha as a meaningful system.[106] This erosion is the culmination of a development that began with Safedian Kabbalah and continued with the Hasidic movement in a centrifugal process whereby anomian tendencies gradually moved from the margin to the center. The rise of antinomian trends may also reflect the crisis of halakhism versus modernism. In the Israeli context, one might even venture to suggest that the Zionist movement has exploited the anti-traditionalist and antinomian potential of the messianic idea, as it existed throughout the generations.[107] As a revolutionary movement, Zionism was, to a large extent, a rebellion against Jewish Halakha as it evolved in the Diaspora. Religious-Zionism, with its dual loyalty to Zionist revolutionism and halakhic tradition, is beset by a basic tension that has accompanied the movement since its inception and is reflected in the persistence of antinomian trends within this movement, as we saw earlier.

It is too early to assess the depths of this crisis, although some indication of the continued vitality of the halakhic world can be found in the works of several contemporary thinkers— R. Joseph Ber Soloveitchik, Abraham Joshua Heschel, Yesh'ayahu Leibowitz, Eliezer Berkowitz, and David Hartman—who highlighted the importance of the halakhic system as a response to the crisis of modernism and the growing popularity of nonhalakhic approaches. The coming decades will tell to what extent their views will survive the upsurge of many nonhalakhic forms of Jewish spirituality in Israel and abroad, such as the widespread study of Torah by secular Jews, study groups formed by "formerly religious" Jews, and similar phenomena.[108] Another possible explanation for the rise of antinomian trends is that halakhic practice, like concrete sacred place, has been eroded in this era of virtual reality, in which the Internet is replacing existing forms of social organization.

From a sociological point of view, the phenomenon of newly observant Jews has influenced the development of anomian trends in the religious world, particularly in recent generations. What may have begun as the encroachment of the religious world on the secular world has, in time, become a kind of Trojan horse in which newly observant Jews, such as Yitzchak Ginsburgh and Pinḥas Raḥlin, have become spiritual leaders. Indeed, when the Ḥazara bi-Teshuva movement gained ground in the 1970s and 1980s, some ultraorthodox circles warned of the danger this might represent to the ultraorthodox world.

In conclusion, the rise of nonhalakhic trends in twentieth-century Kabbalah must be viewed in a broader comparative context, and anomianism on the individual level must be viewed as an expression of the intensification of anomian trends on a global level. For example, modern Western Sufism, unlike traditional Sufism, does not emphasize the importance of the Shari'a (Islamic law). Whereas classical Muslim mystics, such as Muḥyi al-Din ibn 'Arabi, were legalists and even decisors, modern leaders such as Idris Shah, Abdullah Dougan, or Reshad Feild are not.[109] Feild states (in the name of his master, Rauf Bulent, the founder of an important Sufi center in Britain), "We are not involved with the form of religion. We are concerned with the truths that lie silent, waiting to be revealed, within all religions."[110] These mystics are part of the phenomenon of the spread of Sufi centers in the Western world, partly as a result of the suppression of Sufism in the Islamic world by fundamentalist currents, on the one hand, and modernist currents, on the other.

It is not surprising, therefore, that Western Sufis, such as Peter Wilson (also known as Ḥakim Bey), a Sufi researcher and anarchist, are given to making antinomian statements.[111] However, even the more traditional spiritual leaders have been influenced by Western trends, such as feminism and criticism of the external forms of religion. Thus, for example, Sheikh Muhammad al-Jamal al-Rifa'i al-Shadili, a Sufi master who officiates in Ḥaram al-Sharif (the Dome of the Rock), criticizes those who "obey the Shari'a without examining its significance." The example he cites is the demand for the segregation of the sexes during prayer services. Al-Jamal rejects this demand, stating that a woman's face reflects the face of Allah, and that "there is no male or female in the essence of Allah's reality," emphasizing that his aim is to smash the "idols" created by the proponents of segregation.[112]

In the Christian world, too, key figures such as G. I. Gurdjieff in Eastern Christianity and Rudolf Steiner in Western Christianity emphasized the personal rather than ritual.[113] In the 1960s, the whole of Western Christianity was stunned when priests such as John Robinson in England advocated antinomian conduct, particularly in regard to sexual behavior.[114] Thinkers such as Robinson were influenced by "Situation Ethics," which advocated action based on intuition rather than on absolutes (somewhat on the lines of the doctrine advocated by the author of *Mei Ha-Shiloaḥ*).

This process was even more marked in Tibetan Buddhism. The forced transition of the Tibetan Buddhists to the West in the mid-twentieth century (following the brutal Chinese occupation) signaled the transition of broad sections of Tibetan spirituality from an emphasis on the ritual to an emphasis on the individual-psychological, as we see, for example, in the writings of Chögyam Trungpa or Tarthang Tulku. Note the parallel between the intensification of the psychological factor in Tibetan Buddhism and its intensification in twentieth-century Kabbalah—a phenomenon I have referred to throughout the book. Trungpa, for example, decided to translate Buddhist terminology and practice into terms of Western psychological discourse. As one of his senior students, Carolyn Rose Gimian, wrote, "His use of psychological terminology helped westerners in general to realize that Buddhist meditation was not a religious discipline as such, having nothing to do with God, and that Buddhist teachings were concerned with human experience, not the relationship between human beings and the divine." Gimian also quotes Trungpa himself in an interview on the future of Buddhism in America: "If it becomes a Church it will be a failure; if it is spiritual practice it will have strong influence in all areas—art, music and psychology."[115] (Trungpa's latter prediction indeed transpired.) Although atheistic rhetoric also exists in classical Buddhist texts, what we witness here is a conscious transition to a nontraditional—especially psychological—emphasis, as part of the rehabilitation of the Tibetan world in the West.

In this chapter, we saw a correlation between the rise of psychological-individualistic discourse and the decline of Halakha in contemporary Kabbalah. In Chapter 5 we saw how the individualistic principle that placed greater emphasis on the person of the Tzaddiq also sowed the seeds for the dissociation from sacred space (at least in the classical sense). Furthermore, the perception of the Tzaddiq is itself tied up with psychological perceptions of power, as we saw earlier. The interconnectedness of these issues indicates that they are not isolated but rather part of a process that evolved over the twentieth century. This development, which has brought about a change in the place of mysticism within the Jewish religion, is what distinguishes twentieth-century Kabbalah from classical Kabbalah.

7

THE UPSURGE OF MYSTICISM AS A JEWISH AND GLOBAL PHENOMENON

In this final chapter I focus on three processes in the development of Jewish mysticism from the start of the twenty-first century: the global process (that is, the rise of the New Age movement), changes taking place in Israel and the Jewish world in general, and changes within Jewish religious society in Israel and the world. Although I differentiate between these processes, globalization and increasing ties between Israeli society and the Jewish Diaspora have to some extent blurred the distinctions between them.

Let us first consider the global process. The globalization of spirituality, known as the New Age movement, is clearly a product of the global society that emerged after the Second World War, especially in the last decades of the twentieth century. The New Age movement embraces a vast and eclectic range of mystical, magical, and mythical trends that have become a significant feature of contemporary global culture. This is evident both in "high culture" (as testified by a growing body of research on mysticism and the influence of mysticism on famous writers such as Umberto Eco) and in "popular culture" (such as television and cinema, advertising, the Internet, fantasy and juvenile literature, self-help literature, fashion, nutrition and so on).[1] As researchers have already indicated, globalization entails the flow of cultural products between countries, especially in light of the increasing focus on the production of leisure goods in the Late Capitalist era. In this sense, the New Age can be considered a cultural import of sorts, especially from the United States.[2]

I believe that while the New Age movement has a certain degree of autonomy, it is also part of a wider process involving the weakening of the modernist metanarrative in the postmodernist era. The undermining of the supremacy of the rationalist narrative has triggered a chain reaction of sorts that has also affected modernistic forms of religion, which were to a large extent influenced by this supremacy.[3] The erosion of the rationalist narrative facilitated the emergence of a variety of religious phenomena that did not obey the dictates of rationality. Robert Forman, a leading researcher into mysticism, alluded to this phenomenon in referring to the emergence of a "grassroots spirituality" that circumvented the religious establishment and created an informal network of millions of individuals and groups involved in mystical practices. The New Age movement, therefore, is a movement that lacks central institutions, leaders, and even a shared platform. Paradoxically, the emergence of this movement has, to a large extent, been facilitated by modern information technologies, particularly the Internet.[4]

The New Age movement, thus, is one of many reactions to the decline of the modernist metanarrative. In a certain sense it is also a manifestation of the phenomenon of multiculturalism that accompanied that decline. I am referring not only to the existence of large immigrant populations from Third World countries in Western metropolises but also, and principally, to cultural imports from Third World countries to the West. As Mircea Eliade, the well-known historian of religion, pointed out several decades ago, the main feature of contemporary global religion is the loss of hegemony by the classical Western monotheistic religions in favor of an upsurge of religious phenomena, many of which originated from countries previously under Western colonial rule.[5] In its consciousness, content, style, and sources, the New Age movement reflects this evolving multicultural mosaic. No wonder, then, that mysticism in Israel today eclectically combines Jewish themes and ideas with practices originating mainly from Eastern religions.

Even the war waged by ever-declining sections of the Israeli elite against mystical and magical phenomena can be placed in this global context.[6] Zionism was part of the project of the Jews' reinstatement in the family of Western nations. The dominant Zionist cultural position is evident in its attitude toward Arab culture and immigrants from Arab countries.[7] (The Zionist movement led to the abandonment of Arabic as one of the most widely spoken languages of the Jewish public.)[8] This is not to detract from certain achievements the Zionist movement has reached in other areas.

The cultural hegemony achieved by the Israeli elites is currently facing an existential crisis because of the rise of sectorialism within Israeli society.[9] The decline of this cultural hegemony goes hand in hand with the phenomenon known as post-Zionism—namely, the erosion of Israeli society's common sociocultural agenda. The rise of popular magical Kabbalah (especially among immigrants from Arab countries) is one of the salient features of this growing threat to existing forms of cultural hegemony in Israel. National mysticism, too, with its intense particularism, threatens the "historical pact" between moderate Religious Zionism and the ruling elites in Israeli society.[10] This pact explains the ties (which are not self-evident) between large sections of Religious Zionism and rationalist trends within modern orthodoxy.[11] Religious Zionism had no choice but to join rationalist and "universalistic" (that is, Western) trends as part of its affiliation with Zionism as a Western movement. Clearly, national mysticism threatens these already frayed ties.

Thus, the new mysticism in Israel is simultaneously an expression of global processes and the reflection of a specific crisis within Israeli society. As an agent of globalization, the New Age movement in Israel imports ideas and practices that are prevalent in the Western and Jewish world. It has specific import channels, such as "spiritual" tourism to the Far East. Ties with Jews abroad or even with the many Israelis living abroad help this "flow of knowledge." On the technological level, the Internet plays a decisive role in this process. At the same time, Israel has also become an "exporter" of mystical and alternative techniques (the Feldenkrais, Paula, and Avi Greenberg systems, to name but a few). Israelis and former Israelis have become spiritual masters in India and elsewhere. National mysticism, by contrast, would like to curb the globalization process in favor of a separatist cultural position.[12]

Apart from the global context, there is a specifically Israeli context to the rise of the new mysticism in Israel. As well as the general collapse of the modernist metanarrative as a result of multiculturalism, there are a number of local factors accounting for the decline of the unifying Zionist narrative and the rise of a variety of sectors, including the religious ones. One such factor is the influence of Russian immigrants on the development of the New Age movement in Israel. Ḥamutal Bar-Yosef has already pointed out the correlation between Russian immigration and the upsurge of interest in mysticism in Israel at the start of the twentieth century.[13] Certainly, this sector exhibits a great interest in mysticism nowadays. Under Soviet rule, mystical practices were banned, and works on yoga and meditation were distributed clandestinely (although the KGB and other related institutions are known to have researched paranormal phenomena for military and intelligence purposes, and this information percolated through to the broader population).[14] The collapse of the Soviet regime was followed by a huge upsurge of interest in religion in general, and in mysticism in particular, as one of the expressions of the new freedom. The mass immigration from Russia and its sister states created a very large community of people interested in the New Age, some of whom saw it as an opportunity for rapid social mobility. It is not surprising, therefore, that many spiritual masters and healers originate from the former Soviet Union.

The empowerment of the religious public in Israel since the late 1960s and the various sociocultural processes that accompanied this empowerment also created a fertile soil for the dissemination of mystical ideas. The more confident this public became, the less it felt the need to hide the nonmodern aspects of its religiosity. Formerly, the religious world had been on the defensive and even engaged in a struggle for survival, rendering it difficult to criticize the basic assumptions of modernity. Religious writing had apologetic undertones and attempted to show that religious thought was compatible with scientific achievements and the demands of the times.

However, with the diminishing self-confidence of the ruling secular elites and the growing public legitimization of religious perceptions, premodernist (mythical, magical, and mystical) perceptions were presented more openly. Thus, the rise of Israeli mysticism can be seen as yet another expression of the collapse of the Zionist ethos of the "normalization" of the Jewish people through incorporation into the modern world. This trend goes hand in hand with the growing schism between Israeli society and academic, media, and political circles in the West, particularly in Europe, partly because of the rise of nationalist elements in Israel.

In addition to this general overview of global and Israeli processes, the rise of mysticism in Israel must be seen in the context of ongoing changes that are taking place within religious society—changes that are undermining existing structures of knowledge, power, and social organization. One of these changes is the emergence of communities on the fringes of orthodoxy, such as networks of no-longer observant Jews who continue to study Judaism and joint-study frameworks for the secular and religious (such frameworks have already been in existence for several generations and include the Shalom Hartman Institute, Elul, 'Alma College, Saḥarit, Qolot, and so on).[15] In line with Forman's analysis, these are not institutional structures as such but rather a network of associations revolving around the study of texts, frequently mystical texts.[16] In addition, the participation of many religious youngsters in New Age festivals contributes to the blurring of the boundaries of religious society and to the decline of institutions that had formerly been the focus of religious identity, such as the Yeshiva and synagogue.

As already stated, the role of newly observant leaders, such as 'Adin Steinsaltz, Yitzchak Ginsburgh, Yehoshu'a Zuckerman, Pinḥas Raḥlin, Avraham Zagdon, Ohad Ezraḥi, and others, in the contemporary Jewish mystical world should not be underestimated. The "return to Judaism" of tens of thousands of Jews since the 1970s has led to a growing preoccupation with the "internal" dimensions of Judaism. The creation of a leadership stratum of newly observant Jews has shifted power within religious society from the learned-halahkic leadership to the mystical one.[17] Furthermore, the fact that many newly observant Jews have, to some extent, remained within the secular world has also contributed to the blurring of the distinction between secular and religious society, as has the increasing religiosity of traditional populations on the periphery.[18]

The blurring of the distinction between the religious and secular sectors has been paralleled by a blurring of distinctions within the religious public itself. For example, today many Ashkenazim study with Sephardic kabbalists and seek their blessings, many Bratzlav Hasidim (such as the followers of R. Eli'ezer Berland) support Shas, and many Religious-Zionist youths study with Ginsburgh, who is affiliated with Habad. (In addition, it should be noted that Ginsburgh himself has written a commentary on a work of Sephardic Kabbalah).[19] Consequently, the phenomenon known as Ḥabakkuk (an acronym of Habad, Bratzlav, and Kook) has evolved.[20] The amalgamation of various streams in the religious world has also contributed to the penetration of mystical elements into circles that were not previously open to this kind of thinking. Examples include the influence of the Hasidic world on the Lithuanian world and the kabbalization of R. 'Ovadia Yosef, as described in the first chapter.[21]

Although academic research has dealt extensively with the phenomenon of secularization, it has not adequately considered the influence of the newly observant on Israeli society, especially in light of similar trends in the West, such as the born-again Christians in the United States.[22] In my opinion, the mass return to religion after generations of secularization is one of the most important phenomena of twentieth-century Jewish history. In practice, this phenomenon was anticipated already in the first part of the century by R. Avraham Yizḥaq Ha-Kohen Kook, who considered himself "the Poet of Return" and predicted that the material development of the land would lead to a "spiritual rebellion" that would restore the Jewish spirit to the Zionist movement.[23] Similarly, R. Hillel Zeitlin saw his journey "on the border of two worlds" (from faith to heresy and back to faith) as a paradigm of sorts for a new kind of religious creativity.[24]

Another change within contemporary religious society relates to the curriculum in Yeshivot. Yeshivot not only are major national institutions but also constitute fertile ground for the spread of new trends and leaders. As noted in Chapter 1, in certain Yeshivot there has been a significant transition from a curriculum based on the study of Halakha to one based on the study of mystical texts.[25] Kabbalah and Hasidism, one could say, have usurped the place not only of the study of Mussar but also of the analytical study of Talmud as foci of spiritual enlightenment. Another innovation in the Yeshiva world is the emergence of poetry and creative-writing workshops, some of which exhibit a certain political, religious, and even sexual audacity. (The poet Yonadav Qaploun, a former student of Ginsburgh's, has been instrumental in this process.)[26] An increasing number of religious pedagogues call for the inclusion of yoga or meditation in the curriculum of State-run religious schools and even in their prayer services. Likewise, many educators conduct "soul talks" with their pupils, a practice that was not formerly prevalent in these frameworks.[27] Such phenomena, which indicate a shift toward the psychological and individual, constitute fertile soil for the assimilation of twentieth-century Kabbalah, in which, as we have seen, these elements predominate.

Religious society is not content to passively assimilate mystical elements from the global New Age movement. As well as the active participation by many religious youths in courses on alternative medicine, alternative festivals, and the like, considerable effort is expended into channeling the New Age movement into more "Jewish" channels, by exploiting the great interest in Kabbalah and Hasidism by secular Jews.[28] The dissociation of Kabbalah from halakhic commitment (see Chapter 6) has rendered contemporary Jewish mysticism more palatable to the secular elites. The New Age movement has helped the religious public penetrate the foci of power controlled by these elites, especially the media.

For example, efforts are being made to provide Israeli backpackers in India with a Jewish experience.[29] Religious thinkers such as Ezraḥi write about Kabbalah in New Age journals, such as *Ḥayyim Aḥerim*.[30] More recently, mystical leaflets on the weekly Torah portion are being distributed in synagogues.[31] Rebbes and kabbalists try to meet with spiritual masters from the East and sometimes even create a common language.[32] The many newly observant disseminators of New Age practices claim that the study of tai chi or Chinese medicine will inevitably lead to the study of Torah and performance of the mitzvot.[33] The fact that religious and secular youths, male and female alike, are brought together by shared New Age activities also contributes to the erosion of sociocultural boundaries between religious and secular society in contemporary Israel.

The "proselytization" of the New Age movement in Israel can be viewed as part of a more general attempt by the Religious-Zionist sector to penetrate centers of power. Spiritual ideas that are not constrained by Torah and mitzvot are perceived as effective in bringing secular society closer to Judaism.[34] The prevalence of kabbalistic and Hasidic ideas is part of the religious public's ongoing and successful campaign to carve themselves a niche in the media, which it considers an important focus of power.

It is my contention that the New Age movement is a new sector that crosses the boundaries between existing sectors and is characterized by new forms of social organization.[35] This sector is currently competing with other sectors to penetrate the social, cultural, and economic fabric of contemporary life in Israel.[36] Social movements are usually engaged in a struggle over management of resources. In postindustrial society, as has already been claimed by scholars, these resources are mostly symbolic and even, to some extent, virtual. Thus, despite the establishment of parties such as the Law of Nature party and the Green Leaf party, the New Age movement (like the Kook circle) does not aspire to political or military hegemony, but instead wishes to penetrate Israeli consciousness and to achieve maximum representation.[37] One of the more obvious signs of the New Age's wish to penetrate the centers of cultural hegemony is the way it uses science to back its claims. Thus, various authors have attempted to demonstrate an affiliation between the new physics and mystical "truths," including the Kabbalah.[38] These attempts are designed to grant mystical ideas the same cultural aura that science enjoys. More recently, the declining popularity of science fiction literature and the growing popularity of fantasy literature indicates that the New Age movement no longer feels a strong need for scientific legitimacy and that it already feels that it has carved a niche for itself in the cultural world.

The New Mysticism: Social and Economic Dimensions

> The Dharma is used for personal gain
> And the river of materialism has burst its banks.
> —Chögyam Trungpa, *The Sadhana of Mahamudra*

The New Age has a clearly social as well as ideological dimension. In view of Forman's aforementioned analysis, a brief overview of the new social networks that make up the New Age movement is in order. It should be noted that, given the relative lack of systematic research on the social psychology of the New Age movement, the following analysis is to a large extent original.[39] Many examples in the discussion that follows are taken from the Israeli context, in accordance with the book's general focus. However, it is in the social dimensions of the new mysticism that the phenomenon of globalization is most evident. Therefore, it is impossible to distinguish between local and global trends in this discussion.[40]

The New Age movement is composed of social networks that may be termed microcircles, such as study groups, classes, therapeutic encounters of various sorts, workshops, and encounters with channelers or spiritual masters. These groups are often advertised in New Age journals, in health food stores, or on the Internet, and sometimes by word of mouth.[41] When a group is set up, it usually establishes branches in multiple cities, where advanced students teach. In the formative phase, ties are usually established with masters or an institution abroad that sends masters over to conduct follow-up workshops or award certificates. Often, independent Internet sites are opened at this stage.

The group feeling is reinforced by visual symbols (such as AZ stickers for followers of Zagdon, and "Na Naḥ Naḥma Naḥman me-Uman" stickers for followers of R. Yisro'el Odesser, the Ba'al Ha-Peteq), the creation of an internal lexicon, and the dissemination of "internal" written material and stories about the masters (and their masters), which together form a kind of group lore.[42] The establishment of mystical groups within the New Age movement is, effectively, the realization of the ambition of more traditional personalities in the early twentieth century, such as Zeitlin or R. Qalonymus Qalman Shapira, to set up mystical fellowships.

These networks, in turn, create wider circles. Sometimes they are incorporated into schools of alternative medicine or journals, such as *Ḥayyim Aḥerim*, that have tens of thousands of readers.[43] The articles published in these journals differ from the run-of-the-mill journalistic writing in that they are almost always upbeat, in the positive spirit of the New Age movement. The New Age festivals, at which "spiritual" music is played, crystals, CDs, and books are sold, and workshops are conducted, also constitute a wider circle. At these events, which are attended by scores of Israelis, social (including romantic) and economic ties are established between groups and individuals.

A common denominator of all these circles is the transition from an "ordinary" identity to a "mystical" or "spiritual" one.[44] The activities of these circles strengthen the psychological and social legitimacy of a new way of life. As part of this spiritual journey, members of the circles begin incorporating various spiritual techniques into their daily lives. (To this end, they may reduce time spent at work or on media consumption, political activity, and social and family ties.) Members of the New Age movement change their mode of attire and nutritional habits and often prefer alternative medicine to conventional medicine. They change their patterns of consumption (they tend to purchase mystical products) and their written and spoken vocabulary. Expressions such as "tuning in," "flowing with," "being Shanti" (or "being peaceful," the equivalent of "becoming stronger [in religion]"), "being in return [to Judaism]," and "seeing the light" have become catchwords of the New Age movement, together with a "looser" body language. This vocabulary, it should be noted, has also filtered through to circles that do not necessarily share these spiritual concerns.[45]

These changes in social identity and behavior sometimes have political repercussions: The newly observant (or religious neophytes) tend to support right-wing and religious parties, while many members of secular New Age circles refrain from voting altogether or support fringe parties such as the Law of Nature party or the Green Leaf party, which do not even reach the threshold for winning a legislative seat.[46] Political changes of this kind are the expression of a certain dissociation from the ordinary public arena—a dissociation that begins with cumulative changes in day-to-day life and social behavior.

I will now turn to the politics of information and power that characterizes the social structure of the New Age movement.[47] In public discourse, some New Age movements (such as Emin and Scientology) are often referred to as sects, because they advocate social seclusion, economic subjugation, and a leadership cult. It is sometimes difficult to determine the exact boundaries between a sect, a new religious movement, or any other spiritual movement.[48] Many New Age movements have sectarian elements. Although the New Age rhetoric preaches being true to oneself and discarding patterns and molds forced on one by family, society, or the establishment, many mystical movements preach some degree of obedience to the "master" or even to "senior students." (This emphasis on the leader's power is evident in many of the texts discussed in the kabbalistic context, as we saw in Chapters 4 and 5.)

Similarly, despite general criticism of the establishment and of Western culture, and despite a general commitment to promoting nature, harmony, and peace, the movements' spiritual activity is not generally translated into a political agenda. On the contrary, the emphasis is on the internal, and the external-political plane is seen as a kind of illusion. While we observed this emphasis on the internal in relation to the Kook movement, it is also a feature of many secular circles. These circles frequently claim that "peace begins within," and that, therefore, spiritual, not public, activity is the solution to political and social problems.

Alongside this apolitical position, the search for an authority figure is accompanied by a desire for leadership based on the personal power of the "One," the "King," or the "Sorcerer" (as in *The Matrix*, *The Lord of the Rings* [particularly *The*

Return of the King], *Harry Potter*, and other popular myths).[49] This search for an authority figure would seem to reflect a consensus that Western democracy is morally bankrupt and unable to provide "spiritual" leaders or answers to existing problems—hence the strong correlation between mysticism and radical politics we observed in the Kook and Habad circles and, on the global level, the similarities often found between New Age circles and neo-Fascist movements.[50] While the political repercussions of the new mysticism are discussed below in the economic context, here I will focus on the sociopsychological dimensions of abandoning "normal politics" in favor of "mystical politics."

The attempt to achieve the status of "master" or "healer" is an important stage in the process of acquiring a mystical identity. One of the characteristics of the New Age movement is the relatively easy transition from the status of pupil or consumer to a higher status, although usually a clear hierarchy is preserved between experienced masters and novices. In certain New Age groups, there even seem to be more masters than seekers. While the attempt to climb the mystical hierarchy obviously has economic repercussions, it also has a bearing on the issue of identity. Frequently, entry to the New Age world is motivated by the wish to create a new identity that is respected and has status, and being awarded various titles in the course of one's mystical pursuits helps implement this desire.[51]

The stages of the process can be clearly demonstrated on a global plane by the example of Steven Russell, a London-born Jew who began his career as a practitioner of Chinese medicine and has become a media guru, particularly in England, where he is known as the "barefoot doctor." Russell writes a column in one of England's foremost papers (*The Observer*), appears frequently on popular television shows, runs a sophisticated Web site, produces music CDs and DVDs, has written a number of best sellers, and markets "natural" products.[52] His clients include celebrities such as Madonna. In his books, Russell presents his success as an example of how the use of "Daoist" tools helps one achieve wealth and fame.[53] Such tools include the use of a variety of media channels that advertise and market each other, and the consolidation of a fluid media image (in his case, he is helped by his "trade name," which paradoxically suggests simplicity).

Despite this example, we must avoid the facile conclusion that the construction of a new mystical identity is a smooth linear process. The dissociation from previous reference groups and from habitual ways of life entails many crises. A quantitative and qualitative psychological study is needed to examine the special psychological problems that accompany the sharp transition to intensive spiritual activity in New Age circles, and the effects that this transition has on family life.[54] There is a certain parallel here to the process of "returning to religion," despite obvious differences (the New Age movement is not a religion in the ordinary sense). The crises that may accompany the process of acquiring a new identity, and the antagonism former social reference groups may exhibit, make the group even more important for the success of this project.

The transformation of identity brings us to the psychological component of the New Age experience. In Foucault's language, New Age practices can be seen as "technologies of the self" that create personality structures of a new kind.[55] Since, as yet, no detailed and comprehensive analysis has been written of the social psychology of the New Age movement, the discussion that follows is tentative rather than empirical. To the best of my knowledge, there is no substantial body of published research of this kind, apart from Philip Wexler's pioneering study (and brief observations by others), so I cannot refer much to existing research.[56] In this particular case, the research field itself is still being formed.

Commentators who sympathize with the New Age movement describe it as an authentic answer to the alienation, loneliness, and confusion experienced by contemporary Westerners.[57] This analysis ties in with studies that emphasize the "empty self" of the contemporary personality and see the New Age as an attempt to fill this existential vacuum.[58] Less sympathetic commentators tend to see it as part of "the culture of narcissism" that has overtaken members of the middle classes who discard social and political responsibility in favor of "self-development."[59]

This interpretation is supported by the status that entertainment enjoys within New Age culture. An advertisement for a new coffee house in Jerusalem recently promised "Kabbalah, Hasidism, Zionism, Judaism, and Fun." One wonders how R. Ḥayyim of Volozhin (who wrote, "The test of whether a person is acting sincerely, or is being led astray by his baser impulses, is whether the thing he wants to do offers no pleasure or prestige, and seems to him a mitzva") or the second rebbe of Habad, R. Dov Baer (who condemned the glorification of enthusiasm stemming from "the life of the flesh") would have reacted to this advertisement.[60] Be that as it may, the hedonist nature of the postmodernist world has led to a significant change in contemporary Kabbalah's attitude toward pleasure. Perhaps the foundations of this change were laid by R. Yehuda Leib Ha-Levi Ashlag, who developed a theurgy of pleasure, and by Kook, who emphasized the "pleasure principle" in his writings.[61]

Ascetic spiritual leaders, such as R. Dov Kook of Tiberias, R. Eli'ezer Berland, and R. Don Segal, do exist today, too, although they are not generally identified with kabbalistic discourse.[62] This metamorphosis of the nature of kabbalistic practice is part of "the economics of pleasure" in late capitalism, in which the impetus for consumerism establishes a "pleasure imperative."[63] Pleasure has become a hallmark of success, and it is not fortuitous that the singer who declared that she was a "Material Girl" and produced the album *Erotica* (in which she asks her lover "to put me into a [sexual] trance") now dabbles in Kabbalah.

The emphasis on pleasure goes hand in hand with the emphasis on the body and cultivation of the body within the New Age culture. In contemporary spiritual and mystical practices, physical exercise is perceived as more or less vital, in contrast to the strongly ascetic imperative of freedom from—or even suppression of—the body often prevalent in classical mysticism. Alongside the large-scale importation of physical and sexual techniques from the East (such as tantra, yoga, chi gong, and tai chi), the New Age has created numerous innovative movement techniques, body therapies, and body awareness techniques (such as bioenergetics, holistic massage, Feldenkrais, and Rolfing, to name but a few).[64] Kabbalah also played a part in this process, as testified by Kook's endorsement of physical exercise (see Chapter 3), which has influenced contemporary discourse regarding the body and is disseminated by writers such as Ohad Ezraḥi and Dvora Nov.[65]

There is also a passive dimension to New Age–type spirituality. The popularity of "channeling" and other automatic writing and speaking techniques testifies to the yearning for possession-trance situations in which the individual becomes a kind of vessel or conduit for subconscious or other forces.[66] Likewise, the widespread use of drugs and other psychotropic substances, which was particularly prevalent in the 1960s (and is still popular in certain circles), testifies to the wish to lose control and blur the boundaries of self.[67] The use of self-possession techniques and psychotropic substances are both related to the growing popularity of Shamanism, as we saw in Chapter 5.

A psychological analysis of the new mysticism must take into account the centrality of psychological discourse in twentieth-century Kabbalah and in the New Age. In this context, it should be noted that, unlike the claim (which is erroneous, in my opinion) that Sigmund Freud's doctrine was influenced by Kabbalah, solid historical proof exists to the effect that Freud influenced the fifth Habad rebbe, R. Shalom Baer Shneurson, at the start of the century. R. Shalom Baer's conversations with the father of psychoanalysis evidently influenced Habad Hasidism's transition from study to action.[68] By contrast, the influence of Kabbalah on Jung, who documents a vision in which he appears as the Zoharic hero R. Shimon Bar Yoḥai, is well known.[69] Note also the contemporary attempts to create a synthesis between selections from kabbalistic discourse and Jungian theories (Micha Ankori) or other psychological theories (Mordekhai Rottenberg). The neo-Hasidic thinker R. Zalman Shalomi-Schachter even wrote a book proposing a model of spiritual and psychological counseling based on Hasidism.[70] To these should be added the Jungian writings of Shimon Ben Ze'ev Halevi (previously Warren Kenton), who is affiliated with Christian Kabbalah, which include a detailed analysis of social psychology according to the Kabbalah.[71] The discourse on psychology and Kabbalah can be compared to the copious discourse on psychology and Buddhism in the United States (see, especially, Daniel Goleman's works).

Finally, a review of the political economy of the New Age movement is in order. Current research has not yet given due importance to the economic dimension of the New Age movement in general, and of the new Israeli mysticism in particular. Kabbalah has become a kind of springboard for megastars wishing to enhance their public image. Conversely, organizations with a commercial interest, such as the Kabbalah Center, use the names of these celebrities in order to boost the reputation of the product known as Kabbalah. The weighty economic interests invested in the New Age advertise and market "mystical products" such as festivals, books, CDs, journals, lectures, therapies, schools of alternative studies, workshops, magical objects (for example, crystals), and the like.[72] Sometimes these economic interests exist autonomously, but in most cases they are linked to other economic interests.

Mystical practices such as yoga, chi gong, and meditation appear in advertisements. Mystical and magical themes appear in television shows and movies (such as *The X-Files* and *The Sixth Sense*).[73] Lectures on mysticism occupy an important place in the huge industry of para-academic enrichment and count as in-service training for teachers and civil servants. Various capitalists use New Age ideas in order to further their economic interests, the most famous Israeli example being tycoon Sherri Erison, who, according to media reports, even pressured the staff of Bank Hapoalim to participate in "Peace Begins within Me" workshops.[74] The interplay between mysticism and economics has even given rise to a new cadre of "spiritual coaches," who counsel high-tech tycoons and media stars in the spirit of the New Age.

Several "mystical empires" exist in the early twenty-first century capitalist economy, such as the Osho Rajyoga Meditation Center in Poona, India, and its branches; the various organizations established by Chögyam Trungpa; and the extremely lucrative activities of the Daoist master Mantak Chia. This prolific economic activity cannot fail to deflect the focus in organizations of this kind from spiritual practice to financial, consumerist, organizational, and marketing activities.[75] It is interesting that Trungpa himself, who founded organizations of this kind, warned against the dangers of "spiritual materialism" back in the 1970s. Trungpa used this phrase to refer not only to the commercialization of ideas or spiritual practices but also to the more covert practice of using spirituality to enhance one's ego and "shopping" in the spiritual world. Trungpa alluded to the fact that the sincere desire for spirituality is exploited by charlatans to obtain money and fame.[76]

It is no wonder, then, that some researchers describe the New Age as "the spiritual logic of late Capitalism."[77] Nor is it surprising that researchers of culture in France, such as Ilias Yocaris, in attempting to analyze the enormous commercial success of books such as the *Harry Potter* series, have exposed the promotion of private initiative in literature of this kind.[78] The claim being made here, which has been brought to the Israeli public in popular articles by Gadi Taub among others, is that the new spirituality is an individualistic and even egocentric escape from the disintegrating public domain, which serves the interests of advocates of privatization.

Because of the connection between capital and mysticism, the New Age has created a kind of class-based stratification, whereby the poor and marginal members of society turn to popular (usually Oriental) kabbalists while the affluent members of society resort to more expensive and prestigious organizations, such as the Kabbalah Center.[79] Various kinds of mystical activities are effectively restricted to high-income, highly educated people because they entail a high financial investment, such as trips abroad to attend courses; participation in masters' workshops in Israel that are taught in English, where the participants pay the cost of the master's trip and stay; and the purchase of pricey books and other imported products.[80]

Some New Age organizations (such as those that teach the Reiki technique) provide expensive but usually brief "training," thereby fulfilling the need for instant satisfaction that is a feature of the capitalist age.[81] In other circles (such as some branches of the Kabbalah Center or representatives of Ouspensky's Fourth Way in Israel), participation in "inner circles" is rumored to be conditional on the "contribution" of a fixed percentage of one's salary. (In the spirit of the New Age belief in the influence of mind over matter, those who are deterred by these steep fees are considered as having an internal problem.)

In a certain sense, the New Age has created a new kind of social and class mobility. Training in alternative medicine, channeling, spiritual counseling, and so on opens the way for bypassing the conventional and complex structures that provide symbolic and real capital. In this way, it is possible to climb the economic ladder without higher education or professional training, sometimes simply by taking a few weekend courses. Many members of the middle class have acquired a second career in one of the New Age "professions," which supplements and sometimes even replaces an unsatisfactory or unprofitable job. Working in the field of New Age therapies and techniques suits the growing trend of working from home. For many youngsters, the study of alternative medicine, the martial arts, or meditation in Israel and elsewhere have become attractive alternatives to a university degree, which is perceived as irrelevant and bureaucratic.

The New Age movement also has a prominent gender dimension because of the prevalence of female teachers, as Forman has pointed out. Evidently, the New Age movement has opened up new channels of mobility for women.[82] Entire New Age professions (such as channeling or aromatherapy) are effectively "gendered" and monopolized by women. This trend has even penetrated the new Kabbalah: as well as the spiritual teachers ordained by R. Shlomo Carlebach, there was a popular female Kabbalah teacher, Yemima Avital, whose technique became known as the "Yemima method." This represents a departure from a long tradition that almost totally barred women from teaching Kabbalah.[83] This trend has also percolated into ostensibly traditional circles. For example, the seventh rebbe of Habad encouraged teaching "the interiority of the Torah" to women, in the framework of the messianic belief that the rising status of women was one of the precursors of redemption.[84] As far as discourse is concerned, the plethora of women who are researching and even teaching mysticism has intensified and propagated the debate on "the female aspect of divinity," or the Shekhina, in the Jewish context.[85] Thus, the new mysticism has enabled not only class mobility but also gender mobility.[86]

Although attempts by the authorities (in conjunction with institutes of alternative medicine) to regulate the field of alternative medicine reflect the economic establishment's concern with this trend, these attempts are unlikely to halt the phenomenon. The flexibility and informality of the New Age movement enables it to elude regulation of its activities. Thus, if the establishment decides to regulate "healing" activities, these simply become "counseling" activities ("co-counseling," for example), and if the establishment decides to regulate "counseling" activities, these would simply be renamed "advice" or even "spiritual conversations."

In contrast to this analysis, scholars such as Forman and Wexler have presented a more positive picture of the sociology of the new mysticism. They describe the New Age as an alternative form of social organization based on networks, which circumvents standard forms of public and political activity. Wexler sees the New Age movement as a revitalization trend designed to meet needs arising from the decline of the modernist social structure.[87] As such, the new mysticism may be seen as an emergent practice that rejects modern social structures (as reflected in dress, health, language, bodily movement, work, identity, and the like). At the psychological level, Wexler claims that the new spiritual movements revitalize the self that has been eroded by the mechanistic production processes of the capitalist economy. He even views the practice of investing a guru or master with special powers in a positive light, since, according to his book, these powers have a reciprocal effect on their followers and revitalize them.

Others still, basing their views on the doctrine of Herbert Marcuse (of the Frankfurt school of social criticism), argue that even if the New Age movement began as an organized protest against existing structures of knowledge and power, it has been swiftly co-opted by market forces, which have managed to turn mysticism into a commodity and neutralize any threat it might present to the existing socioeconomic order. Thus, fast-food chains offer "health menus," fitness clubs offer yoga classes, and cable television offers "mystical" channels—all backed by capitalists. According to this analysis, the growing incursion of mystical ideas and practices into the medical system, the education system, and the workplace (and even into academic research) is a double-edged sword.[88] As well as reflecting the mysticization of society, it may also reflect the co-option and containment of the radical and innovative elements that are inherent in the mystical experience.

I will conclude this discussion with a short review of the relationship between the New Age movement and traditional religion. Despite the new mysticism's penetration of classical religious institutions such as Yeshivot and synagogues (in the Jewish context), there is still much tension between the ancient and emergent forms of social organization. Criticism of the dissemination of Kabbalah in various circles (see Chapter 1) is one expression of this tension. In 2003, the Vatican published a report condemning the New Age movement, which it described as the revival of the Gnostic heresy.[89] This report is one of many attacks on the New Age movement by Christians. Conversely, New Age circles flaunt the slogan "ABC (Anything But Church)" and openly express their desire for a return to pagan forms of religiosity.[90] Many teachers in the New Age movement claim to have had personal revelations and to therefore no longer require tradition or a standard religion.[91] In Chapter 6, I quoted similar ideas espoused by individuals who were averse to established Jewish religiosity, such as the followers of Zagdon or the hilltop youth.

The New Age and Postmodernism

In the introduction to this chapter, I pointed out the interrelationship between the rise in mysticism and the erosion of rationalist, modernist metanarratives. On this matter, I share the view of a number of researchers, such as Slavoj Žižek, that the sociocultural structures that emerged in the postmodern reality constituted fertile soil for New Age therapies.[92] In particular, postmodern relativism helped promote the eclecticism of the New Age movement. This eclecticism enables postmodernism to entertain yearnings for premodernist forms of belief or social organization, such as magic and monarchism. In my opinion, therefore, postmodernism should not be seen as a form of fascism, as has sometimes been claimed, simply because it challenges the prevailing beliefs of modernism. By definition, postmodernism cannot be encapsulated by a single definition.

The analysis that links the New Age and postmodernism has been endorsed also by some proponents of the new Jewish mysticism, such as R. Shimon Gershon Rosenberg ("Shagar"), head of the Siaḥ Yizḥaq Yeshiva and an influential figure in the National-Religious sector. Shagar not only maintained that there is a link between the New Age and postmodernism but even entertained the possibility that the new mysticism and postmodernism may bring about the revitalization of the Jewish religion,[93] as the following text indicates: "The postmodernist (and post-Zionist) crisis shall, in my opinion, open the way to the renewal of mysticism. This is the point where neo-Hasidism links up with R. Kook's vision of the renewal of prophecy in Eretz Israel. . . . Part of this process . . . is entailed in the far-reaching social changes that humanity is undergoing, such as globalization and feminization. . . . As believing Jews, we explain these changes in the context of the prophetic-kabbalistic vision of redemption. . . . I foresee, in the not too distant future, a spiritual explosion of an intensity and significance that matches the explosion of Hasidism itself in the period of the Ba'al Shem Tov and his disciples."[94]

The assumption in this text (and in Shagar's entire book) is that the collapse of the modernist narratives will usher in a spiritual era of greater openness toward mystical beliefs and experiences, enabling the revitalization of the religious world. Therefore, he saw the rebellion of young people who wish "to discover and realize themselves" in the spirit of the New Age as a protest against "a halakhic existence that is shackled by absolute, black-and-white ideologies"—a protest that "is encouraged by the [postmodernist] spirit of the times that does not trust any one ideology." Again, Shagar saw this protest as containing positive seeds, since it is "the nihilistic trend in this generation" that "leads to mysticism." In other words, "the internalization of postmodernist pluralism has fertilized the mystical elements of Religious Zionism and infused them with the breath of life." Despite the apparent contradiction between postmodernism—a movement that was created by secular intellectuals—and the new mysticism, Shagar saw a "close relationship" between the two.[95]

Shagar introduced a kabbalistic dimension into this dialectic process: "Postmodernist deconstructionism 'breaks the vessels' by claiming that reality is simply a cultural construct. But according to the kabalistic explanation, it is this very 'breaking of the vessels' that renders them more refined and fluid." Since Kabbalah "has always described alternative worlds," Shagar found a connection between the kabbalistic perception of the world and contemporary themes in fantasy literature, and concluded that "only a slight mental trigger is required to effect the transition from postmodern literature to mystical concepts." According to him, "the evolving pluralistic and illusory environment creates a fertile soil for the spread of mysticism."[96] This approach can be described as a mystical constructivism that co-opts postmodernism.

As stated, Shagar drew a parallel between the contemporary mystical awakening and the mystical awakening that preceded Hasidism, and therefore was not troubled by its anomian and antinomian manifestations. Nor was he deterred by the fact that some members of the "successor generation" and the hilltop youth in the territories "are seeking Indian 'Shanti' seasoned with mysticism, sometimes even through drugs, as they themselves admit."[97] Shagar's tolerance of antinomian phenomena that are a product, to his way of thinking, of the interplay between the New Age and postmodernism was dictated by his sense that the postmodern situation favors the development of mysticism more than classical modernity.[98] These ideas constitute the germ of a "postmodern Jewish mysticism" that provides a clearer formulation of the feelings that are reflected in the variety of social and ideological phenomena spawned by the postmodern reality. In my opinion, Shagar's thinking is closer to the spirit of postmodernism as a social fabric than the rationalist thinkers whom some researchers saw as a response to postmodernism.[99]

By contrast, members of the fourth generation of the Kook circle are far less positive about postmodernism. R. Yosef Kelner, a disciple and friend of R. Tzevi Yisra'el Tau's who wields great influence in the premilitary academies in Judea and Samaria (Yesha), wrote a tract condemning postmodernism. He describes postmodernist relativism as a "disease," the antithesis of the "absolutism" of Kook's national or "general" spirit.[100] Kelner bases this view on his national psychological perception, as discussed throughout this book. Indeed, his allusion to postmodernism as a disease is based on the claim that pluralism goes hand in hand with "a lack of spiritual depth and the absence of a firm foundation in the depths of one's soul."[101] Obviously, Kelner belongs to the proponents of "absolute, black-and-white ideologies" whom Shagar condemned.[102]

Again, unlike the assumptions of both Shagar and Kelner, I view postmodernism less as a system of ideas than as a kind of socioeconomic organization, or as a social and psychological "habitus" (in the sense that Pierre Bourdieu gave the term).[103] In other words, modernism gave rise to a set of personal and social behaviors, while technological, economic, and social changes have undermined these behaviors. The New Age provides one alternative, out of many, to the modernist social-psychological construct.

The New Age and Twentieth-Century Kabbalah

The main sanctity and importance of the study of Kabbalah is to speak [to the realms] above, not below.

—Shlomo Elyashiv

In this section I will consider the question of continuity between late twentieth-century Kabbalistic phenomena associated with the New Age movement and early twentieth-century Kabbalistic trends associated with the more classical and conservative forms of kabbalistic discourse. In other words, what is the relationship between postmodernist Kabbalah and the modernist Kabbalah of the early century, which was to a greater extent a continuation of the Kabbalah of previous centuries? As far as the Ashlag circle is concerned, the link between the beginning and end of the century is fairly clear. Members of the third generation of this circle continue to disseminate Kabbalah and subject it to the psychological insights of their founder, even if the latter would not have approved of the commercialization that has accompanied this process. Some of Kook's successors, by contrast, categorically deny any connection between their founder's doctrine and contemporary mysticism, and constitute the vanguard of the opposition to the New Age movement. Others, however, such as Shagar and his followers, see the penetration of the New Age into the National-Religious camp as the clear implementation of Kook's vision. Based on our analysis of the antinomian and individualistic elements in Kook's doctrine, it would be hard to completely reject such an interpretation.

Moreover, the preference of the inner realm to the political realm, and the belief in the mind's ability to affect the external reality that characterized the third generation of the Kook circle, closely resembles processes occurring within New Age circles, despite also reflecting Kook's ideas. It is not surprising, therefore, that prior to the disengagement from the Katif settlement bloc, pamphlets were distributed there offering relaxation techniques in the spirit of meditation and yoga.[104] Ginsburgh's kabbalistic doctrine, too, while innovative, also continued the insights of the last few rebbes of Habad at the start of the century. Conversely, antinomian and individualistic New Age circles, such as the followers of Carlebach, resort to earlier texts, such as the writings of R. Qalonymus Qalman Shapira or even *Mei Ha-Shiloaḥ*, a late nineteenth-century work.

In summarizing the continuity-innovation dichotomy in twentieth-century Kabbalah, I would like to draw the reader's attention to several distinctions. We already saw that twentieth-century Kabbalah is not, on the whole, theurgical in its orientation. I suggested several reasons for this, the main one being its dissociation from the halakhic system. In kabbalistic works of this period, there are hardly any attempts by kabbalists to explain Talmudic-Halakhic literature through the

Kabbalah (as, for example, R. Nathan of Nemirov did in *Liqutei Halakhot*). This trend is particularly evident today, as certain kabbalistic circles turn to the secular and even non-Jewish worlds—a phenomenon that may yet facilitate a synthesis between Jewish and non-Jewish forms of kabbalistic writing.[105] Twentieth-century Kabbalah has not only moved away from theurgy, it has likewise steered clear of theosophy. Apart from R. Shlomo Elyashiv and certain Sephardic kabbalists, most twentieth-century Jewish mystics have replaced the kabbalistic interpretation of the structure of the heavenly realm with a psychological or political interpretation. Thus, Elyashiv's staunch assertion at the start of this section, according to which the sanctity of Kabbalah arises precisely from its focus on the heavenly realm rather than on the human realm, still belongs to classical Kabbalah.

The decline of the theurgical-theosophical aspect of Kabbalah is paralleled by a growing focus on ecstasy and mystical experience in twentieth-century Kabbalah, as witnessed by the renewed interest in R. Abraham Abulafia in Israel and elsewhere, both among academics and kabbalists.[106] Indeed, this tremendous interest in Abulafia has turned him into a kind of cultural hero, who "stars" in *Foucault's Pendulum* by Umberto Eco and *Bee Season* by Myla Goldberg, among other works. The psychological focus in much of twentieth-century kabbalistic writing has also contributed to the popularity of Abulafia's works, which contain self-transformation techniques, psychological experiences, autobiographical testimonies, and a psychological interpretation of kabbalistic terms. Note that the kabbalists' traditional aversion to self-exposure (with the exception of ecstatic Kabbalists) had substantially subsided by the twentieth century, as testified by the diaries and letters of Kook, Ashlag, R. David Kohen ("Ha-Nazir"), Zeitlin, and others, which describe personal and even intimate experiences. Even when contemporary kabbalists do not write in an autobiographical style, they are frequently the subjects of their own works, as in the case of Zagdon.

The intensification of the ecstatic element in contemporary Kabbalah has been paralleled by the intensification of the magical element, too. Although important early-century kabbalists, such as Kook and Ashlag, did not give much attention to "practical Kabbalah" in their works or lives, toward the end of the century amulets, blessings, and other magical practices became extremely popular. This trend was not restricted to Sephardic or Hasidic Kabbalah; even Lithuanian sages, such as R. Ya'aqov Kanievsky and his son, R. Ḥayyim Kanievsky, became a dispenser of blessings for those seeking "children, health, and livelihood." This development testifies to the pragmatic nature of our generation, which has also had a part to play in the decline of the more theurgical and abstract study of theosophical structures.[107]

Thus, it is clear that twentieth-century Kabbalah has become increasingly exoteric.[108] Despite a certain ambivalence on the part of early-century kabbalists toward the exposure of the esoteric, and despite the continued prevalence of censored or internal works, phenomena such as the publication of Kook's diaries point to an almost total victory for the exoteric trend, which is fueled by the drive to disseminate Kabbalah. This trend parallels similar phenomena within global mysticism. In recent decades, esoteric doctrines such as Shingon (Japanese Tantric Buddhism) and secret material of the Trungpa circle have been divulged to the West.[109] Naturally, the progress of academic scholarship, advanced information technologies, and globalization processes plays an important part in the disclosure and dissemination of information.

Twentieth-century Kabbalah has rejected the traditional interest in reward and punishment in the world to come in favor of terrestrial, political, and psychological emphases in the here and now. This trend, too, exists in global mysticism: Trungpa's interpretation of *The Tibetan Book of the Dead* situates the *Bardo*, or median state, in the psychological present rather than in the afterlife (as the traditional interpretation has it).[110] Similarly, New Age circles, especially those espousing Daoism, have largely replaced the belief in an afterlife with belief in immortality. Indeed, various economic elites in Israel are associated with The Physical Immortality Movement, whose slogan is "We are together in order to live forever" (a slogan belied by the death of some of the movement's leaders).

Thus, while rejecting the view that the twentieth century was a post-kabbalistic period, and despite the existence of a degree of continuity between twentieth-century and classical Kabbalah, twentieth-century Kabbalah has certain "neo-kabbalistic" elements.[111] Be that as it may, it has certainly succeeded in carving out a niche for itself and, therefore, requires slightly different research tools than does earlier kabbalistic literature. Finally, the works of twentieth-century kabbalists, including Kook, reflect awareness of the need to revitalize kabbalistic language in our generation, especially in the wake of the return to Eretz Israel and of scientific and technological innovations.[112]

Toward a Twenty-First-Century Kabbalah

In conclusion, I would like to emphasize that I do not share the view that spiritual choices can be reduced to social or sociological factors. I believe that the upsurge of interest in mysticism stems also from the internal force of the ideas it represents. Although the demise of the modernist rationalist metanarrative (both secular and religious) may have helped disseminate mysticism, by the same token the force of mystical thought may have triggered the challenge to the modernist metanarrative. It is also possible that mystical forces that were formerly repressed or diverted now enjoy free expression. According to this line of reasoning, Kook's literary and contemplative treasures, which are becoming increasingly evident with the publication of his hidden works, have a force of their own that contributes to the dissemination and popularity of his works. The same process is occurring within contemporary Hasidic literature, where early works such as *Esh Qodesh* or *Mei Ha-Shiloaḥ* are fertilizing the neo-Hasidic renaissance. As for magic, it is older than all the religious and ideological phenomena mentioned in this book and shall probably outlive them.[113]

Gershom Scholem anticipated that Jewish mysticism would resurface, and he therefore wrote at the end of his monumental work *Major Trends*, "The story has not yet ended, it has not yet become history, and the secret life it enfolds may surface tomorrow in you or me."[114] Today we are witnessing the realization of this prophecy. Indeed, Scholem himself proposed on a few occasions the possibility of a secular mysticism.[115] The New Age movement, which operates mainly outside the religious establishment and frequently without any religious belief in the accepted sense, is the effective realization of this option.[116] We may, therefore, anticipate the development of a secular Kabbalah devoid of religious affiliations, along the lines of the Kabbalah offered by the Kabbalah Center. Michael Laitman, the leader of Bnei Barukh, claims that "it is almost impossible to approach Kabbalah from religion," and that it is easier for the secular public to embrace Kabbalah, since, according to him, "Kabbalah relates solely to the internal dimension of divine worship within man."[117] From a sociological perspective, the secularization of mysticism may take many forms, from religious organizations masquerading as secular ones to spiritual activities by the formerly religious.[118]

Alongside the secularization of Kabbalah, we see a growing schism between Kabbalah and Jewish identity—a trend even more marked than the schism between Kabbalah and halakhic Judaism (see Chapter 6). The overtures of the Ashlag circle to the non-Jewish world and the burgeoning of Christian Kabbalah are manifestations of the globalization of Kabbalah within an eclectic culture that is unaffiliated with any specific religion. Even contemporary Christian Kabbalah has a more psychological flavor than a Christian one. The growing rift between neo-Kabbalah and Jewish traditions should permit a merger of Jewish and Christian forms of Kabbalah.

These qualitative changes may trigger quantitative changes, some of which we are already witnessing, such as the establishment of Kabbalah centers in countries that formerly had little kabbalistic activity, such as England, Australia, and South Africa.[119] This trend, which should bring about new kinds of kabbalistic writing, reflects the globalization of Kabbalah and the return to Judaism that is taking place within these communities.

Although I am not sure that Forman is right in categorizing the new mysticism a "civilizational" change, it certainly represents an extremely profound social and spiritual transformation, which is no longer in its infancy. In writing this book, therefore, I have attempted not only to write "a history of the present," in the spirit of Foucault's appeal, but also to pave the way for the writing of a history of the future.[120] In this context, it is worth quoting Joseph Dan's statement that the New Age movement was not only "the most sweeping phenomenon of the late twentieth century" but also one "that shows us very clearly what to expect in the next century."[121]

POSTSCRIPT

In Chapter 7 I proposed a sociopolitical review of the proliferation of contemporary mysticism. This review does not detract from the reasonable assumption that mystical practice and experience may effect a transformation in many individuals. This transformation in turn may lead to a deeper investigation of the profundity and mystery of the human experience. It is precisely because of this possibility that we must restrict the commercialization and popularization of contemporary mystical discourse. I do not wish to hide my aversion to these trends behind a screen of academic "objectivity."

In conclusion, I wish to add that it is somewhat frustrating, although also exciting, to write a book that is already out-of-date even as it is being written. In addition, there are many existing topics that I have not touched on, such as apocalyptic prophecies that surfaced toward the end of the century.[1] Nevertheless, the arguments proposed here on issues such as exotericism, power, nationalism, the psychologization of mysticism, the status of space, the status of the leader, and the attitude to law, among others, provide an overall picture of twentieth-century Kabbalah in the context of global mysticism. I hope that by referring to processes connected with these motifs, I will help those who wish to conduct similar research in other contexts. An attempt has been made here not only to describe the development of Kabbalah in the twentieth century but also to chart its development and orientations for the coming decades.

NOTES

Introduction

1. As well as many other books, such as those by Stephen Donaldson and Ursula Le Guin. A magical dimension exists also in Stephen King's best sellers, some of which were made into films. Neil Gaiman's novels and comics, steeped in mystical and magical themes, have been widely acclaimed in the United States. In addition, the Gnostic and Shamanic myths in Philip Pullman's works should be noted. Usually, Kabbalah does not play a major role in this literature, but see Stroud, *The Golem's Eye*; Piercy, *He, She and It*; Jones, *Chrestomanci*, p. 127. Also worth mentioning are the descriptions of contemporary Christian mysticism and magic in the works of Susan Howatch. The following statistics demonstrate the importance of research into this kind of literature: Stephen Donaldson's *Thomas Covenant* series, which is second-rate

fantasy literature (both qualitatively and in terms of sales), has so far (eight books in) sold about ten million copies—a number larger than the entire Israeli population. Mythical-magical fantasy literature has replaced science fiction, reflecting the shift of the popular imagination away from scientific themes in favor of New Age themes. Yet science fiction also made some use—albeit minor—of quasi-kabbalistic motifs, such as the "miraculous abridgments of journeys" in Frank Herbert's *Dune* novels. One should also note the centrality of mystical, mythical, and magical dimensions in many other movies, such as the *Matrix* series, *The Sixth Sense*, or the Japanese series *Neon Genesis Evanglion* (in which kabbalistic symbolism is prominent). Throughout the book I shall frequently refer to movies, since I believe that the cinema is the nearest thing to a joint cultural language in the postmodern world.

2. For the source of this term, see Aveni, *Behind the Crystal Ball*, p. 249. Of the many studies on the New Age, only a few are mentioned here. According to various estimates, one-fifth to one-third of the U.S. population is affiliated with New Age circles. See Forman, *Grassroots Spirituality*, pp. 8–23. See also data in Heelas, *New Age Movement*, pp. 107–113; and see Heelas and Woodhead, *Spiritual Revolution*. An example of how certain researchers disregard the scope of the phenomenon can be found in Hobsbawm, *Age of Extremes*, p. 494. Hobsbawm seeks to estimate the number of people who seek refuge in beliefs whose very lack of rationality contributes to their power. Since he totally disregards the New Age movement and focuses on sects only, he claims that only 5 percent of the population is affected.
3. See Dan, *Apocalypse*, pp. 338–339. Forman (*Grassroots Spirituality*, p. 26) claims that this may be the first case of a major religion without a founding leader.
4. See Forman, *Grassroots Spirituality*; Castells, *Power of Identity*, p. 362, for a broader discussion of the "reticular" nature of the contemporary social structure. See also Chapter 7 of the present book. On the economy of the new network, see Barabasi, *Linked*, pp. 202–217. Localities in Israel include Hararit (Transcendental Meditation), Yodfat (Shechterian Commune and the Gurdjieff school), Neot Smadar (Yosef Safra Commune), Harduf (Anthroposophy), inter alia.
5. On the Kabbalah in the world of Madonna, see Huss, "All You Need Is LAV." See also S. Lev-Ari, "One Needs to Know How to Receive," *Ha'aretz*, 24 Sept. 2004.
6. Foucault, *Archeology of Knowledge*, pp. 21, 23.
7. Note, too, that there is scant research on other trends in Jewish religion in this century, such as the Mussar movement or the analytical method of Talmud study introduced by R. Ḥayyim Soleveitchik of Brisk.
8. Huss, "To Ask No Questions," p. 61, 64. Of all Huss's claims, the latter appears to have the least textual basis.
9. Note there is no guarantee, either, that the classical kabbalistic texts available to us are of the top caliber. On the contrary, quite possibly more popular works survived better and reached later generations.
10. However, see now Ashkenazy, *Secret of the Hebrew*; Ashkenazy, *Eulogy for the Messiah?*; Ashkenazy, *Secret of the Holy Tongue*. In this context, note also the prolific writings of R.

Yizḥaq Hutner, author of the *Paḥad Yizḥaq* series, which includes many kabbalistic themes (see Chapter 1 of the present book).

11. A significant step toward the study of unpublished works was the establishment of the Institute of Microfilmed Hebrew Manuscripts in Jerusalem soon after the establishment of the State of Israel. For a historical summary of Kabbalah research in Israel, see Idel, "Academic Studies of Kabbalah."
12. On the phenomenon of "internal" works (intended only for in-group distribution) and its social function, see Chapter 7. This phenomenon is the archenemy of the researcher seeking to present his readers with the full range of kabbalistic texts, especially since frequently it is the internal texts that are particularly interesting. On the importance of oral traditions in Kabbalah research, see Idel, *Kabbalah*, pp. 20–22. This, naturally, further highlights the need to research the Kabbalah of recent generations.
13. On the need for contact of this kind, see Idel, *Kabbalah*, pp. 25–27.
14. Bilu, "Studying Folk Culture." On the new anthropology, see the seminal works Marcus and Fischer, *Anthropology as Cultural Critique*; Clifford and Marcus, *Writing Culture*.
15. On researchers having mystical experiences, see, for example, Halit Yeshurun's interview with Ḥaviva Pedaya, *Ḥadarim* 15 (2003–2004), pp. 169–190. (See also, however, Huss, "Authorized Guardians.") This phenomenon is not peculiar to the study of Jewish mysticism. On the contrary, in other fields, such as the study of Sufism, Daoism, or Tibetan Buddhism, the phenomenon of researchers who are actively involved in the practices of the group they are studying is far more prevalent. See, for example, Hermansen, "American Sufi Movements," p. 55. The desire to combine research with mystical experience existed also in the first part of the century, as reflected in Gershom Scholem's yearning for an experience of this kind (see Idel, *Kabbalah*, p. 30).
16. See Liebes, "New Directions"; Idel, *Kabbalah*.
17. See, for example, Brown, "Primal Faith"; Liebes, "The Ultraorthodox"; Belcove-Shalin, *New World Hasidism*; Levine, *Mystics, Mavericks, and Merrymakers*; as well as the works discussed below. See also the Foreword for recent studies.
18. From 2002 to 2007 alone, dozens of doctorates in the field of Kabbalah were authorized in Israel and abroad. Approximately 5 percent of doctorates approved in the Hebrew University in 2004 were on this topic.
19. See, respectively, Amnon Gross's introduction to *The Key of Wisdom* (Jerusalem, 2001), pp. 1–2, as well as Barnai, *Sabbateanism*, pp. 138–139.
20. The dissemination of Kabbalah research is not restricted to Israel, as testified by the many studies conducted abroad, particularly Professor Daniel Matt's marathon project of translating the Zohar into English. To this one may add the many English translations of Israeli studies. See, for example, the series of popular books on Kabbalah published by Shambala Press of Colorado, which specializes in mystical literature, such as Bonder, *Kabbalah of Envy* and *Kabbalah of Money*. Evidently, the expression "The Kabbalah of" mimics the popular title found in New Age books, "The Tao of."

21. See Hanegraaff, *New Age Religion*, pp. 395–396; Bloom, *Omens of the Millennium*, pp. 31–32.
22. A patent example is Rachlevsky, *Messiah's Donkey*. Evidently, the writings of R. Yitzchak Ginsburgh have hardly been studied for this reason. Since the rise of radical doctrines on both the right and the left is a feature of the past century (which, not for nothing, was dubbed by the "Age of Extremes" by the historian Hobsbawm), anyone researching the history of ideas in this century cannot avoid studying these kinds of opinions.
23. Aḥituv, "Strange Revival." For my response, see Garb, "The Understandable Revival."
24. For a preliminary mapping of the cultural history of postmodernism, see, for example, Huyssen, "Mapping the Post-modern."
25. Hobsbawm, in *Age of Extremes*, gives an alternative periodization (based on a Marxist analysis) of the twentieth century, beginning with the outbreak of the First World War (1914) and closing with the end of the Cold War (1991). In my opinion, 1914 is a late date, since the First World War was the apex, not the starting point (see Tuchman, *The Proud Tower*).
26. See Roszak, *Making of a Counter-Culture*; Bishop, *Dreams of Power*; Clarke, *Tao of the West*; Fields, *How the Swans Came*. On the development of the New Age movement from the 1950s to today, see Forman, *Grassroots Spirituality*, pp. 115–118, and sources quoted there; Heelas, *The New Age Movement*, pp. 49–54.
27. Contemporary attempts to bridge the gap between Kabbalah and Islamic mysticism, including the research of Paul Fenton and Avraham Elqayam or the poetry of Binyamin Shvili, are a continuation of this trend.

CHAPTER 1. JEWISH MYSTICISM IN THE TWENTIETH CENTURY

1. Scholem, *Major Trends*, p. 34; see also pp. 324–325.
2. This opinion is reflected in attitudes such as that of Piekarz (*Ideological Trends in Hasidism*, pp. 50–80), who views Hasidism in the twentieth century as losing its mystical energy in favor of more conservative positions.
3. On the dissemination of magic (or, as he puts it, occultism) in Israel today, see Beit-Hallahmi, *Despair and Deliverance*, pp. 73–99.
4. Some masters teach only in their country and in Israel. A striking example is Ryokyu Endo, one of the top Shiatsu practitioners in the world, who adopts a Daoistic approach. (On his problematic encounter with the Israeli public, see W. Favan, "When East Sometimes Meets West: Impressions of a Dao-Shiatshu Workshop Conducted by Ryokyu Endo," *Ḥayyim Aḥerim*, January 1999, pp. 14–16).
5. There is room here to review only a small portion of this literature. An empirical study is needed to determine what types of literature are translated and imported, and the ways in which this literature is disseminated.
6. Only a few of which will be cited here.
7. 'Isbei Ha-Sadeh is particularly popular among the radical "hilltop youth" in the territories. One could also mention 'Adi Ran (whose lyrics formed the basis for the soundtrack of the film *Ushpizin*, produced by G. Dar in 2004) and the Israeli trance group Astral Projection, which won international acclaim. The band's name is in

itself taken from the New Age lexicon, and the cover of one album has an image of the kabbalistic Tree of Life (containing the ten Sefirot).

8. On the infiltration of kabbalistic themes into literature, see Bar-Yosef, "Introduction to Mysticism." An example of kabbalistic themes in film is *Ushpizin*, which deals with the world of Bratzlav Hasidim. See also Chapter 7.
9. See Bilu, "Modern Saints"; Bilu, "Sanctification of Place," pp. 75–79; Gonen, *Pilgrimate and Hilulot in Israel*; Huss, "Holy Place, Holy Time, Holy Book."
10. See, respectively, Bloom, *American Religion*; Csordas, *Sacred Self*; Cupitt, "Post-Christianity."
11. For a short description of Roth's group, see Scholem, *Explications and Implications*, p. 79. This sect, known as Reb Aralach, is better known for its uncompromising anti-Zionist stance. For a summary of Shapira's doctrine, see Polen, *Holy Fire*; see also Farbstein, "Voice of God."
12. See the book of the same name (Tel Aviv, 1989) and compare with R. Hillel Zeitlin's attempt to set up a mystical group named Bnei Yavneh, close in time and place to Shapira's group (see Bar-Sella, *Between the Storm*, p. 123; Hallamish, "The Concept of the Land of Israel," p. 204).
13. The influential R. Yizḥaq Moshe Erlanger, author of the *Sheva' 'Enayim* series, is supposedly connected to these circles.
14. See Wacks, "Emotion and Enthusiasm," p. 73. On this phenomenon and on the influence of the book *Esh Qodesh* today, see Y. Sheleg, "I Have No More Strength to Give You," *Ha'aretz*, 18 Apr. 2004.
15. See Magid, *Hasidism on the Margin*; Brill, *Thinking God*.
16. Recently, a prolific "panegyric literature" has grown up around Carlebach, and many of his own works are now being published. See, for example, the popular pamphlet *The Depth of the Heart*. Several Internet sites, containing much interesting material, are dedicated to his teachings.
17. Rumor has it that the elders of this sect were ridiculed when they built the large synagogue of the Bratzlav community in Mea Shearim, but that they retorted, "The day will yet come when the place will be too small to contain the masses of worshippers."
18. See Piekarz, *Studies in Bratzlav Hasidism*, pp. 200–205, 210–218.
19. The book, Shatil, *Psychologist in a Yeshiva*, was written about this Yeshiva. Politically, this is the "right-wing faction" of contemporary Bratzlav Hasidism.
20. See Assaf, *Bratzlav*, pp. 231–239; Piekarz, *Studies in Bratzlav Hasidism*. Some of these trends will probably be discussed in a future study by 'Eran Sabag.
21. The works of R. Menaḥem Mendel include many collections of articles and talks. A database of the entire corpus can be found at the Habad Web site, www.otzar770.com. For an uncensored bibliography of R. Menaḥem Mendel, see Deutsch, *Larger than Life*.
22. A fair amount has been written about this fascinating personality. See, for example, Bar-Sella, "Hillel Zeitlin"; Green, "Three Warsaw Mystics." For a detailed and up-to-date summary of the literature on Zeitlin, see Meir, "Hillel Zeitlin's Zohar"; Meir,

Rabbi Nahman of Bratzlav. Hallamish ("The Concept of the Land of Israel," p. 212) is nonetheless right in saying that his special contribution has not yet been assessed within wider discussions on Zionism and Religious Zionism, and this is true also in the context of discussions on twentieth-century Kabbalah. On Zeitlin and Kook see Meir, "Hillel Zeitlin's Zohar"; Meir, "Longing of Souls."

23. On this Hasidic perspective, see Piekarz, *Ideological Trends in Hasidism*, pp. 85–93. The following anecdote sheds light on the extent of the kabbalization of the Lithuanian public. In 2001, news spread in this community that a distinctly non-kabbalistic leader from the previous generation, the Brisker Rov, came in a dream to one of the present-day Torah luminaries and informed him that the al-Aqsa Intifada was the result of the imprisonment of ultraorthodox Shas political leader Aryeh Der'i.

24. See Chapter 2 on the positive attitude of the nineteenth-century Lithuanian kabbalist R. Yizḥaq Ḥaver toward the dissemination of Kabbalah. On the study of Kabbalah in the Volozhin Yeshiva—the archetype of Lithuanian Yeshivas—see Stampfer, *Lithuanian Yeshiva*, pp. 56, 58 (and see also Schuchat, "Lithuanian Kabbalah," p. 202). On the other hand, see the testimony of the fifth rebbe of Habad on decision makers in the Lithuanian world who disparage Kabbalah (quoted in Friedman, "Messiah and Messianism," p. 181). Although this testimony comes from an interested party (the rebbe was involved in the establishment of a Yeshiva that would match up to the Lithuanian Yeshivas), we should not reject it out of hand. As we shall see in the next chapter, even portions of the Lithuanian public—including some members of the Mussar movement—entertained reservations about the study of Kabbalah. In any case, until recently, this public has most fervently upheld halakhic constraints concerning the study of Kabbalah.

25. On Karelitz's reservations concerning Kabbalah, see Brown, "Ḥazon Ish," appendix 3. For Kanievsky's writings, see his book *Ḥayye 'Olam.*

26. See Etkes, *Rabbi Israel Salanter*, pp. 102–104. For a literary description of the tension between students of Kabbalah and students of Mussar in a Lithuanian Yeshiva in the 1950s, see Segal, *Ne'ila*, p. 146.

27. See Bloch, *Shi'urei Da'at*, vol. 1, p. 59, for incisive criticism of the "fools" who oppose Kabbalah (from the context, he was apparently referring to the Yemenite rabbi R. Yiḥya Kappaḥ); see also ibid., vol. 2, pp. 19–20, for Bloch's dialogue with R. Shlomo Elyashiv on kabbalistic issues.

28. See, for example, Friedlander, *Treasures of Ramḥal.* Freidlander's talks in the Yeshiva, collected in the multivolume series *Siftei Ḥayyim*, which started to appear in 1989 and is still being published, also contain much kabbalistic material. Luzzatto's Kabbalah is today disseminated by, inter alia, the Ramḥal Institute in Jerusalem, which held a gala event in his honor in 2007, attended by numerous ultraorthodox leaders. Evidently, opposition to the study of his writings, following suspicions of his Sabbatian leanings, disappeared completely in the course of the twentieth century. Further books by Wolbe, as well as letters containing kabbalistic material, have been published recently.

29. *Ha-Sulam* (Jerusalem, 1945–1953 [and subsequent numerous editions]).
30. For an insider's account of the history of Ashlag and his son, see Gottlieb, *Ha-Sulam*. The process of transferring leadership was problematic. Another of Ashlag's sons, R. Shlomo Benyamin Ashlag, created a separate faction, distinct from R. Barukh's faction, and his heir today is his son, R. Yeḥezkel Ashlag. See also Lavi, "Idea of Cosmogony," p. 11.
31. During a recent trip to Israel, Madonna even went on a pilgrimage to Ashlag's tomb in Jerusalem.
32. See Kaplan, *Meditation and Kabbalah*.
33. It should be noted, however, that in the previous research generation, a number of researchers published and analyzed the writings of the kabbalists of North Africa, Syria, and Turkey.
34. The sociologist Dr. André Levy proposed a similar formulation in a lecture delivered at a conference on Israeli Kabbalah at the Van Leer Institute in Jerusalem in 2000. See also Huss, "Gershom Scholem," p. 65. Levy's claim notwithstanding, it is true that Oriental Kabbalah tended to deal with the complex structures of Lurianic Kabbalah and deliberately refrained from the attempts at national or psychological interpretations that typified Ashkenazi Kabbalah. See Schuchat, "Lithuanian Kabbalah," p. 185. As we shall see throughout the book, this exegesis typifies the ideational innovation of twentieth-century Kabbalah. For an up-to-date and moderate formulation of the Sephardic stance see Hillel, *Shorshei Ha-Yam*, p. 167.
35. On kabbalistic Yeshivas in the twentieth century, see Breuer, *Oholei Torah*, pp. 162–262.
36. See in particular Fischer, "The Shas Movement."
37. In addition to the Shas-controlled Council of the Wise, which is modeled on the ultraorthodox party Agudat Yisra'el's Council of Torah Sages (which has effectively become a Hasidic organization), a Council of Kabbalists, affiliated with Shas, is apparently in the pipeline. On Kabbalah in Yosef's decisions, see Lau, *Rav 'Ovadia Yosef*, pp. 269–324; Picard, *Philosophy of Rabbi 'Ovadia Yosef*, pp. 214–216.
38. See Alush, *Amazing Story*; Sheleg, *New Religious Jews*, pp. 204–205.
39. For a positive evaluation of *Faith and Folly*, see the review by Neriyah Gutel, a star alumnus of the Merkaz Ha-Rav Yeshiva, in *Ha'aretz*'s Book Column, 17 May 2000. On opposition to magic in the Kook circle, see the end of Chapter 2.
40. See, for example, Ish-Shalom, *Rabbi Abraham Isaac Kook*, particularly p. 26, and cf. Avivi, "History as Divine Prescription." For a more recent summary of this issue, see Pachter, "Faith-Heresy in Rav Kook's Thought," and sources cited there. See also Gellman, "Teshuva in Kabbalah," which makes an important contribution to the evaluation of the place of Kabbalah in Kook's writings.
41. I accept the methodological hypothesis that Kook and his students should be considered members of a mystical circle; see Dov Schwartz, "Methods of Research" (and other works), and cf. Cherlow, "The Circle of Rav Kook." The following text by Kook testifies to the circle's way of thinking (*Shmona Qevatzim*, vol. 1, par. 307): "There is one kind of tzaddiq who needs great and pious students, people of genius and caliber,

and only then will he realize his true potential." See, however, Meir's important critique of this model, "Lights and Vessels."

42. See Garb, "Ideological Roots of Gush Emunim," pp. 181–182; Schwartz, "National Messianic Thought," pp. 77–81; Sheleg, *New Religious Jews*, pp. 31–36; and cf. Aran, "From Pioneering."
43. See Y. Sheleg, "Rabbi Tau on Conscientious Objection," *Ha'aretz*, 15 Sept. 2004.
44. The rise of this leadership stratum was one of the factors behind the schism that took place in the late century in the Merkaz Ha-Rav Yeshiva set up by Kook; see Rosen-Zvi, "Creation of Metaphysics."
45. In this context, note Eliyahu's influence on Sephardic Members of Knesset of the National Religious Party, which evidently prevented the party's inclusion in the unity government of 2001–2003. On Nir Ben-Artzi, see A. Golan, "The Rural Saint," *Ha'aretz*, 14 May 1999. Golan states that rabbis of the Kook circle, principally Shlomo Aviner, objected to this magical-messianic figure.
46. See Kaplan and Dresner, *Abraham Joshua Heschel*. On his attitude toward Kabbalah, see Green, "Three Warsaw Mystics," pp. 36–56.
47. See, for example, Heschel, *Passion for Truth*.
48. For a preliminary discussion, see Hanegraaff, *New Age Religion*, p. 396. Hanegraaff claims that the specific contribution of Christian and post-Christian Kabbalah to the New Age religion is fairly marginal. My opinion is that in-depth research into this topic would refute this assertion. See his discussion (p. 453) of the place of kabbalistic texts in the theosophist movement of the early century. On the interest in general and Jewish mysticism in the West in the early century, see Mendes-Flohr, "Fin-de-siècle."
49. Chapter 6 describes a similar process in the neo-Hasidic movement.
50. For more about Ashkenazy, see Charvit, "Identity and History." As I pointed out in the Introduction, most of his writings have yet to be published. For Ashkenazy's analysis of Kook's doctrine and its leaning toward Kabbalah, see Ashkenazy, "Kabbalistic Concepts."
51. Levinas was influenced by R. Ḥayyim of Volozhin (see Hand, *The Levinas Reader*, pp. 227–234); Neher by the Maharal of Prague (see Neher, *Le Puits de l'exil*).
52. See Idel, *Absorbing Perfections*, pp. 416–422; Bloom, *Kabbalah and Criticism*; Bloom, *Omens of the Millennium*.
53. In this context, note that the influence of Kabbalah is not limited to the West. I was presented with a book by a Malaysian author, Ong An-Taat, dealing with the relationship between Kabbalah and the Chinese "Bagua" system.

Chapter 2. The Drive to Disseminate Kabbalah

1. Such as Shaul Bumyan's *Key to the Wisdom of Truth* (*Mafteaḥ Ḥokhmat Ha-Emmet*) and the anonymous work *Introductory Principles of Wisdom* (*Klalei Hatḥalat Ha-Ḥokhma*).
2. See Tishby, *Studies in Kabbalah*, p. 108; Idel, *Messianic Mystics*, p. 129; Elior, "Messianic Expectations." See also the many primary sources cited in R. Mordekhai 'Attiya's article, referred to later in this chapter.

3. Tishby, *Studies in Kabbalah*, pp. 139–182; Idel, *Kabbalah*, pp. 253–260; Hundert, *Jews in Poland-Lithuania*, pp. 119–130. See also Garb, *Manifestations of Power*, pp. 262–263, and sources cited there.
4. See Liebes, *Studies in the Zohar*, pp. 1–84.
5. This is especially true of German Jewry, as Gershom Scholem testifies (see Weiner, *Nine and a Half Mystics*, p. 60). For the change in German Jewry's attitude toward Kabbalah, see Horowitz, "Revelation in Jewish Philosophy," p. 258, and cf. Magid, "Deconstructing the Mystical," p. 38n51, and sources cited there, for R. Yizḥaq Breuer's attitude to Kabbalah. In general, German Jewry's social achievements before the Holocaust did not act as a catalyst for kabbalistic discourse, as happened, for example, in Spain's Golden Age or in the Italian Renaissance.
6. On the reservations entertained by R. Menaḥem Mendel of Kotzk, the famous nineteenth-century Hasidic teacher, toward the study of Kabbalah, see Heschel, *Passion for Truth*, pp. 78–80.
7. There is prolific research and Torah literature on Kook, only some of which will be cited here. It should be noted that "the Rav's house" (*Beit Ha-Rav*) on R. Kook Street, Jerusalem, contains an archive with a collection of bibliographical items relating to Kook.
8. See Kook, *Orot Ha-Torah*, pp. 30–32. There is a certain similarity here to the attitude expressed by the seventh rebbe of Habad, namely that the very decline of the generation necessitates the revelation of the esoteric aspects of Torah (see Ratzabi, "Rabbi Shalom Dov Baer," pp. 99–100), although there the dialectic dimension present in Kook's thinking is absent.
9. Kook, *Orot Ha-Qodesh*, vol. 1, p. 141.
10. Kook, *Letters*, vol. 1, letter 43.
11. Ibid., vol. 2, letter 147.
12. See *Ḥagiga* 2a and cf. *Berakhot* 54a.
13. This issue is discussed at length by my predecessors. See, for example, Schweid, "Renewed Prophecy," pp. 88–103; Schweid, *Prophets for Their People*, pp. 190–214; Rosenak, "Rav Kook's Hidden Treatises," pp. 261–262; Rosenak, "Prophetic Halakha and Reality," pp. 595–599; Rosenak, "Education and Meta-Halakha," p. 102. See also Rosenak, *Prophetic Halakha*.
14. On this subject, see Garb, "Rabbi Kook." Compare to the term *mystical nationalism* in Schwartz, "National Messianic Thought," p. 65. On Kook's mystical-ecstatic experience, see Cherlow, "The Tzaddiq"; Cherlow, "Ha-Ahavah."
15. The censored texts themselves demonstrate an awareness of the need to restrict public access to Kook's intimate thoughts. See, for example, Kook, *Shmona Qevatzim*, vol. 1, par. 567.
16. See Rosenak, "Rav Kook's Hidden Treatises"; Schwartz, *Challenge and Crisis*, especially p. 146n1; Abromovitz, "The Publication of the Notebooks"; Avivi, "Source of Lights"; as well as my articles mentioned here. Recently, Merkaz Ha-Rav circles have published a new collection of manuscripts—*Pinkas Yud-Gimel*—as part of the trend toward pub-

lication of censored texts (see publisher's preface), but even these were partly censored (see publisher's admission that they were publishing "most" of the notebook). These texts have now been published in uncensored form, together with other important texts, in the collection *Qevatzim Mi-Ktav Yad Qodsho* (2 vols., Jerusalem, 2006–2008).

17. See Rosenak, "Rav Kook's Hidden Treatises," pp. 268–270. For more examples, see Kook, *Shmona Qevatzim*, vol. 7, par. 193, and cf. Kook, *Orot Ha-Qodesh*, vol. 1, pp. 110–111. See also Kook, *Shmona Qevatzim* vol. 1, par. 315; Kook, *Orot Ha-Qodesh*, vol. 2, p. 446.
18. This is especially noticeable in the collection entitled *Ḥadarav: Personal Chapters*, which focuses, as its name suggests, on personal phases in Kook's writing (see also Fischer, "Radical Religious-Zionist Thought"). I quote at length from this collection, particularly from the addenda that came with the new and expanded edition (2002).
19. Kook, *Ḥadarav*, pp. 74, 15; Kook, *Shmona Qevatzim*, vol. 6, par. 34.
20. Kook, *Shmona Qevatzim*, vol. 6, par. 161. This is not the place to examine the kabbalistic meaning of the text, which, in my opinion, provides a national and psychological exegesis of the Lurianic concept of *birur* (the extraction of divine sparks from the husks).
21. Despite the official position of halakhic Judaism that prophecy ceased after the destruction of the Temple, there are many testimonies of the continuation of the prophetic consciousness throughout the generations (see, for example, Heschel, "Inspiration in the Middle Ages"). This question in particular preoccupied Kook's disciple R. David Kohen ("Ha-Nazir"), as we see from his main work, *Qol Ha-Nevu'a*. See in particular pp. 5, 7, 145, 158, 218.
22. See, for example, Kook, *Orot*, pp. 95–96. See also Schwartz, *Israel in Religious Zionist Thought*, p. 73. Compare to pp. 111–112; Schwartz, *Religious Zionism*, p. 166 and 195, concerning the Western Wall (and see Kook, *Shmona Qevatzim*, vol. 6, par. 85). For the similar attitude of another major student, R. Ya'aqov Moshe Ḥarlap, see the texts cited in Schwartz, *Israel in Religious Zionist Thought*, p. 50. Concerning Kook's son, R. Tzevi Yehuda Ha-Kohen Kook ("Ratzia"), see p. 108. See also Shagar, *Broken Vessels*, p. 122, for proof that a student of Kook's disciples (rumored to be R. Yehoshu'a Zuckerman) defined the Yeshiva as a School of Prophecy.
23. This sentiment is echoed by R. Hillel Zeitlin, a contemporary and acquaintance of Kook's: "One who feels a true leaning . . . toward esoterics" (*The Book of the Few*, cited by Bar-Sella, "Hillel Zeitlin," p. 122). In *Orot Ha-Qodesh* (vol. 1, p. 36), Kook explains that those who master exoterics feel a mystical richness, while those who master esoterics feel satiated in the field of exoterics. Cf. the classical kabbalistic model (see Vital, *Sha'ar Ha-Gilgulim*, p. 126), whereby those who studied exoterics in a former incarnation are reincarnated in order to study esoterics.
24. Texts such as *Shmona Qevatzim* show that the claim that great souls (such as Kook himself) are the source of many other souls can be traced back to personal experiences and visions. Once again we see a correlation between Kook's self-perception and his understanding of his place in the redemptive processes of his generation. In

Kook, *Shmona Qevatzim* (vol. 5, par. 252), the wording is "on the degree of one's holiness and on the degree of one's humility." The censors may have attempted to play down Kook's high self-esteem as revealed here by emphasizing the quality of humility.

25. See Kook, *Ḥadarav*, pp. 16–17, 123–124; Kook, *Shmona Qevatzim*, vol. 6, par. 69. See also Rosenak, "Rav Kook's Hidden Treatises," p. 283.
26. Kook, *Orot Ha-Qodesh*, vol. 1, pp. 88–89. See also Kook, *Ḥadarav*, pp. 102–103.
27. Kook, *'Arphilei Tohar*, pp. 31–32.
28. Kook, *Pinkas Yud-Gimel*, p. 26: "Public leaders and special individuals resemble the Shabbat. They are great people who do not need public approval." On the antinomian implications of comparing the chosen individual to the Shabbat, see Chapter 6 of the present book.
29. Kook, *Shmona Qevatzim*, vol. 6, par. 69.
30. Ibid., p. 45.
31. See, for example, Kook, *Ḥadarav*, p. 100. The contrast between personal calling and social conventions also fueled Kook's antinomian doctrine.
32. On Kook's perception of the function of literary writing in general, and poetic writing in particular, see Garb, "Rabbi Kook," and sources cited there.
33. Kook, *Ḥadarav*, p. 99. On the need for a critical approach when studying Kabbalah, see Kook, *Orot Ha-Torah*, p. 31. This was one of the restrictions Kook placed on the dissemination of Kabbalah.
34. Kook, *Orot Ha-Torah*, pp. 33–35, and cf. p. 36. Also cf. another poem on the dissemination of his doctrine that ends, "And from country to country, the voice of my yearnings shall be heard." This poem appears in Ofan, *Nafshi Taqshiv Shiro*, p. 73, an anthology containing personal and censored poems by Kook. Its publication was in itself part of the general process described earlier.
35. On Kook's disciples as "the masses," see Pedaya, "Space, Time, and Eretz Israel," p. 590.
36. Kook, *Ḥadarav*, p. 48 (my emphasis). Compare the liturgical phrase "a new light shall shine forth on Zion" to the line of his poem "shall illumine all sides."
37. For testimony by students of Kook's disciples on his prophetic powers, see Sussman, "Letters," p. 19 (my thanks to Jonatan Meir for having drawn my attention to this source). For similar testimonies in relation to R. Ashlag, see Lavi, "Idea of Cosmogony," p. 6.
38. See Kook, *Ḥadarav*, pp. 30–31, 64. On Kook's extreme suffering, see pp. 36–37, 196; see also Cherlow, "The Tzaddiq," pp. 129, 168, 213, and especially p. 231 on "the pain of expression." On Kook's attempt to reach harmony in his inner life, see Kook, *Ḥadarav*, p. 119, as well as Rosenak, "Torah of Eretz Israel," pp. 49–50.
39. Kook, *Ḥadarav*, p. 70, and related adjoining passages, particularly pp. 68–69. See also the text cited in Rosenak, "Rav Kook's Hidden Treatises," p. 284.
40. See Kook, *Orot Ha-Qodesh*, vol. 1, p. 199, on the correlation between the "messianic light" initiated by the redemption of thought and the light emanating from his own

doctrine, as stated in the aforementioned texts. On Kook's quasi-messianic consciousness, see Chapter 6 of the present book.

41. Kook, *Ḥadarav*, p. 19.
42. See Avivi, "History as Divine Prescription"; Avivi, "Source of Lights."
43. Kook, *Orot Ha-Qodesh*, vol. 1, p. 83.
44. *Magen Ve-Tzina*, published in Ḥaver, *Treasures*, p. 14.
45. See Lavi, "Idea of Cosmogony," p. 3; Hansel, "The Origin in Rabbi Ashlag," p. 39.
46. On the exegetical literature, see Hansel, "The Origin in Rabbi Ashlag." There is still much room for research into Ashlag's interpretation of earlier kabbalistic sources, which could well be more radical than is presently acknowledged.
47. Ashlag, *Pri Ḥakham*, vol. 2, pp. 112, 120. See also pp. 107, 114, 122. For more on Ashlag's self-perception as the expounder of Lurianic Kabbalah, see Lavi, "Idea of Creation," p. 261.
48. Ibid., p. 121. This is not the last case of identification with Luria among twentieth-century kabbalists. In 2004, a book was published (Israeli, *You Shall Enter*) by an author who claimed she "channeled" Luria. According to her, Luria began to communicate in "archaic" language, and then switched to late-century Hebrew. Predictably, Luria expressed religious and political ideas that tied in with the view of secular left-wing Israelis. In general, the growth of the phenomenon of "channeling" (with aliens, the souls of the deceased, angels, etc.) in Jewish and general mysticism in the twentieth century is a sign of the ascendancy of the "passive" model and the weakening of the modern, active ego (see also Chapter 7 of the present book).
49. See Ashlag, *Pri Ḥakham*, vol. 2, p. 122. On the ties between Ashlag and Kook, see Meir, "Longing of Souls"; Meir, "Hillel Zeitlin's Zohar," p. 127n74, and sources cited there. R. Yehuda Léon Ashkenazy also wrote a short pamphlet comparing these two thinkers (*Science of Kabbalah*). See also Schweid, *Ruin to Salvation*, pp. 197–198.
50. As we will see in the following two chapters, the theme of evolution plays a large part in Kook's doctrine (see also Ben-Shlomo, "Perfection and Perfectibility"; Ross, "Elite and Masses"). Note that this is a common theme in twentieth-century mysticism in general, as in the doctrine of the Christian mystic Teilhard de Chardin or the Indian mystic Sri Aurobindo (see Garb, "Working Out as Divine Work," p. 8). For more on the subject of evolution in Ashlag's teachings, see Lavi, "Idea of Creation," vol. 1, p. 158.
51. Ashlag, *Pri Ḥakham*, vol. 1, p. 158. This argument complemented the more common argument that dissemination of Kabbalah helps hasten the redemption (see next paragraph on this theme). See Ashlag, *Sefer Ha-Haqdamot*, pp. 9–11. Another fairly common argument is that the dissemination of Kabbalah is possible because of our proximity to the year 6000 (2240) in the Jewish calendar (see ibid., p. 90). This is frequently linked to statements in the Zohar (vol. 1, p. 117a) on the revelation of wisdom after the year 5600 (1840).
52. *Ashlag, Sefer Ha-Haqdamot*, pp. 159–160. On p. 207, Ashlag provides an inflated historical description, whereby after the appearance of the Ari Ha-Qadosh (Luria) "all sages

of ensuing generations . . . unanimously abandoned all books and works that preceded him, whether the Kabbalah of the Ramak [R. Moses Cordovero] or the Kabbalah of the Early Sages [*Rishonim*] . . . and devoted all their spiritual life to his wisdom only." To his credit it should be said that some researchers agree with this assertion. For an opposing view, see Idel, *Hasidism*, pp. 33–43. In Ashlag's description of the history of Kabbalah, he assigns a large place to Hasidism, one of his main sources of inspiration. According to him, Luria saved the people from drowning "via the mind" and the Ba'al Shem Tov saved them "via the heart." However, since the light of the Ba'al Shem Tov was blocked, Ashlag took it upon himself to reveal the light of Luria.

53. Ashlag, *Pri Ḥakham*, vol. 1, pp. 160–161, 169.
54. Ibid., p. 192. Kook's thinking is mirrored in the dialectic statement that the very decadence of this generation completes the "divine stature" and therefore, paradoxically, enables the revelation of spiritual light (*Sefer Ha-Haqdamot*, p. 90).
55. Ibid., p. 89.
56. Ibid., pp. 2, 9–11. According to Ashlag, Exile is a consequence of selfish worship, and therefore redemption is dependent specifically on the dissemination of Kabbalah. For more on the relationship between selfless worship and Kabbalah, see Lavi, "Idea of Creation," pp. 315–316.
57. One national element is the emphasis on studying Kabbalah specifically in the Land of Israel.
58. Ashlag, *Sefer Ha-Haqdamot*, p. 91.
59. Ibid., p. 92. See also Lavi, "Idea of Creation," pp. 331–332; see Aḥituv, "Rav Ashlag." By contrast, see Schweid's allegation (*Ruin to Salvation*, p. 195) that Ashlag did not mention, or even allude to, the Holocaust. See Fisch, *Points of Light*, p. 334, on the correlation between the failure to study Kabbalah and the suffering of Exile (this kabbalist is one of R. Mordekhai Scheinberger's disciples). On adherence to figures such as Ashlag as a means of avoiding suffering, see Chapter 7 of the present book.
60. See Shapira, *Esh Kodesh*, pp. 139, 148. See also Schweid, *Ruin to Salvation*, pp. 105–154; Goldberg, "The Rebbe." On the Kook circle see Rosen-Zvi, "Justifying the Holocaust," in connection with Ratzia; Greenberg, "Death of History," pp. 104–106, in connection with Ḥarlap. For Ashkenazy's response, see "In the Latter Days." On R. Yosef Yizḥaq Shneurson's response to the Holocaust, see Friedman, "Messiah and Messianism," pp. 210–214; Elior, "Messianic Resurgence," pp. 390–391. For Slonim, see Brezovsky, *Kuntras Ha-Haruga 'Alayikh*. For more information on the responses of the various branches of Hasidism to the Holocaust, see Schindler, *Hasidic Responses*.
61. See, for example, Fisch, *Points of Light*, p. 1, who claimed that before Ashlag, it was not possible to study Kabbalah from books.
62. For a description of this circle's activities, see Weiner, *Nine and a Half Mystics*, pp. 96–101.
63. For Sheinberger's covert criticism of other disseminators of Ashlag's doctrine, see Berkowitz, "Interview with R. Sheinberger," p. 24.
64. See E. Salpeter, "Excuse Me: Where Could I Find a Jewish T-shirt?" *Ha'aretz*, 14 July

2004; Y. Bar-Moha, "Bargain Kabbalists," *Ha'aretz*, 29 May 1998. On the commercialization of Kabbalah, see also Chapter 7 of the present book.

65. See Ashlag, *Sefer Ha-Haqdamot*, p. 35, on how the study of Kabbalah as such, even when one does not understand it, awakens the unconscious or "universal" forces of the soul.
66. Ibid., pp. 203–208. For a similar statement concerning the use of magic, see the end of Chapter 4 of the present book.
67. See also the letters at the end of B. Ashlag, *Sham'ati*, p. 39, which state that one who wishes to hide his work from others is sincere, while one who wishes to publicize his work to others is not sincere. On Ashlag's reservations concerning the dissemination of his doctrine, see Lavi, "Idea of Cosmogony," p. 8.
68. See, for example, Kook's endorsement to the 1930 edition of Ashlag's book *Or Ha-Bahir*. See also the endorsement by the High Rabbinical Court in Ashlag, *Introduction to the Science of Kabbalah*.
69. For a clear example, see Ashlag, *Pri Ḥakham*, vol. 2, pp. 183–184.
70. Ibid., pp. 118, 122.
71. Ibid., p. 96. On pp. 119–120, Ashlag wrote that Vital was young and did not fully understand Luria's works; he had a similar opinion of another of Luria's disciples, R. Israel Sarug (see p. 112). This criticism pales in comparison to an opinion I heard from a Hasidic rebbe, that because Vital was Sephardic he was unable to understand the works of the Ashkenazi Luria.
72. See Meir, "Hillel Zeitlin's Zohar," p. 137. For a text that was interpreted by Ashlag's successors as expressing doubts about Zeitlin, see Lavi, "Idea of Cosmogony," p. 8. However, Meir ("Wrestling with the Esoteric," pp. 619–621) rejects this interpretation.
73. See, for example, the endorsement by R. Ḥayyim Shaul Dwik Kohen to the 1930 edition of Ashlag, *Or Ha-Bahir*, and in particular his statement that the dissemination of Kabbalah (as advocated by Ashlag) brought the redemption closer.
74. The article appears as the preface to an edition of *Pardes Rimonim* by R. Moses Cordovero, published in his Yeshiva. All other quotes by 'Attiya are from this source.
75. See Lau, "Holy Land," pp. 174–175. For a similar attitude by R. 'Ovadia Haddaya, see the preface to *Yaskil 'Avdi*, vol. 5, p. 5.
76. See Haddaya's preface to *Va-Yiqaḥ 'Ovadyahu*, vol. 3, p. 4. In the early century, R. Yosef Ḥayyim from Baghdad (who immigrated to Jerusalem toward the end of his life), one of the most important halakhic and kabbalistic leaders of the Sephardic community (and teacher of the almost equally famous R. Yehuda Petaya), wrote a semipopular introduction to Kabbalah (*Da'at U-Tvuna*). In its preface (p. 2 of the 1911 Jerusalem edition), he discussed the possibility of the revelation of the Kabbalah in the sixth millennium of the Jewish era, and the obligation of "every Torah scholar in Israel" to study esoterics.
77. Hillel, *Shorshei Ha-Yam*, vol. 1, pp. 28–30. See also Meir, "The Revealed."
78. On the ideology of the mass dissemination of Hasidic doctrine in Bratzlav circles today, see Piekarz, *Studies in Bratzlav Hasidism*, pp. 202, 215.

79. See Friedman, "Messiah and Messianism," pp. 178–186. On earlier roots of this ideology, see pp. 187–188. On R. Shalom Baer as a source of inspiration for the seventh rebbe (R. Menaḥem Mendel Shneurson) regarding the dissemination of Torah mysticism, see Ratzabi, "Rabbi Shalom Dov Baer," pp. 99–100.
80. This practice of using information technologies had begun already under R. Shalom Baer; see Friedman, "Messiah and Messianism," p. 186. On R. Menaḥem Mendel's ideology of disseminating Kabbalah, see, for example, Goldberg, "The Zaddik's Soul," pp. 256–257.
81. See, for example, Steinsaltz, *The Candle of God.*
82. See Loewenthal, "Mysticism and Modernity," pp. 251–257. A striking example of such a spiritual guide in our time is R. Yosef Yizḥaq Ofen.
83. For the debate concerning the study of Kabbalah among adherents of the school of R. Elijah of Vilna, see Nadler, *Faith of the Mitnagdim*, pp. 39–46. For earlier sources on opposition to Kabbalah, see Ravitzky, "Insanity of Amulet Writers."
84. See Shashar, *Talks with Leibowitz*, p. 95; and see pp. 93–95 for his debate with Kook.
85. For a critical discussion of Hartman's attitude toward Kabbalah, see Garb, "Joy of Torah."
86. See Tobi, "Emunat Ha-Shem," and sources cited there. See also ibid., p. 89, on the responses of Kook and Zeitlin to Kappaḥ's attack on Kabbalah.
87. Yosef, *Yeḥave Da'at*, vol. 4, p. 245. In general, this responsum indicates the rabbi's reservations toward the widespread dissemination of Kabbalah. On opposition to the Kabbalah Center in the United States, see Y. Ben-Ami, "Kabbalah American Style," *Ha'aretz*, 5 Nov. 2004.
88. Dessler, *Mikhtav Me-Eliyahu*, vol. 4, p. 9.
89. Ibid., vol. 2, p. 94. Even Dessler's works, however, contain some kabbalistic themes (see, for example, vol. 4, pp. 304–306).
90. For the negative responses of various Religious-Zionist rabbis to Madonna's visit in 2004, see the report in *Ha'aretz*, 20 Sept. 2004.
91. For a rationale of this curricular practice, see Tzevi Yehuda Kook, "Study of Torah," *Talks of Rabbi Tzevi Yehuda*, vol. 2 (Jerusalem, undated).
92. "Secrets of Torah," *Talks of Rabbi Tzevi Yehuda* (Jerusalem, undated), pp. 2, 4; see also p. 7.
93. On his opposition to the widespread study of Kabbalah, see Tau, *Le-Emunat 'Itenu*, vol. 3, pp. 127–129.
94. Ibid., p. 17. See p. 160 for his condemnation of ecstasy.
95. Ibid., pp. 202–203. For similar reservations vis-à-vis alternative medicine, see Aviner, "Alternative Medicine"; Aviner, "Complementary Medicine."

CHAPTER 3. THE CONCEPT OF POWER IN NATIONAL MYSTICISM

1. The relationship between mysticism and nationalism in the twentieth century deserves a broader comparative study. For the time being see, for example, Victoria, *Zen War Stories*, pp. 15, 41.
2. On Maharal and Kook, see Rosenak, "Theory of Unity of Opposites," p. 276. For

more on the origins of national mysticism, see Garb, "Rabbi Kook and His Sources"; Garb, "On the Kabbalists of Prague"; Garb, "Alien Culture."

3. See Williams, *Keywords*.
4. Garb, *Manifestations of Power*.
5. See Biale, *Power and Powerlessness*; Ezrahi, *Rubber Bullets*, pp. 176–178; Mopsik, *Les Grands Textes de la Cabale*, p. 642.
6. See Shapira, *Land and Power*.
7. On the ultraorthodox view, see for example, Ravitzky, *Messianism, Zionism, and Religious Radicalism*, pp. 40–78, 145–180. On "power" in Religious-Zionist thought, see Luz, *Wrestle at Jabbok*, pp. 362–392; Schwartz, *Religious Zionism*, pp. 28–32; Holzer, "Nationalism and Morality."
8. See, for example, Schwartz, *Israel in Religious Zionist Thought*, pp. 228–230; Schwartz, *Theology of the Religious-Zionist Movement*, pp. 14–15. However, see Schwartz, *Religious Zionism*, p. 131n73.
9. On this process, see Garb, "Ideological Roots of Gush Emunim." On Eitam's quasi-messianic self-perception, see A. Shavit, "A Leader Awaiting a Sign," *Ha'aretz*, 22 March 2002.
10. In order to focus the debate on the twentieth century, this historical review must be brief. I hope to discuss this subject in more detail in future studies.
11. For a similar process with messianism, see Idel, *Messianic Mystics*, pp. 236–240, 288–289.
12. There is much research on this topic; see, for example, Elior, "*Yesh* and *'Ayin*."
13. See Idel, *Hasidism*, pp. 208–230. On the personal model of power, see Garb, *Manifestations of Power*.
14. For the sources and debate, see Avivi, *Zohar Ramḥal*, particularly pp. 109–114, 117, 122, 136–143, 177.
15. See Avivi, *The Kabbalah of the Gra*, pp. 93, 102–103, and cf. Morgenstern, *Messianism and Settlement*, pp. 109–111, 158; Morgenstern, *Redemption through Return*, pp. 263–327 (but see Barnai, *Historiography and Nationalism*, p. 169; Bartal, *Exile in the Homeland*, pp. 250–295). Luzzatto's historiosophical doctrine and its continuation in the Kabbalah of R. Elijah of Vilna are discussed by Schuchat, "Historiosophy of the Vilna Gaon"; Schuchat, "Doctrine of Redemption" (see also Avivi, "History").
16. For a general description of this school, see Schuchat, "Lithuanian Kabbalah." On Kook and the Kabbalah of R. Elijah of Vilna, see Neria, *Siḥot Ha-Re'iah*, pp. 196–213. On Kook and Luzzatto, see Kohen, *Qol Ha-Nevu'a*, pp. 315–318. On Elyashiv, whom Kook described as "the leading kabbalist of the generation" (Kook, *Letters*, vol. 2, p. 463), see Wacks, "R. Elyashiv"; Baumgarten, "History and Historiosophy." For more on Kook's ties with him, see Neria, *Siḥot Ha-Re'iah*, pp. 159–166; Sussman, "Letters," p. 23 (and pp. 31–32 for their disputes). For Hertz and Kook, see Morgenstern, "Place of the Ten Tribes," p. 228n2. Hertz was Kook's predecessor in the Jaffa rabbinate. His book *Brit 'Olam* was published in an expanded edition in 2001. The correspondence between

Hertz and Elyashiv (incorporated in the 2006 edition of *Mishnat Hasidim* by R. Emmanuel Ḥai Ricci) proves that mutual ties existed between these Lithuanian kabbalists.

17. According to the testimony of R. David Kohen ("Ha-Nazir") in his introduction to *Orot Ha-Qodesh*, p. 21. On the personality of the Tzaddiq in Kook's doctrine, see Avivi, "History as Divine Prescription," pp. 740–741; Rosenak, "Rav Kook's Hidden Treatises," p. 265; Cherlow, "The Tzaddiq."
18. Kook, *Orot*, p. 146; see also pp. 147, 149.
19. Kook, *Shmona Qevatzim*, vol. 2, par. 140; ibid., vol. 8, par. 83; Kook, *Me'orot Ha-Re'iah*, p. 20; Garb, "Rabbi Kook and His Sources," pp. 86–89. These findings challenge claims by researchers and kabbalists that Kook was close to Hasidism (Fine, "Rabbi Abraham Isaac Kook," pp. 36–37; Zeitlin, *Book of the Few*, p. 237). On the issue of Kook's ambivalence toward Hasidism, see Kook, *Articles*, pp. 6–7, and cf. Ross, "Rabbi Kook," pp. 165–166. Clearly, the views of Kook's son, R. Tzevi Yehuda Ha-Kohen Kook ("Ratzia"), were distinctly anti-Hasidic (see T. Y. Kook, "Ḥasidim Ve-Mitnagdim," and see also Remer, *Gadol Shimusha*, pp. 132–134). R. Ya'aqov Moshe Ḥarlap's attitude was more complex; for a kabbalistic analysis of the advantages and disadvantages of Hasidism by this prominent student of Kook's, see Ḥarlap, "Opposition and Hasidism." For reservations about Hasidism in the third generation of the Kook circle, see Aviner, "Hasidim and Mitnagdim."
20. Following the categories I presented in my work on power, Cherlow also analyzed the place of power in Kook's thinking ("The Tzaddiq," pp. 314–315n773, 339).
21. See, for example, Kook, *Orot Ha-Qodesh*, vol. 2, p. 482; ibid., vol. 3, pp. 41–43, 61, 75–81. For a passage that seems to recommend reading Nietzsche, see Kook, *Shmona Qevatzim*, vol. 1, par. 767. See also Rosenberg, "R. Kook and the Blind Serpent"; Gellman, "Aesthetics." R. David Kohen has already pointed out the relationship between Kook and Bergson; see his introduction to Kook, *Orot Ha-Qodesh*, pp. 34–36. See also Bergman, *Philosophical Essays*, pp. 350–358. On Bergson's influence on R. Hillel Zeitlin, see Meir, "Hillel Zeitlin's Zohar," p. 135. For Schopenhauer, see Rosenberg, "Thought of Rav Kook."
22. For a summary, see Garb, *Manifestations of Power*, pp. 16–21.
23. See Garb, "Alien Culture," on the similarity between the position of Kook on this issue and those of his son, Ratzia, and of Ḥarlap. These thinkers viewed rejection of the alien influence as an integral part of the national-psychological makeup of the emergent Jewish nation in its land, and even attributed this influence to the "impure atmosphere" of foreign countries. See, for example, Kook, *Shmona Qevatzim*, vol. 7, par. 10; ibid., vol. 8, par. 124; Tzevi Yehuda Kook, *Li-Ntivot Yisra'el*, vol. 1, pp. 5–11; Ḥarlap, *Ma'yanei Ha-Yeshu'a*, pp. 122–123; Schwartz, *Challenge and Crisis*, pp. 254–256.
24. On this concept, see Rosenberg, *Good and Evil*, pp. 62–64; Cherlow, "Boldness and Modesty," pp. 62–64. On the theurgical action of "the spiritually powerful," see Kook, *Orot Ha-Qodesh*, vol. 3, pp. 338–339.
25. See Kook, *Orot Ha-Qodesh*, vol. 1, p. 86. This text, which deserves a discussion in its

own right, challenges the necessity of external-social action on the part of the Chosen (see also Kook, *Shmona Qevatzim* vol. 1, par. 669; ibid., vol. 4, par. 67; Kook, *Pinkas Yud-Gimel*, p. 27). For a similar attitude on the part of Ḥarlap, see *Yishlaḥ mi-Marom*, p. 32. On this attitude in successive generations of the Kook circle, see Schwartz, *Challenge and Crisis*, pp. 48–50, 78–83, 92–98, 191–192; Tau, *Le-Emunat 'Itenu*, vol. 1, p. 104; ibid., vol. 3, 138, 145; ibid. vol. 4, p. 58; Kelner, *Pluralism*, pp. 60–61. For a similar attitude within the Ashlag circle, see Berkowitz, "Interview with R. Sheinberger," p. 22. For an in-depth review of the concept of internalization in Jewish mysticism, see Margolin, *The Human Temple*.

26. Ḥarlap, *Pure Sayings*, p. 44. Note the expression "clear and direct vision" (*mitokh aspaklaria me'ira*), used by the Talmud (*Sukka* 45b) to describe the *Lamed Vav Tzaddiqim* (thirty-six righteous Jews).
27. On the issue of holy volition and power, see Kook, *'Olat Re'iah*, vol. 2, pp. 5–6. On "the internal subjugation" of the world to the power of the Tzaddiq, see Kook, *Orot Ha-Qodesh*, vol. 1, p. 147. For more on the power of the Tzaddiq, see the antinomian passage in Kook, *'Arphilei Tohar*, p. 15 (see also Kook, *Mussar Avikha*, pp. 148–149).
28. Kook, *Orot*, pp. 13–17. See also Kook's text in Pedaya, "Space, Time, and Eretz Israel," p. 592.
29. For purpose of comparison, it should be noted that a far more antimilitant, antipolitical, and antimilitaristic view can be found among other early twentieth-century mystics, some of whom had ties with Kook, notably A. S. Tamrat (see Rosenberg, *Good and Evil*, pp. 62–64; Shragai, "Letters of Tamrat") and R. Avraham Ḥen (see Meir, "Longing of Souls"; Weiner, *Nine and a Half Mystics*, pp. 269–272). Yet Kook effectively supported a somewhat "hawkish" policy toward the "Arab Problem" (this issue deserves an in-depth study; for the time being, see Lanir, "Rabbi Kook and Zionism," pp. 378–379).
30. Kook, *Orot*, pp. 78–79. This passage was not censored despite a general tendency on the part of his editors to modify passages that spoke of Kook's visions. For his mystical vision on war and courage, see Kook, *Orot Ha-Qodesh*, vol. 3, p. 131. For more of Kook's visions, see, for example, Kook, *Ḥadarav*, pp. 85–86, 159–160. For more on the prophet Elijah in Kook's works, see Cherlow, "The Tzaddiq," p. 349, and sources cited there.
31. See, for example, Kook, *Orot*, pp. 15, 63, 79. Even his pluralistic perspective, as set forth in his famous essay on the "Three Forces" (*Orot*, pp. 70–72), is linked to his view of revival as the awakening of the nation's powers (see also pp. 44–45 and Kook, *'Olat Re'iah*, vol. 1, pp. 330–331). On the awakening of the nation's powers, see also Kook, *Orot Ha-Qodesh*, vol. 1, p. 149.
32. Kook, *Orot*, p. 80. For his views on "physical might" and "the might of the sanctified flesh," see ibid. and also Kook, *'Olat Re'iah*, vol. 1, pp. 375–376; Kook, *Orot Ha-Qodesh*, vol. 3, p. 78; Ross, "Rav Kook's Concept of God," pp. 53–54. For more on the issue of physical exercise and power in the context of national mysticism, see Garb, "Working Out as Divine Work," where I also discuss the current schism between the "gentle"

approach to the body that characterizes the circles of religious renewal in the spirit of Kook (see, for example, Nov, "The Body in Movement," pp. 65–70) and the "harsh" militaristic approach to the body that is prevalent in premilitary academies in Judea and Samaria. On Ratzia's attempts to censor, see Even-Ḥen, *Rabbi and Leader*, p. 399; Agnon, *Book, Writer, Story*, p. 352.

33. Kook, *Hadarav*, pp. 91–92. On the doctrine of the Tzaddiq as a redeemer of souls, see Cherlow, "Tzaddiq," particularly p. 118. For the relationship between prayer and power, see Kook, *Orot Ha-Qodesh*, vol. 3, pp. 48, 59–60; Kook, *Shmona Qevatzim*, vol. 1, pars. 73, 173.
34. See Sussman, "Letters," p. 18.
35. See Kook, *Ḥadarav*, pp. 90–93; Kook, *Pinkas Yud-Gimel*, p. 5 (lightly censored).
36. For a text that expresses a very strong perception of self-aggrandizement, see Rosenak, "Rav Kook's Hidden Treatises," p. 261n21.
37. Kook, *Ḥadarav*, p. 47. The relationship in Kook's writings between the theme of freedom and those of volition and power requires clarification. On the connection between freedom and volition, see Ish-Shalom, "R. Kook, Spinoza, Goethe," pp. 101, 162–163; Rosenberg, "R. Kook and the Blind Serpent," p. 332.
38. See the poem describing the power of Kook in Ofan, *Nafshi Taqshiv Shiro*, p. 51. See also Kook, *Ḥadarav*, pp. 80–81. For a Nietzschean view of the superior man, see Kook, *Orot Ha-Qodesh*, vol. 3, p. 239; cf. ibid., p. 154, concerning the power of the superior soul. The concept of soul in Kook's writings shall be discussed in a future study. See Kook, *Shmona Qevatzim*, vol. 6, par. 98, regarding his anguish at not allowing the power of thought to expand. See also Kook, *Ḥadarav*, p. 146, and cf. Ashlag, *Or Ha-Bahir*, p. 293.
39. See Kook, *Ḥadarav*, pp. 99, 151–153, 163. R. David Kohen also wondered if his physical and internal powers would stand by him in his striving for prophecy. See Schwartz, *Religious Zionism*, p. 178.
40. See, for example, Ratzia's perception of his father as someone whose mission was to rectify the generation, in an interview published in *Ha-Ma'or: A Journal for the Study of R. Kook's Doctrine* (Jerusalem, 1994), pp. 34–41; cf. the allusion to Kook's messianic mission in T. Y. Kook, *Li-Ntivot Yisra'el*, vol. 2, p. 47.
41. On the editing of Kook's works, see Meir's important study "Lights and Vessels."
42. This claim can be found in his introduction to the book.
43. On this episode, see Schwartz, *Religious Zionism*, pp. 198–233; Rosenak, "Rav Kook's Hidden Treatises," pp. 289–290.
44. See Schwartz, *Religious Zionism*, pp. 174–186; and see also the expressions "and the voice is strong and bold" (p. 175) and "for a long time, my soul has been yearning for prophecy, for the revelation of the spirit in its full force and might" (p. 177). See also the passage cited on p. 191. On the "passive" model of power, see Garb, *Manifestations of Power*, pp. 64–71, 76, 160, 200, 224, 228, 234, 266, 278.
45. Cited by Schwartz, *Religious Zionism*, p. 156. See also Kohen's Nietzschean self-description: "The genius is not dependent on the opinion of people around him. . . .

On the contrary, the inner soul walks firmly with contempt and derision for all pettiness in the environment" (ibid., p. 170). This description parallels expressions of the Tzaddiq's hatred and contempt of mediocrity in the writings of Kook.

46. T. Y. Kook, *Or Li-Ntivati*, pp. 90–91. See also ibid., p. 59–65; T. Y. Kook, *Li-Ntivot Yisra'el*, vol. 1, 74, 115; Schwartz, *Challenge and Crisis*, p. 260; Schwartz, *Theology of the Religious-Zionist Movement*, p. 69. For a similar parallel between political-military power and divine power, see Ḥarlap's statement in Schwartz, *Theology of the Religious-Zionist Movement*, p. 92. For the way the spiritual leaders of Gush Emunim perceived power, see Schwartz, *Israel in Religious Zionist Thought*, pp. 105, 109, 114, 115, 117n58; Ravitzky, *Messianism, Zionism, and Religious Radicalism*, p. 132. R. Tzevi Yisra'el Tau's perception of power deserves a study in its own right; for the time being, see *Le-Emunat 'Itenu*, vol. 1, pp. 182–183; vol. 3, pp. 45, 63; vol. 4, pp. 7–52.
47. On the tension between Kohen and Ratzia, see Meir, "Lights and Vessels"; Meir, "Longing of Souls."
48. For a critique of power in the new literature of the Religious-Zionist circles, see Grienberg, *Almost a Bride*, particularly pp. 97–99.
49. Kook, *Me'orot Ha-Re'iah*, pp. 16–17. See also later in this chapter for the disparity between the ideal state and the real state in Kook's writings.
50. See Kook, *Shmona Qevatzim*, vol. 3, pars. 1–2.
51. Garb, "Religious Zionism." See also Don-Yehiya, "The Book and the Sword." On this affair, see also Gal-Or, *Jewish Underground*, which focuses on the political dimension. The debate on the ideological dimension, on the other hand, is based almost entirely on secondary or journalistic sources.
52. But also in the Kabbalah of R. Elijah of Vilna's disciples. See, for example, Menaḥem Mendel of Shklov, *Derekh Ha-Qodesh*, pp. 37–38: "Alas, for our many sins, power has been granted to the external princes, the princes of the Nations of the World. And they enter the inner sanctuary, the secret of the Holy of Holies and Jerusalem the holy city. . . . and now that you are in exile, seek the peace of the city, because in its peace you will find peace. The source of the blessings that emanated from the Holy of Holies . . . which is the source of all blessings, are now being divided among Shem, Ham and Japheth, the sons of Noah. . . . And then [in the time of redemption] they shall all merge in love and peace and shall encompass the might that, for our many sins, was granted to the princes of the Nations of the World. . . . And God shall unleash His storm upon the heads of the wicked." The Temple Mount was perceived as the source of blessing, and the dominion over the Sanctuary by the Nations of the World severed the attribute of "might" from other attributes and transformed it into a source of power for the Nations of the World. According to the messianic expectation, the Sanctuary will be returned to the Jewish people, and the attribute of might will reunite with the other attributes and be directed against the Nations of the World.
53. See Segal, *Dear Brothers*, p. 56.
54. Regarding the term *It'aruta Di-Le-Tata*, see, for example, Zohar, vol. 3, p. 92.
55. From Segal, *Dear Brothers*, p. 276.

56. In accordance with Ratzia's famous comparison of the leader of the State to the "king" of Israel. On "the kingdom of Israel" as an expression of God's sovereignty, see, for example, T. Y. Kook, *Li-Ntivot Yisra'el*, vol. 2, p. 513.
57. Zuckerman, "Interview."
58. Segal, *Dear Brothers*, p. 218.
59. Kook, *Orot*, p. 160. See Zuckerman, "Interview," and also Bin-Nun, "In Favor of Stocktaking," p. 14. Consequently, the Underground was presented by its opponents as a departure from Kook's path.
60. See Kook, *Me'orot Ha-Re'iah*, p. 30, which argues that Israeli nationalism mirrors the celestial world, just as the earthly Temple mirrors the heavenly Temple, and therefore "its ways are far superior" to those of regular nationalism.
61. Ari'el, "Rebellion in Halakha," p. 16. See also Don-Yehiya, "The Book and the Sword," pp. 211–212; 'Etzion, "Mi-Degel Yerushalayim," p. 28.
62. 'Etzion, "Mi-Degel Yerushalayim," p. 9.
63. Segal, *Dear Brothers*, p. 235. See p. 58 for Tau's paradoxical statement that the fact that gentiles trample the Temple Mount is an indication that it belongs to the Jewish people. See also p. 232. For a vigorous rejection of the focus on the Temple Mount, see Tau, *Le-Emunat 'Itenu*, vol. 5, p. 158. See also Don-Yehiya, "The Book and the Sword," pp. 213–214.
64. See Bowman and Woolf, "Literacy and Power," p. 6.
65. See, for example, Kelner's claim in *Pluralism*, pp. 44–45, that those who disagree with Kook's doctrine simply do not understand it. Clearly he is implying that such an understanding is channeled through members of the Kook circle, who claim that those who wish to study his writings require "instruction."
66. On the tension between the Kook circle and more "activist" circles, in Gush Emunim in particular and Religious Zionism in general, see Sheleg, *New Religious Jews*, pp. 46–53.
67. Nonetheless, there were Sephardic kabbalists, chiefly the "Holy Grandfather" (*Ha-Saba Qadisha*), R. Shlomo Eli'ezer Alfandari, who strongly opposed Zionism. See Ravitzky, *Messianism, Zionism, and Religious Radicalism*, pp. 57–58.
68. Such racism is evident in the following quote, for example: "The gentile in this world is the embodiment of the *Sitra Aḥra* from which he is fashioned; thievery, robbery and adultery and all kinds of abominations in the world" (Haddaya, *Yaskil 'Avdi, Yoreh De'ah*, section 43). On Haddaya's political doctrine, see Zohar, "Zionism and Israel." On Haddaya's response to the establishment of the State, see Garb, "Kabbalah outside the Walls."
69. See Neria, *Bi-Sde Ha-Re'iah*, p. 265. For more on cooperation between Sephardic kabbalists and members of the Kook circle, see Shapiro, "Note on Practical Kabbalah." Earlier in this chapter, we also saw the support that Yeshu'a Ben Shushan, a Sephardic kabbalistic member of the Jewish Underground received from fellow Sephardic kabbalists for his program to rid the Temple Mount of mosques.
70. For Habad Hasidism's adoption of militaristic terminology in the period of R. Shalom Baer, see Friedman, "Messiah and Messianism," pp. 189–191. It was in this period

that the interpretation of the acronym "HaBaD" as *Ḥayalei Beit David*, or soldiers of the House of David, was added to the existing *Ḥokhma, Bina ve-Da'at* to designate this branch of Hasidism (see also p. 179). The messianic implications of the added acronym should be noted. For a kabbalistic debate on the symbolism of the Habad youth movement "God's army," see Shneurson, *Ba'ti le-Gani*, vol. 1, pp. 226–227. See also Goldberg, "The Zaddik's Soul," p. 217. For a discussion of Habad "militarism" as a symbol of the ultraorthodox public's growing interest in power and as an indication of its growing political and social power, see Menaḥem Friedman in A. Golan, "The Level of Threat and Rejection," *Ha'aretz*, 16 Jan. 1998.

71. See the booklet *The Truth about the Habad Movement*, published in Brooklyn in the 1980s by Moshe Moshkovitch.
72. See Loewenthal, "Habad Approaches"; Friedman, "Messiah and Messianism," pp. 210–215, 220–221.
73. For earlier positions of Habad, see Alfasi, "Hasidism." For R. Shalom Baer's opinion, see Selzer, *Zionism Reconsidered*, pp. 11–18; Ratzabi, "Rabbi Shalom Dov Baer"; Friedman, "Messiah and Messianism," pp. 191–195; Pedaya, "Space, Time, and Eretz Israel," pp. 587–597.
74. Militaristic attitudes toward the Israeli-Arab conflict prevailed in Habad circles by the 1940s; see Greenberg, "Redemption after Holocaust," pp. 73–74. For a summary of Habad's attitudes toward Zionism, messianism, and activism, see Ravitzky, *Messianism, Zionism, and Religious Radicalism*, pp. 181–206.
75. For a different perspective on the processes that took place in Habad in the period of R. Shalom Baer, see Loewenthal, "Mysticism and Modernity" (and cf. Loewenthal, "Habad Approaches," pp. 298–300). However, Loewenthal, too, agrees that the fifth rebbe introduced significant changes in Habad's patterns of activity in response to modernization. For a discussion of this process from another perspective, see Idel, *Messianic Mystics*, p. 278. From a panoramic perspective of the evolution of Jewish mysticism, it is worth noting the early sources of the transition from study to action in Jewish thought, and the role of the concept of power in this transition. See Garb, *Manifestations of Power*, pp. 175, 270–272, and sources cited there.
76. See Kraus, *Messianism in Habad*.
77. See A. Golan, "The Turn of Rabbi Ginsburgh," *Ha'aretz*, 27 Nov. 1998.
78. Qarpel is the author of the book *The Revolution of Faith*.
79. For a summary of his views, see the pamphlet entitled *Root Treatment: The Need of the Hour*, published by Ginsburgh in 2001.
80. See Ginsburgh, *Kuntras Barukh Ha-Gever*. Goldstein's act is described as a manifestation of the divine attribute of "might" (p. 3). See also Ginsburgh, *Ha-Hitqashrut*, p. 19: "Might expresses the power [of God] more than any other positive attribute."
81. It is not surprising, therefore, that Yehuda 'Etzion of the Jewish Underground also had ties with the Jewish Leadership Movement. Ginsburgh also taught Kabbalah to Underground members while they served their prison sentence.

82. Ginsburgh, *Aleph Beit*, p. 2. The structure and contents of this book may have been influenced by Kook's *Reish Milin*, inter alia.
83. See, in particular, Ginsburgh, *Spirit of the Messiah*, pp. 238–240, on the power to conquer Eretz Israel, as well as Ginsburgh, *Yesod*.
84. See, for example, Leiner, *Mei Ha-Siloaḥ*, vol. 1, pp. 54, 55, 179, 190; vol. 2, p. 73. For his concept of power, see, for example, vol. 2, p. 52.
85. Ibid., vol. 1, p. 170. The prohibition on "precipitating the end" is one of the "Three Oaths."
86. See Hadari, "Two High Priests"; Cherlow, "Rav Kook," p. 237.
87. On the significance of the year 2000, see Ryback, *'Al Qetz*, p. 514. Also, regarding Ryback's work, see Wolfson, *Venturing Beyond*, pp. 124–126.
88. Ryback, *'Al Qetz*, pp. 401, 450. This is not the first time that the kabbalists of the twentieth century predicted that the redemption would come at a time when suffering actually increased. R. Elazar Shapiro, the rebbe of Munkacz, predicted that the redemption would come in 1941 (see Nadler, "War on Modernity," p. 237). An anonymous kabbalist, apparently a follower of R. Elijah of Vilna, reckoned that the end would come in 1939, the year the Second World War broke out (see Garb, "Kabbalah outside the Walls"). Ryback himself warned that extra caution was necessary during this momentous period of heightened retribution (*'Al Qetz*, p. 465), and that the forces of the *Sitra Aḥra* (literally The Other Side, evil force) were conspiring to obtain "an extension" beyond the year 2000 (p. 550). Ryback also wrote that the events of the First Intifada (the rioting of "Arab gangs," as he put it), which began in 1988, were simply "a taste of things to come" (p. 521, and also see there for the "power of retribution"). According to him, the Arabs, like the Soviets and Nazis, belonged to the "root" of Amaleq (see, for example, pp. 477, 524).
89. Ibid., pp. 525, 567. See also p. 594 for a condemnation of the withdrawal from Sinai. See also Ginsburgh's (critical) kabbalistic analysis of the Oslo Process in Ginsburgh, *Ḥasdei David*, vol. 1, pp. 106–108.
90. See, for example, Ryback, *'Al Qetz*, pp. 398–399. See also pp. 434 and 446, which state that the Jewish people's "secret weapon" is Torah and Kabbalah, and p. 459, which criticizes the "opponents" of Hasidism, who do not contribute to the dissemination of Kabbalah. (According to Ryback, opposition to Habad strengthens the power of the Sitra Aḥra [p. 551]). The doctrine of the Tzaddiq also occupies an important place in Ryback's book, as in other twentieth-century kabbalistic works (see, for example, pp. 537, 542).
91. See ibid., pp. 510, 545.
92. See Charvit, "Identity and History," and sources cited there. Other examples of a historiosophical-nationalist discourse that are also based on the doctrine of the Maharal of Prague include R. Yizḥaq Hutner's series, *Paḥad Yizḥaq*; R. Yisra'el Eliyahu Weintraub's series, *Be-Sod Yesharim*; and R. Moshe Shapira's series *Afiqei Mayim*, all of which originated from the Lithuanian world.

93. Ashkenazy, "Jews in Exile," p. 91. See also his statement (ibid., p. 87) that R. Judah Loew of Prague followed the Sephardic tradition. As proof, Ashkenazy invokes the influence of Sephardic Kabbalah on his thought. See also his assertion that the Sephardic theology was the authentic one (p. 90).
94. Ryback, *'Al Qetz*, p. 591.

CHAPTER 4. PSYCHOLOGICAL NOTIONS OF POWER

1. For Ashlag's emphasis, à la Luzzatto, on the need to practically demonstrate that there is no power other than God's, see B. Ashlag, *Sham'ati*, pp. 1–2, and see also Lavi, "Idea of Creation," p. 259.
2. His son, R. Barukh Ashlag, by contrast, had no qualms about identifying "the wish to receive" with the gentiles (letters at the end of *Sham'ati*, p. 47).
3. Schweid's contention (*Ruin to Salvation*, p. 194) that "obviously" the central axis of R. Ashlag's writings was historiosophical, and that its main theme was the response to the Holocaust, is questionable.
4. See the famous "declaration" that "all of mankind, whether black, white or yellow, without any distinction," is subject to the "purpose of the creation" and that the choice of the Jewish people was simply "a transitional step" toward the universal rectification (*tiqqun*) of the world (Ashlag, *Sefer Matan Torah*, pp. 40, 41, and see also p. 38). Nevertheless, some members of the circle had reservations about studying Kabbalah outside Eretz Israel. See Laitman, *The Kabbalah Experience*, pp. 60, 206. Not all of these statements were included in the English adaptation of this work.
5. In light of the findings of this chapter, there is reason to challenge Brill's contention (*Thinking God*, p. 371) that Jewish psychology ended in the late nineteenth century and has only recently been revived.
6. For an analysis of the more technical kabbalistic concepts relating to this doctrine, see Hansel, "The Origin in Rabbi Ashlag," pp. 42–46; Lavi, "Idea of Creation," pp. 56–63. For the influence of this doctrine on Mussar thinker R. Eliyahu Dessler, see Gottlieb, *Ha-Sulam*, p. 147.
7. B. Ashlag, *Sham'ati*, p. 66. See also Ashlag, *Pri Ḥakham*, vol. 1, p. 31; Lavi, "Idea of Creation," p. 284.
8. Ashlag, *Pri Ḥakham*, vol. 2, p. 29. See B. Ashlag, *Sham'ati*, p. 174, for a definition of spirituality as an incorporeal force, and cf. Ashlag, *Sefer Ha-Haqdamot*, p. 81.
9. B. Ashlag, *Sham'ati*, p. 58. Cf. p. 136.
10. See Ashlag, *Pri Ḥakham*, vol. 2, p. 3. On the pleasure of giving, see Ashlag, *Or Ha-Bahir*, p. 352. For a Hasidic text that defines the Tzaddiq as one who strives to give pleasure to God, see, for example, Elior, "Innovation of Hasidism," p. 398.
11. Ashlag, *Sefer Ha-Haqdamot*, pp. 50, 80. According to him, the purpose of the Torah is to foster the desire to give (p. 83).
12. On "vessels" in Ashlag's thinking, see Lavi, "Idea of Creation," pp. 277–281, 284–285, 300.

13. Ashlag, *Sefer Ha-Haqdamot*, pp. 57, 77; Ashlag, *Or Ha-Bahir*, p. 353. See also, Lavi, "Idea of Creation," p. 311.
14. Ashlag, *Introduction to the Science of Kabbalah*, pp. 24–25. For more on the concept of purification in Ashlag's thinking, see Lavi, "Idea of Creation," pp. 300–302, 313. On the screen as a force that filters light in order to purify the recipient, see ibid., pp. 88, 204. On the "force of attraction" and "force of repulsion," see Fisch, *Points of Light*, p. 103.
15. Ashlag, *Introduction to the Science of Kabbalah*, p. 83. On the relationship between the concepts of the vessel, the desire to receive, and the body, see Ashlag, *Pri Ḥakham*, vol. 1, p. 179. According to this text, the desire to receive is the main force of Creation. As we will see, it is also viewed as the natural force, which is rooted in the godhead itself. See also Ashlag, *Sefer Ha-Haqdamot*, p. 78, on turning the body from a vessel that receives into a vessel that gives. For more on the body in Ashlag's doctrine, see Lavi, "Idea of Creation," p. 288.
16. See, respectively, Mark, *Mysticism and Madness*, pp. 115–134; B. Ashlag, *Sham'ati*, pp. 54, 75. However, see also R. Mordekhai Sheinberger's argument in Berkowitz, "Interview with R. Sheinberger," p. 21.
17. B. Ashlag, *Sham'ati*, pp. 109, 114, 135.
18. On the importance of "the group" for Ashlag himself, see *Pri Ḥakham*, vol. 2, p. 147.
19. Ibid., p. 61.
20. Ibid., p. 161.
21. See ibid., pp. 151, 162, 170.
22. See ibid., p. 171. On how Eretz Israel is currently subject to the dominion of "the husk [*qelipa*] of Canaan," see p. 122. Obviously, the Ashlag circle's perception of the place of the sacred was totally different than that of the Kook circle. See also Ashlag, *Sefer Matan Torah*, p. 136.
23. Laitman, *Interview with the Future*, p. 118. Similarly, Laitman psychologizes the difference between Jew and gentile, when he speaks of the internal "Jew" as against the internal "gentile" and even "Arab," who is responsible for writing new textbooks "from the perspective of the Jews' enemies" (pp. 125–127).
24. Ginsburgh, *Divine Worship*, pp. 3, 6. This booklet was reworked in his *Lev la-Da'at* (Kfar Habad, Israel, 1990). See also Ginsburgh, *Ha-Hitqashrut*, p. 15.
25. Ginsburgh, *Divine Worship*, p. 9.
26. Compare the development of the Hasidic paradigm of "submission, differentiation, mitigation" (Ashlag, *Pri Ḥakham*, vol. 1, p. 102; and cf. the political application of this doctrine in Ginsburgh, *Kingdom of Israel*, vol. 4, pp. 5–8), or the model of "dot, line, area" (Ashlag, *Pri Ḥakham*, vol. 1, pp. 141–142, as against Ginsburgh, *Kingdom of Israel*, vol. 1, pp. 159–175). The thesis that man's actions—at least post factum—are predetermined and not based on choice is highly developed in the late Hasidic work by Leiner, *Mei Ha-Shiloaḥ* (see, for example, vol. 1, pp. 25, 27, 47, and cf. vol. 1, p. 45; see also Elior, "Innovation of Hasidism," pp. 410–411). In general, the passive model of power is extremely prevalent in Hasidic thinking.

27. Shapira, *Esh Qodesh*, p. 158. See also there the role of suffering (mainly during the Holocaust, since this book is based on his sermons during this period) in conquering "human knowledge." This view is also reminiscent of Ashlag's doctrine.
28. B. Ashlag, *Sham'ati*, p. 88.
29. Ashlag, *Pri Ḥakham*, vol. 2, p. 30. See also Lavi, "Idea of Creation," p. 258.
30. The letters of R. Barukh at the end of *Sham'ati*, p. 9. For a similar complexity in the doctrine of R. Naḥman of Bratzlav, see Mark, *Mysticism and Madness*, pp. 162–174, 345–356.
31. Ashlag, *Pri Ḥakham*, vol. 1, pp. 29, 36–37, and cf. p. 36 on restricting the masses' right to curb the individual's freedom. On the masses as a quantitative force, and the Tzaddiqim as a qualitative force, see Ashlag, *Sefer Ha-Haqdamot*, p. 221.
32. Ashlag's book *Pri Ḥakham* (vol. 1, pp. 39, 33) also endorses the possibility of the transmission of piety from generation to generation, since spiritual "property" is inherited. It is equally possible that this article alludes to Ashlag's prophetic consciousness, which resembled that of Kook. See p. 50 on how the prophets bring celestial light down to this earth, and p. 47 on how prophecy can be brought down to this earth through combinations of letters. (Note the probable influence of R. Abraham Abulafia's prophetic doctrine, which influenced Kook's disciple R. David Kohen ["Ha-Nazir"], too. See Schwartz, *Religious Zionism*, pp. 176–181.)
33. Ashlag, *Pri Ḥakham*, vol. 1, pp. 66–67.
34. Ibid., pp. 69–70. I would be cautious, however, of sweepingly defining Ashlag's doctrine as socialist, even though some claim that certain writings published by Ashlag in the early 1940s were banned by the British Mandate authorities because of its Marxist tendencies (see Gottlieb, *Ha-Sulam*, p. 120). To the best of my knowledge, the research publications on this subject have not reprinted this ban, or any other British document relating to this affair. By contrast, see, for example, Ashlag, *Sefer Ha-Haqdamot*, p. 220, which presents a somewhat caste-like social structure, in which the world is divided into the classical hierarchy of "mineral, plant, animal, and human" (for this hierarchy in Ashlag's doctrine, see Lavi, "Idea of Creation," pp. 260, 294–299), and subdivided into the masses, the affluent, heroes, and sages, depending on the talents with which different people are endowed. The claim of Bick in *Hem U-Mishnatom*, pp. 78–86, concerning Ashlag's "socialism" is based more on testimonies (important in themselves) and on conversations by various personalities with Ashlag on this issue than on his writings as such. Possibly, future research on the topic will uncover more solid textual evidence. Huss, "Altruistic Communism," discusses Ashlag's article "A Critique of Marxism," published in his journal *Ha-Uma*, which expressed great sympathy for socialist ideas and demonstrates a clear link between the Marxist dialectic and Ashlag's own doctrine of dialectic development. Aḥituv, "Rav Ashlag," also presented additional material on the issue of socialism in Ashlag's world. As Huss notes, these findings have also been reinforced by the publication of a collection of political treatises recently edited and published in Michael Laitman's *The Future Generation* (Thornhill, Canada, 2006). Nonetheless, there is still room for exam-

ining the role of Socialism in the broader context of Ashlag's works. On Kook's attitude toward socialism and anarchism, see Rosenberg, "Thought of Rav Kook," pp. 59–61; Cherlow, "The Tzaddiq," p. 139.

35. Ashlag, *Pri Ḥakham*, vol. 1, pp. 71–72, 74–75. See also p. 73 for an analysis of power along the lines of Hegel's "master-slave dialectic" (see Klein, *Master-Slave Dialectic*). According to Ashlag, power is in the hands of those who are prepared to risk their lives for their truths. On the conflict between kindness and truth in Hasidism, see Heschel, *Passion for Truth*, p. 132.
36. Ashlag, *Pri Ḥakham*, vol. 1, p. 78.
37. Ashlag, *Pri Ḥakham*, vol. 1, pp. 77, 117. In these ideas, as elsewhere in Ashlagian Kabbalah, the influence of R. Moshe Ḥayyim Luzzatto, one of the founders of modern Kabbalah, can be discerned.
38. Ashlag, *Pri Ḥakham*, vol. 1, p. 63. Cf. Kook, *Orot*, discussed at the end of Chapter 6 of the present book.
39. Ashlag, *Pri Ḥakham*, vol. 1, p. 65. Cf. pp. 36–37, and Ashlag, *Sefer Ha-Haqdamot*, p. 207. A possible source for this doctrine can be found in the work of R. Shlomo Elyashiv (see, for example, *Leshem Shvo Ve-Aḥlama*, vol. 1, chap. 6). Even though Ashlag does not quote Elyashiv, he refers often to R. Naftali Hertz, whose correspondence with Elyashiv was published in 2006. (For such references, see *Sefer Ha-Haqdamot*, pp. 23, 33, 35, 201; indeed, apart from the Ari, Hertz is the most often quoted in Ashlag's book.)
40. Ashlag, *Sefer Ha-Haqdamot*, pp. 79–80. For more on Ashlag's "path of suffering," see Lavi, "Idea of Creation," p. 310.
41. Laitman, *Interview with the Future*, pp. 129–130, and cf. pp. 110–113. See also the political application, where it is argued that returning parts of Eretz Israel will cause "terrible suffering" (p. 118).
42. See Garb, "Mysticism and Magic," pp. 106–107.
43. See, respectively, Ashlag, *Pri Ḥakham*, vol. 1, p. 190; B. Ashlag, *Sham'ati*, p. 75. For a similar formulation in sixteenth-century Kabbalah, see Yehuda Albotini, *Sulam Ha-'Aliya*, p. 70.
44. See Ashlag, *Sefer Ha-Haqdamot*, p. 221, regarding the idea that someone who is on a physical level imagines the redemption in terms of physical control over people. For a Sephardic parallel, see Haddaya, *Va-Yiqaḥ 'Ovadyahu*, vol. 4, p. 192, on Torah scholars as the center of the "divine cosmic body" (*shi'ur qoma*).
45. Leet, *Kabbalah of the Soul*, pp. 185–193, 263–272. On personal power in the New Age culture, see Garb, *Manifestations of Power*, pp. 12–13; Garb, "New Age Kabbalah."
46. For the concept of power in Avraham Zagdon's thinking, see, for example, *Or Ha-Ganuz*, pp. 49–50; *Ilu Yeda'tiv*, vol. 1, pp. 218, 223. The concept of power also occupies an important place in many other works, such as the *Shiv'a 'Einayim* series by R. Yizḥaq Moshe Erlanger, the works of R. Shmuel Toledano (*Nifl'aot Torat Hashem*, Jerusalem, 1989), or Eli'ezer Mordekhai Théon (Argaman Circle, *Secrets of Contemplation*, pp. 9, 12–13, 15–16).
47. Ginsburgh, *Transforming Darkness*, p. 6; see also pp. 117–119 on the exposure of the

"spark of the Messiah" in each person through the psychotherapeutic process. On the Hasidic concept, see Idel, *Messianic Mystics*, pp. 236–242.

48. Ginsburgh, *Ḥasdei David*, vol. 1, p. 6.
49. See, for example, the pamphlet *The Seeds of the Fall*, which is an abstract of Raḥlin's book *The War with the Evil Impulse*. Much material can be found at his Internet site, www.rachlin.org.il. Raḥlin also publishes *Teguva*, a weekly bulletin on current affairs.
50. Schechter, *Ve-Nikhtav Ba-Sefer*, vol. 1, p. 33. Cf. similar formulations of the late rebbe of Slonim, another Hasidic mentor who analyzed psychological issues in depth (Brezovsky, *Netivot Shalom*, vol. 1, 78–83).
51. Schechter, *Ve-Nikhtav Ba-Sefer*, p. 35. Schechter's psychological doctrine is extremely interesting and deserves a study in its own right.
52. Wolbe, *'Alei Shur*, vol. 1, pp. 146–147.
53. Ibid., pp. 150–153, 160.
54. Ibid., p. 165.
55. Wolbe, *'Alei Shur*, p. 167.
56. See Leibowitz, *Da'at Ḥokhma U-Mussar*, vol. 1, p. 184. The various uses of the term *power* by this original thinker deserve a study in their own right.

CHAPTER 5. SACRED SPACE AND SACRED PERSONS

1. On secular-Zionist "holy places" in Israel, see Bilu, "Sanctification of Place," pp. 65–74.
2. The doctrine of the Tzaddiq has also infiltrated the Mussar movement. See Dessler, *Mikhtav Me-Eliyahu*, part 4.
3. Nonetheless, neo-Hasidic circles also internalized the concept of the sacred person. For example, R. Zalman Shalomi-Schachter claims that anyone can be a Tzaddiq in certain situations, and that the Tzaddiq does not have to be a specific person (see Magid, "Rainbow Hasidism," pp. 38–39).
4. For a similar differentiation of sacred space in Zionist discourse, see Gurevtich and Aran, "On Place." Extensive research has focused on sacred space. See Garb, "Models of Sacred Space," and the sources cited there.
5. *Ketubot* 111a.
6. It is not surprising that this issue served both proponents and opponents of the commandment of settling the land throughout the generations.
7. For a general characterization of these two trends see Idel, *Kabbalah*, pp. 8–16. This, naturally, is only one typology of the extremely prolific Kabbalah literature. For a critical review of this issue, see Garb, *Manifestations of Power*, p. 61, and cf. Pedaya, *Vision and Speech*, pp. 31–32, 39.
8. Critique of Maimonides' *Sefer Ha-Mitzvot*, Positive Commandments 4.
9. *Otzar Ha-Ḥayyim*, cited in Idel, *Studies in Ecstatic Kabbalah*, p. 100n40.
10. See Idel, "Land of Israel," pp. 212, 213; Idel, *Hasidism*, pp. 39–40.
11. For a broader discussion of Eretz Israel's status in the thinking of the Kook circle, see Schwartz, *Israel in Religious Zionist Thought*, pp. 62–127.
12. Ḥarlap, *Ma'yanei Ha-Yeshu'a*, p. 282.

13. Ḥarlap, *Ma'yanei Ha-Yeshu'a*, p. 234. (On the air of Eretz Israel making people wise, see *Baba Batra* 158b.) See also Schwartz, *Israel in Religious Zionist Thought*, pp. 95–97.
14. For a similar argument regarding the affiliation between Eretz Israel and the Ein Sof, see text by R. Hillel Zeitlin cited by Hallamish in "Hasidism," p. 211.
15. See Chapter 3. The allegation that Kook did not effectively add anything new to the kabbalistic understanding of the status of Eretz Israel is raised in Schwartz, *Israel in Religious Zionist Thought*, p. 76. On the extremely close correlation between the people of Israel and the Land of Israel in Kook's doctrine, see pp. 65, 72.
16. For more on Kohen, see Schwartz, *Religious Zionism*, pp. 191–197; Schwartz, *Israel in Religious Zionist Thought*, pp. 111–112. For Ḥarlap, see *Ḥed Harim*, p. 69. For Kook, see Rosenak, "Torah of Eretz Israel," p. 32; Schwartz, *Israel in Religious Zionist Thought*, p. 73. For a similar attitude on the part of Ḥarlap, see texts cited in Schwartz, *Israel in Religious Zionist Thought*, p. 50.
17. See Schwartz, *Israel in Religious Zionist Thought*, p. 68; Schwartz, *Religious Zionism*, p. 165; Rosenak, "Torah of Eretz Israel" (and cf. *Orot Ha-Torah*, pp. 387–40); Kook, *Articles*, pp. 78–80; Kook, *Shmona Qevatzim*, vol. 6, par. 77.
18. There is also an antinomian undercurrent in Kook's assertions regarding the ability of Eretz Israel to convert the permitted into the proscribed (see Schwartz, *Israel in Religious Zionist Thought*, p. 108). Antinomian elements can also be found among halakhic kabbalists, who perceive Eretz Israel literally. As Ravitzky has shown ("Waymarks to Zion," p. 10), underlying the thinking of Naḥmanides, one of the most important kabbalists of this stream, is the radical conclusion that the commandments have full validity in Eretz Israel only. One nonkabbalistic rabbi who implemented the program of an Eretz Israeli Torah was R. Eli'ezer Berkowitz, who claimed that Halakha had to be changed as a result of the return to Eretz Israel and sovereignty over it (cf. Rosenak, "Exile and Eretz Israel," pp. 551–553).
19. Kook, *Shmona Qevatzim*, vol. 7, par. 14. On the revelation of the higher Eretz Israel referred to here, see also vol. 1, par. 745.
20. For the sanctification of the secular in Kook's doctrine, see Ben-Shlomo, "The Sacred and the Profane," pp. 517–518.
21. Cf. Kook, *Shmona Qevatzim*, vol. 6, par. 171.
22. With which Kook identified, as we shall see in Chapter 6.
23. Kook, *Shmona Qevatzim*, vol. 1, par. 395.
24. Further corroboration of this interpretation of the text can be found in ibid., vol. 6, p. 171, where Kook writes, "Despite the sheer drop in spirituality of Ḥutz La-Aretz, we must seek in it the illumination of knowledge. For God is Lord of the Universe, and his Kingship rules over everything. And if we return with assets, these are added to Eretz Israel, and are illuminated by the radiance of the Torah even more forcefully." Here, the sanctification of Ḥutz La-Aretz and the incorporation of its strengths into Eretz Israel are described in the first person (albeit in the plural, referring to the entire Kook circle). This text, which was written in Switzerland, may have been alluding to the difficult experience of spending the First World War abroad, to which Kook also

alludes in a poem from the same period titled "The Depths of My Exile" (see Ofan, *Nafshi Taqshiv Shiro*, p. 54). One of the advantages of the publication of Kook, *Shmona Qevatzim*, was the possibility of reconstructing the original dates—and consequently also the historical and biographical contexts—of Kook's writings. See also Rosenak, "Torah of Eretz Israel," pp. 45–48.

25. Kook, *Shmona Qevatzim*, vol. 8, p. 83. On trends toward identification with, or opposition to, the image of Moses in Jewish mysticism, see Goldreich, "Tikkunei Zohar"; Huss, "Bar Yohai and Moses." On the image of Moses in Kook's thinking, see Cherlow, "The Tzaddiq," p. 350.
26. We should not be too shocked by his self-esteem, since in several places in Kook's writings he verges on self-deification. In the text cited here (Kook, *Shmona Qevatzim*, vol. 8, p. 83), Kook compares his words to those of God: " 'Our word is like as fire, And like a hammer that breaketh the rock in pieces' [Jeremiah 23:29], for it is the word of God. . . . 'Happy is the man that hearkeneth to me' [Proverbs 8:34]." See also Kook's text on the importance of the self, which he ends thus: "I am the Lord" (*Orot Ha-Qodesh*, vol. 3, p. 140, and also Rosenak, "Rav Kook's Hidden Treatises," p. 262). Although Kook emphasizes that his pride is godly pride (see for example, *Ḥadarav*, p. 36), this assertion, too, smacks of self-deification.
27. For a different view, which emphasizes the concrete activity of R. Shneur Zalman on behalf of Eretz Israel and his concrete perception of Eretz Israel, see Hallamish, "Hasidism," especially pp. 243–244.
28. In a response by the third rebbe of the Habad dynasty, the author of the *Tzemaḥ Tzedeq*, to his disciple who wished to immigrate to Eretz Israel (see Ravitzky, *Messianism, Zionism, and Religious Radicalism*, p. 185).
29. See Friedman, "Messiah and Messianism," pp. 194–195. On the opposition of R. Shalom Baer's son, R. Yosef Yizḥaq, to the immigration of his Hasidim to Eretz Israel see p. 199. See also the interesting text presented by Ratzabi, "Rabbi Shalom Dov Baer," p. 84, in which R. Shalom Baer writes that even though Jerusalem is more sacred than Hebron, the fact that Hebron was less exposed to secularism afforded "Hebron greater sanctity than Jerusalem." This text places R. Shalom Baer in the category of those who viewed sacred space as a spiritual concept.
30. See Zorotzkin, "Building the Earthly," pp. 151–159.
31. *Megilla* 29a.
32. Liebes, "Emeq Ha-Melekh," p. 105.
33. See, for example, *Sifrei* on Deuteronomy, Finkelstein edition, section 1; *Mekhilta* on Deuteronomy in *Midrash Tann'aim*, Hoffman edition, p. 61; *Yalqut Shim'oni*, vol. 2, section 503.
34. The seventh rebbe, however, also adopted the spiritual model of sacred space. See his statement that all Jews, in their hearts, are Eretz Israel and sacred space, in a letter printed by Shneurson, *Heikhal Menaḥem*, p. 146. This statement is reminiscent of that by R. Yizḥaq of Acre cited earlier.

35. Menaḥem Mendel Shneurson, *A Minor Temple—Our Rebbe's House in Babylon* (New York, 1992). See also Maman, *Torah of the Messiah*, pp. 123–125; Menaḥem Mendel Shneurson, *Kuntras Tzaddiq La-Melekh* (Kfar Habad, 1992), pp. 27–28.
36. The rebbe's house is the "actual site of the temple in the future," the site where "the temple shall be revealed in the future, and from which it will return to Jerusalem" (Menaḥem Mendel Shneurson, *Kuntras Tzaddiq La-Melekh*). Evidently, it was a perception of this sort that led to the construction of a replica of the rebbe's house in Kfar Habad during the 1980s (see Bilu, "Sanctification of Place," p. 81). On the physical residence of the rebbe in R. Yosef Yizḥaq's doctrine, see Goldberg, "The Zaddik's Soul," pp. 140–141, 147–148.
37. There is room for comprehensive research into messianism in the twentieth century and how it relates to the paradigms of messianism in classical Kabbalah (on these paradigms, see Idel, *Messianic Mystics*). The cornerstone of this research was laid by Ravitzky, *Messianism, Zionism, and Religious Radicalism* (and see more recently Cherlow, "Messianism and the Messiah"). In this context, there is room for a comparative study of the rise of apocalyptic and millenarian expectations toward the end of the century (see, for example, Dan, *Apocalypse*). On messianic expectations for the year 2000, see Chapter 3 of the present book.
38. On Ginsburgh's perception of Eretz Israel, see Shlomo Fischer's important and profound study ("Radical Religious-Zionist Thought"). My thanks to Fischer, who brought the article to my attention while still in press (an abridged version appeared in *Eretz Aḥeret*, 26 [2005]).
39. Ginsburgh, *Ha-Hitqashrut*, p. 14.
40. Fischer, "Nature."
41. Ginsburgh, *Ha-Hitqashrut*, p. 27. Ginsburgh explained the fact that the rebbe himself refrained from visiting Eretz Israel through the classical Hasidic dictum that "you are where your thoughts are," claiming that the rebbe was, in fact, always in Eretz Israel (Ginsburgh, *Ḥasdei David*, vol. 2, p. 14).
42. On these claims, see Elior, "Messianic Resurgence," pp. 397–398; Elior, *Mystical Origins of Hasidism*, pp. 132–134.
43. Ginsburgh, *Ve-Tzaddiq Yesod 'Olam*, pp. 8, 18, 20. Cf. also Ginsburgh, *Ḥasdei David*, vol. 2, p. 47, where he writes that the rebbe is the embodiment of "Adam Qadmon" (primeval man) or a cosmic divine entity in an anthropomorphic form.
44. Ginsburgh, *Ha-Hitqashrut*, pp. 23, 35.
45. Ginsburgh, *Face to Face*, pp. 35–36.
46. Ginsburgh, *Ha-Hitqashrut*, pp. 29–30.
47. See Elior, "Messianic Resurgence"; Dan, *Apocalypse*, pp. 309–323; Friedman, "Messiah and Messianism"; Idel, *Messianic Mystics*, pp. 243–244, 247. (For a similar emphasis on messianism in neo-Bratzlavism, see Piekarz, *Studies in Bratzlav Hasidism*, pp. 209–214.) Berger, in his book *The Rebbe*, discusses the relative lack of opposition to this messianism in the orthodox world. Berger himself laments this phenomenon.

However, in my opinion, this is simply an indication of the power of messianism in the twentieth-century Jewish world, in which the return to the land on the one hand and the Holocaust on the other substantially strengthened messianic expectations.

48. For R. Shneur Zalman of Liadi's aversion to being approached for magical purposes of this kind, see *Tanya*, vol. 4, letter 22.
49. *Igrot Qodesh*, presented in Goldberg, "The Zaddik's Soul," p. 71.
50. *Torat Menaḥem*, p. 241.
51. Quoted in Nathan of Nemirov, *Life of Moharan*, "Talks Related to the Teachings," 15.
52. See Goshen-Gottstein, "The Land of Israel," pp. 281, 285–286, 296; Mark, *Mysticism and Madness*, pp. 208–329.
53. For the rabbinical roots of this halakhic attitude, see Kahane, "Land of Israel," and cf. a similar attitude of halakhic authority by R. Shlomo Aviner, a disciple of Kook's (in the booklet *Ma'yanei Ha-Yeshu'a* 59, 5762). My thanks to Zvi Mark who brought the latter text to my attention.
54. I have heard that even travelers to Uman are uncomfortable about leaving Eretz Israel for the festivals.
55. *Even Shtiya—Clarification concerning the journey from Eretz Israel to Uman* (author, date, and place of publication not specified). According to Assaf, *Bratzlav*, p. 226, it was published in 1991. The pamphlet begins with these words: "Behold, an argument is being raised once again by several of our men to the effect that since our holy rabbi (R. Naḥman), of blessed memory, emphasized the tremendous sanctity of Eretz Israel to an extent that is not found in the holy books, because no-one [in the holy books] speaks as much of the sanctity of the land as does our rabbi, of blessed memory. . . . Therefore, even though Rosh Ha-Shana in Uman is an important and awesome experience, they claim that one must not leave Eretz Israel even for this, or at the very least, there is no obligation to leave Eretz Israel during the Rosh Ha-Shana season." For the main argument, see p. 7. For the halahkic defense, see pp. 16–17. The author of the pamphlet, however, stresses that there is no real need for a halahkic justification, since one could simply rely on the tradition of the disciples of R. Nathan of Nemirov, Naḥman's successor.
56. Naḥman of Bratzlav, *Liqutei Moharan*, *Tanina* 40.
57. Nathan of Nemirov, *Life of Moharan*, section 220.
58. Ibid., section 225. See Mark, "R. Naḥman of Bratzlav's Tiqqunim."
59. Another version of this argument (see pamphlet *Even Shtiya*, p. 8) subordinates the sanctity of the land to that of the people, which is also sustained by the status of the Tzaddiq. According to this version, the sanctity of the land derives from the fact that God glories in the souls of Israel, and the true Tzaddiq is the personification of this glory. R. Naḥman himself adopts a similar approach at times. For example, he writes (*Liqutei Moharan*, *Tanina* 40) that "on Rosh Ha-Shana, when there is the great collectivity, then the glory is even greater due to the multitude of people seeking to get close to the Holy-One-Blessed-Be-He, and thus does the glory and beauty of the Tzaddiq

become enhanced, for he himself is the epitome of this glory." See also Goshen-Gottstein, "The Land of Israel," p. 281.

60. Mark informed me that he is preparing a study of the sacred geography of Uman in the writings of Bratzlav Hasidism.

61. An ethnographic study of the pilgrimage to Uman, similar to that made of the pilgrimage to the house of the rebbe of Habad in New York (Kravel-Tobi, "Tishrei with the Rebbe"), is sorely needed. From a quantitative perspective, tens of thousands of Hasidim and newly observant Jews participate in this event. From a qualitative perspective, several important religious leaders, such as R. Shimon Gershon Rosenberg (also known as Shagar; see Chapter 7 on this figure), have visited Uman.

62. See, for example, Smith, *Taking Place*, pp. 16–23, and also Garb, "Power, Ritual, and Myth," pp. 68–69, and sources cited there.

63. Zagdon, *Or Ha-Ganuz*, p. 23. (I have recently been given reason to believe that large portions of Zagdon's works were, in fact, written by his erstwhile student Shemer Niv, who has recently set up his own subsect and written other works.)

64. Ibid., p. 67. Cf. Zadgon, *Ilu Yeda'tiv*, vol. 1, p. 191.

65. Zagdon performs a similar exercise in relation to sacred time. He claims that while the minutiae of Sabbath laws are the body of the Sabbath, the Tzaddiq is the spirit of the Sabbath. Therefore, the redemption will come only from the Sabbath of the spirit (*Or Ha-Ganuz*, pp. 14–18, and cf. p. 25). He goes on to say that the source of all hardships in the Diaspora is the glorification of the minutiae of Halakha at the expense of the soul: "We do not live the Torah, for we have forgotten the true Sabbath" (p. 20; the antinomian implications of this statement are clear). The true Sabbath is effectively a situation that is beyond time in the usual sense (*Ilu Yeda'tiv*, vol. 1, p. 220). A review of the various concepts of sacred time in twentieth-century Kabbalah is beyond the scope of this book (although the concept of redemption is directly connected to this issue).

66. See Zagdon, *Or Ha-Ganuz*, pp. 64–65.

67. See, for example, ibid., p. 29. Zagdon stresses the importance of the word *AZ* in Kabbalah and Hasidism.

68. Ibid., pp. 12–14.

69. Zagdon (*Ilu Yeda'tiv*, vol. 1, p. 232) identifies the redemption with the actualization of the divinity that is within man. Since he sees himself as the herald of the true redemption, he may have given way to self-deification, rather like Kook and the rebbe of Habad.

70. A parallel phenomenon can be observed in the world of Halakha, namely the epidemic of halakhic discussion on the land, its borders, and its commandments. Naturally, even in the past some works (such as the fourteenth-century *Kaftor Va-Peraḥ* by Ashtori Ha-Parḥi and the nineteenth-century *Pe'at Ha-Shulḥan* by R. Yisra'el of Shklov) dealt with these issues, but they were few and far between and certainly nothing like the spate of journals and books on this subject that appeared in the twentieth century.

71. See Bar-Asher, "Eretz Israel," pp. 220–224; Tobi, "Settlement of Eretz Israel," pp. 191–194. Cf., however, Lau, "Holy Land," pp. 169–172. Likewise, a work that was widely disseminated in the late twentieth century was *Em Ha-Banim Smeḥa* (Jerusalem, 1983), by the Hasidic ideologue Y. S. Teichtel, which traces the merit of the concrete land to many halakhic and kabbalistic sources.
72. Lorberbaum, *Image of God*, pp. 436–468.
73. Cf. the discussion of Eretz Israel as a land of "spiritual ascent" by R. Hillel Zeitlin, in Hallamish, "Hasidism."
74. See Zorotzkin, "Building the Earthly," and previous studies mentioned there.
75. See ibid., p. 161. This is not the place to expatiate on the perception of the Hebrew language in the twentieth century. Suffice it to say that alongside the renewal of the language by the Zionist movement, which was also accompanied by the secularization of the language, many works within the national mystical stream focused on the sanctity of Hebrew and on the fact that it was the source of all languages. See Ginsburgh, *Aleph Beit*, and also Glazerson, *Mystery of Hebrew* (one of his many works). There is a need for a debate on hermeneutic perceptions in twentieth-century Kabbalah, in particular the widespread use of codes allegedly embedded in the Bible, which are also perceived as means for predicting the future.
76. Kook, *Letters*, vol. 1, p. 18.
77. Kook, *Orot*, pp. 71–72.
78. Kook, *Shmona Qevatzim*, vol. 1, par. 573.
79. On the declining status of space in the thought of Abraham Joshua Heschel, for example, see Green, "Three Warsaw Mystics," p. 57. See Saskia Sassen's economic-political research (for example, "Globalization and Denationalization") into the changing status of local space in the era of global communications. See also Bertens, *Idea of the Postmodern*, pp. 209–237.
80. Wexler, *Mystical Society*, pp. 18–21, 28–29.
81. On R. Menaḥem Mendel's close connection with the tomb of his father-in-law and predecessor, R. Yosef Yizḥaq, see Friedman, "Messiah and Messianism," p. 221; Goldberg, "The Zaddik's Soul," pp. 148–150.
82. See Schwartz, *Philosophy of R. Soloveitchik*, pp. 171–178. On this thinker's attitude to Kabbalah, see Garb, "Joy of Torah," pp. 88–91, and sources cited there. For Soloveitchik's critique of the concept of power see Soloveitchik, *Family Redeemed*, pp. 91–103.
83. See Feild, *Last Barrier*.
84. See Dorje, *Dangerous Friend*.
85. Trungpa, *Collected Works*, vol. 4, pp. 290–293. It should be added that for this reason Trungpa cautioned (see, for example, p. 293) against the premature transmission of tantric traditions to the United States. For criticism of the attempt by Western Buddhist circles to tone down messages such as these and to adapt them to democratic perceptions, see Dorje, *Dangerous Friend*, pp. xiv–xviii.
86. Similarly, the sexual element is emphasized in tantric practice in the contemporary

West (see Margot Anand's best sellers). For the classical tradition, see Padoux, "Tantric Guru."

87. The figure of the magician is, naturally, a key figure in the *Lord of the Rings* and *Harry Potter* series, as well as in the books of Ursula Le Guinn, Diana Wynne Jones, or Stephen Donaldson (although in the latter's books, the "antihero" also plays an important part—an unusual phenomenon in literature of this kind). The shaman is the key figure in the film *The Green Mile*, which is in turn an adaptation of Stephen King's best seller. The shaman plays an important role in Philip Pullman's books, too. There is also congruency between developments in popular culture and academic orientations. Following Mircea Eliade's research into the subject, Shamanism has become an important topic in contemporary scholarship (see Garb, *Manifestations of Power*, p. 24). On the response to Shamanism in Israel today, see K. Ben-Simhon, "Full Moon Nights," *Ha'aretz*, 7 Jan. 2005.
88. The above notwithstanding, the media has managed to assimilate the democratic ethos, too, by offering the "ordinary man" the possibility of becoming a star overnight, as in "reality" television shows such as Israel's immensely popular and ever-promoted *A Star Is Born* (*Kochav Nolad*).
89. The media, which seizes on scandals of a psychological or sexual nature, plays here a dual role. By exposing the private lives of stars, it shows that they are ordinary people, while simultaneously feeding the public's obsession with them.
90. As indicated by Scholem, *Major Trends*, pp. 15–17.
91. Famous cases involve Bagwan Rajneesh (also known as Osho), Thomas Rich (Chögyam Trungpa's successor), and Richard Baker (Shunryu Suzuki's successor). On the latter, see Fields, *How the Swans Came*.

CHAPTER 6. CIRCUMVENTION AND VIOLATION OF HALAKHA

1. See Scholem, *On the Kabbalah*, pp. 77–85.
2. On the relationship between Halakha and Kabbalah, see also Katz, *Halakha and Kabbalah*.
3. See Idel, *Kabbalah*, pp. xi–xvi, 74–75, 173–199, 252–253; Mopsik, *Les Grands Textes de la Cabale*; Garb, *Manifestations of Power* (dealing with the concept of theurgy). See also Pedaya, *Vision and Speech*, p. 27.
4. There is plenty of material on anomian and antinomian allusions and implications in medieval philosophical literature. See, for example, Schwartz, "Spiritual-Intellectual Decline."
5. The antinomian element in Sabbatianism has already been comprehensively discussed. See, for example, Scholem's famous essay "A Religious Act Achieved through a Wrongful Deed" (in Scholem, *History of Sabbetianism*, pp. 9–67). On the anomianism of the "prophetic" current of Kabbalah, see Idel, *Mystical Experience*, p. 9. By contrast, see Wolfson, *Abraham Abulafia*, pp. 186–228. For more on the different attitudes toward Halakha in kabbalistic discourse, see Wolfson, *Venturing Beyond*.
6. See Piekarz, *Beginning of Hasidism*.

7. Far be it from me to paint a stereotype of the halakhic world as devoid of spontaneity and personal creativity. In Aggadic (homiletic) works through the generations, one can find a focus on the personal domain that exists within the halakhic system. One cannot deny, however, that a detailed normative prescription of day-to-day behavior, which is one of the distinguishing features of Religious Judaism, regularizes and even standardizes the life of the individual. For more on this subject, see Garb, "Circumventions of Halakha."
8. See Fine, *Physician of the Soul*. This technique was important for one of Kook's sources of inspiration—R. Moshe Ḥayyim Luzzatto, who claimed that he experienced a divine revelation due to the intensive practice of yiḥudim ("almost one yiḥud each quarter of an hour"). See Friedlander, *Treasures of Ramḥal*, p. 315.
9. Kook, *Orot Ha-Qodesh*, vol. 1, pp. 119–120. Cf. Ḥarlap, *Ḥed Harim*, p. 69.
10. Kook, *Orot Ha-Qodesh*, vol. 1, pp. 120–121.
11. Kook, *Shmona Qevatzim*, vol. 2, par. 19. Cf. Kook, *Orot Ha-Qodesh*, vol. 1, p. 115, where the sequence is "exoterics, esoterics, yiḥudim." Note that at the end of this section, Kook states that through the yiḥudim "true life manifests itself in man, the nation, and the universe." Note the order here: man, nation, and universe. Note, too, that this last addition does not appear in Kook, *Shmona Qevatzim*, vol. 8, par. 231. This issue requires further study.
12. See, for example, Kook, *Shmona Qevatzim*, vol. 2, par. 347: "The clarification of ideas and the sanctification of the volition, which is situated in the realm of the Holy of Holies, above any concept of morality, can only be achieved through the holy names, the union [yiḥudim] of higher lights, the marriage of traits, the amalgamation of souls and the integration of universes. . . . It is only through descending several levels and blending with ordinary life that we can find some of their sacred strength in the brightness of the natural requirements of kindness and truth, goodness and honesty, etiquette and beauty, manners and ordinary morality in life."
13. Kook, *Ḥadarav*, pp. 193–194. On Kook's ideas about individualism, see Rosenak, "Individualism and Society."
14. See Rosenak, "Prophetic Halakha and Reality," pp. 595–597; Rosenak, "Torah of Eretz Israel."
15. See Garb, "Joy of Torah," pp. 100–103, and sources cited there (see also Idel, *Hasidism*, p. 34).
16. See Piekarz, *Beginning of Hasidism*; Magid, *Hasidism on the Margin*, p. 254.
17. See, respectively, Grader, *The Yeshiva*, pp. 252–253; Dessler, *Mikhtav Me-Eliyahu*, vol. 4, p. 278.
18. See Shapira, *Derekh Ha-Melekh*, pp. 450–451, for a technique that is clearly influenced by Western hypnosis, and compare with Wacks, "Emotion and Enthusiasm," pp. 82–85. My student Natanel Yeḥieli as well as Daniel Reiser, both of Hebrew University, are writing on R. Menaḥem Eckstein's book *The Psychological Prerequisites for Attaining Hasidism*, written in Galicia in 1921 (translated in English as *Visions of a Compassionate World*). Like Shapira (whom Yeḥieli correctly identifies as one of the book's sources of

inspiration), Eckstein stresses the technique of guided imagery, which was influenced by contemporary hypnotic literature. In my opinion, the book is also influenced by Hillel Zeitlin. In the New Age movement, fairly close ties evolved between hypnotic and mystical practices, a phenomenon I hope someday to discuss further. Meanwhile, see, for example, Silverthorn and Overdurf, *Dreaming Realities;* James and Shephard, *Presenting Magically.*

19. See also Schachter's contribution in the collection published by *Commentary* magazine, *The Condition of Jewish Belief,* pp. 207–215, which heralded the start of his break with orthodoxy. This is an example of the way kabbalistic discourse penetrated the nonorthodox movements in America, which had formerly eschewed this kind of language (see Chapter 1 of the present book on a similar role that Heschel played in the Conservative movement).
20. See Magid, "Rainbow Hassidism"; Prell, *Prayer and Community.*
21. For a short interview with Rabinovitch, see Forman, *Grassroots Spirituality,* pp. 30–34. On similar personalities—Shefa Gold and Lynn Gottlieb—see Kamenetz, *Stalking Elijah,* pp. 40–43, 112–121.
22. In this context it is worth mentioning R. Mordekhai Gafni (the object of much media attention), who operated in Israel and abroad in a similar spirit. On this figure and the polemic he triggered, see Garb, "The Understandable Revival," pp. 186–187.
23. See Forman, *Grassroots Spirituality,* p. 98. According to Forman, it is precisely this relatively comfortable blend of different traditions that corroborates his thesis that the New Age should be considered a single movement rather than an amalgam of different movements, despite its "reticular" and decentralized nature.
24. Another figure closely linked to Native American Shamanism is a former orthodox rabbi, Gershon Winkler (see, for example, *A Jewish Theology*).
25. See Ezraḥi, "Al Da'at Ha-Maqom."
26. One of Ginsburgh's former students, however, the newly observant Nir Malḥi-Zaltzman, is a tai chi expert in Israel and integrates the study of Jewish texts into his courses for tai chi teachers. For amazingly similar attitudes among Muslim clerics (which were also publicized on the Internet), see Z. Barel, "Allah Will Take Pity on the Buddha," *Ha'aretz,* 27 Oct. 2004. More generally, this example demonstrates an interesting blend of two contemporary phenomena. First, we have the transformation of the Internet into a major site for religious discourse, and even a major arena of religious activity, which largely replaces textual study and ritual worship. (This issue has not yet been adequately researched; meanwhile, see Weinstein, "Religious Forums.") Personalities such as R. Yuval Cherlow derive a large degree of their halakhic authority from their "Internet responsa." Second, we have the transformation of Kabbalah or "thought" experts into halakhic authorities of a sort, who deliver "responsa." Both phenomena comprise an anomian element.
27. Y. A. Ozolbo, *Dibur La-'Avarim,* p. 5, and see also pp. 12–13. The book, which is undated, was published in Tel Aviv in 2001 at the latest.
28. See, for example, Ginsburgh, *Sod Hashem,* pp. 398–404.

29. See, Ginsburgh, *Face to Face*, pp. 50–51, 57, 63, 73. Again, there is an allusion here to the messianism of the seventh rebbe of Habad (as well as to Ginsburgh's doctrine of power).
30. However, cf. Ginsburgh, *Be-'Itah Aḥishenah*, p. 111, on an emergency disposition as overriding the usual rules of the Torah and belonging to "a higher form of divine worship."
31. Ginsburgh, *Face to Face*, p. 54.
32. Ginsburgh, *Ha-Hitqashrut*, p. 35. See above for similar themes in the doctrines of Kook and Avraham Zagdon.
33. For other works by Ginsburgh work, see, for example, *Be-Khol Derakhekha* (reprinted in *Teshuvat Ha-Shana* [Kfar Habad, 1997], pp. 253–279), which focuses on the rabbinical interpretation of this verse, with the addition "even for a sin." (The verse itself has always been invoked by those seeking to create an anomian religious space.) Cf. Ginsburgh, *Ha-Hitqashrut*, p. 32, which argues that Eretz Israel lends itself to a broader form of worship—that of knowing God in all one's ways ("Be-kol derakhekha da'ehu")—which frees man from the restrictive "meticulousness" of the commandments. (The linkage of the return to Eretz Israel to anomian trends is influenced by Kook's doctrine, as we shall see.) See also p. 35, on the need for a new Torah that would emanate from God himself (although here, too, Ginsburgh adds the qualification that "of course this new Torah will not be foreign, God forbid, to its predecessor"). For more on the ranking of Kabbalah above Halakha, see Ginsburgh's article "Reality, Halakha, Kabbalah," in Ginsburgh, *Kingdom of Israel*, vol. 4.
34. See Kravel-Tovi, "Tishrei with the Rebbe." On the messianic faction of Habad, see Friedman, "Messiah and Messianism," p. 175 (and on innovations in Habad rituals in the early century, see pp. 186–187).
35. Shach was referring in particular to Habad's practice of getting passersby to lay Tefillin (phylacteries) even in unclean places, as part of their "Tefillin Operation," and Habad's extension of the permit not to perform the ritual of sleeping in the Sukkah (booth in which one dwells during the Tabernacles festival) in the Diaspora to Eretz Israel.
36. This phenomenon will probably be discussed in a future study by 'Eran Sabag.
37. Wolbe, *'Alei Shur*, vol. 2, p. 413.
38. Ibid., p. 415.
39. On rabbinical literature, see Rakover, *Ends That Justify the Means*. For example, "A sin performed with good intentions is greater than a good deed performed without good intentions" (*Nazir* 23b). There is room for more subtle distinctions than that proposed by Magid (*Hasidism on the Margin*, p. 215), between "soft" antinomianism and "hard" antinomianism—a topic I hope to expand on someday.
40. See Faierstein, "The Friday Night Incident."
41. For a general discussion, see Faierstein, *All Is in the Hands of Heaven*, and sources cited there; Gellman, *Fear and Trembling*, pp. 47–54, 62–72. See also Meir's important work "Status of the Mitzvot."

42. See, respectively, Magid, *Hasidism on the Margin* (see pp. 217, 240, for the moderation of Leiner's position by his son, R. Ya'aqov Leiner, author of the book *Beit Ya'aqov*); Brill, *Thinking God* (see also Green, "Three Warsaw Mystics," p. 37 for R. Zadok and Abraham Joshua Heschel).
43. On Kook and Leiner's student Zadok, see end of Chapter 3. On Kook and *Mei Ha-Shiloaḥ*, see Garb, "Rabbi Kook and His Sources," p. 90. Ginsburgh, as stated, delivered a series of classes (which were taped and distributed by the *Gal 'Einai* movement) on Leiner's thought. These classes include moderate antinomian elements, especially in connection with sexuality, which were partly censored when published in one of Ginsburgh's books (*Shekhina*, pp. 148–153).
44. Outstanding examples are the extremely popular classes by Aviva Gottlieb-Zornberg (some of the lectures of which have been published: see Gottlieb-Zornberg, *Genesis* and *Particulars of Rapture*), which give ample room to interpretations of Leiner's thought. On the tremendous international popularity of these talks, see T. Rotem, "From George Eliot to the Garden of Eden," *Ha'aretz*, 10 Sept. 2004.
45. For reservations toward antinomian elements in his writings, see Leiner, *Mei Ha-Shiloaḥ*, vol. 1, pp. 120–121; vol. 2, p. 76.
46. See Leiner, *Mei Ha-Shiloaḥ*, vol. 1, pp. 13–14, 47–48, 50–51, 97–98, 159–160, 170–171, 240–241; vol. 2, pp. 65, 135. See also Elior, "Innovation of Hasidism," pp. 412–413, 415, 417, 423, 427; Magid, *Hasidism on the Margin*, p. 223.
47. Leiner, *Mei Ha-Shiloaḥ*, vol. 1, pp. 25–26, 30, 33–34, 52, 56–57, 137; vol. 2, pp. 44, 69. And see also Elior, *Mystical Origins of Hasidism*, pp. 166–167; Magid, *Hasidism on the Margin*, p. 224.
48. See, for example, ibid., vol. 1, pp. 30, 116–117. On the superiority of the Jews' religious intuition, see vol. 1, pp. 33–34, 158, and compare with the attitude of his son, R. Ya'aqov Leiner, in *Beit Ya'aqov* (Lublin, 1903), p. 37: "In the future . . . the Holy One Blessed-Be-He will discover the depth of heart and reverence with which Israel steadfastly adheres to Him, Blessed-Be-He, and everyone will discern that the Jews are utterly good, and the nations will discern that they are utterly wicked. At such time, there will be other rulings, and they will no longer need 'clarification,' that is, they will no longer have to restrict themselves in any way." Texts such as these attest to a close tie between antinomian doctrines and national mysticism.
49. For a fascinating additional interpretation of the antinomian elements in Kook's doctrine and life (although the word *antinomian* does not appear), see Pedaya, "Space, Time, and Eretz Israel," pp. 585–597. See also Cherlow, "The Tzaddiq," p. 360.
50. Kook, *Orot Ha-Qodesh*, vol. 1, p. 157; Ravitzky, *Messianism, Zionism, and Religious Radicalism*, pp. 119–120; Kook, *Ḥadarav*, p. 90; Kook, *Shmona Qevatzim*, vol. 4, par. 17. For a different analysis of the text, see Cherlow, "The Tzaddiq," pp. 244–247.
51. For use of this expression by R. Elazar Shapira, the rebbe of Munkacz, against rebbes who cooperated with Zionists, see Nadler, "War on Modernity," p. 251.
52. On this trend in Kook's thinking, see Rosenak, "Rav Kook's Hidden Treatises," pp. 263–267; Rosenak, "Individualism and Society," pp. 102–111.

53. Kook, *'Arphilei Tohar*, p. 15; Kook, *Shmona Qevatzim*, vol. 2, par. 30. The censored version is "saddens the heart in itself, but gladdens it in terms of its results." "Long-term" was omitted in the censored version.
54. Kook, *Mishpat Kohen*, p. 345 (*Laws of Kings*, Responsum 144).
55. Kook, *Mishpat Kohen*, pp. 344–345. Cf. the phrase "to marshal their words" as quoted earlier. For more on prophecy and Halakha in Kook's doctrine, see Cherlow, "The Tzaddiq," pp. 153–154. For a discussion on rabbinical sources on this issue, see Shemesh, "Halakha and Prophecy," pp. 930–935.
56. Ḥarlap, *Ḥed Harim*, p. 69, courtesy of Yosef Aḥituv, who drew my attention to this important source. This testimony, together with the fact that Ḥarlap was appointed Kook's first successor as head of the "central world Yeshiva" that he founded, testifies to his great importance in the Kook circle. Nevertheless, there has so far been no systematical research on his attitudes and doctrine. However, see Barak, "Doctrine of Redemption." In Schwartz (*Israel in Religious Zionist Thought; Challenge and Crisis*), too, there are several relatively lengthy discussions on Ḥarlap. See also Greenberg, "Death of History."
57. Cf. the text cited by Schwartz, *Challenge and Crisis*, p. 191.
58. In a passage that was censored by Kohen himself or his editors, R. David Kohen also testifies to Kook's prophetic consciousness. See Kohen, *Nezir Eḥav*, vol. 1, p. 291. See also Cherlow, "The Tzaddiq," pp. 352–353.
59. The possibility of changing Halakha can also be found in Kook's earlier attitude concerning the right to reinstate the Sanhedrin. See Ravitzky, *Messianism, Zionism, and Religious Radicalism*, pp. 85–92. See also the fairly radical debate on the evolution of Halakha in Kook, *Letters*, vol. 1, pp. 89–90.
60. By way of example, see Kook's famous text—which his son, Ratzia, tried in vain to censor (see Agnon, *Book, Writer, Story*, p. 352)—in *Orot*, p. 80. In this passage (also discussed in Chapter 2 of the present book), Kook states that physical training by Jewish youngsters "in order to strengthen their bodies so that they could serve as brave sons of the Nation," even if it had "drawbacks" and "drops of impurity," was a holy act "that raised the Shekhina to ever greater heights, in the same way as the songs and praises that King David wrote in the Book of Psalms did." As I have shown elsewhere (Garb, "Working Out as Divine Work"), his reference to "drawbacks" and "drops of impurity" could be a reference to the desecration of the Sabbath that premilitary sports activities entailed. Another expression of latent antinomianism in Kook's thought is the expression of the yearning to pronounce the Tetragrammaton—known to be the first public antinomian act performed by Shabbetai Tzevi (see Scholem, *Shabbatai Zvi*, vol. 1, pp. 113–114). This yearning was expressed in a censored text that was published in *Ḥadarav*, pp. 25–26. (Cf. text quoted by Idel, *Kabbalah*, pp. 53–54).
61. Kook, *Me'orot Ha-Re'iah*, pp. 76, 80.
62. As Zevin put it (*Ishim Ve-Shitot*, p. 253), "The Rabbi's method of instruction was not to deviate from the path of Halakha as ordained by the standard decision makers." See

also Nehorai, "Rabbinic Rulings of Rav Kook," which in my opinion exaggerates Kook's conservatism. Nehorai turned the *Heter Mekhira* (the sale of farmland to a non-Jew to avoid the prohibition of working the land in Eretz Israel during the Sabbatical year)—a rather daring halakhic tactic—into a stringency (*ḥumra*). (On this issue, see also Malkiel, "Ideology and Halakha"; Rosenak, "Prophetic Halakha and Reality"). On the perplexing change in Kook's thinking in the 1920s, see Meir, "Lights and Vessels."

63. See Aḥituv, "Haredi and National-Haredi Modesty"; Aḥituv, "Modesty: Myth and Ethos"; and see also Rapoport and Garb, "Experience of Religious Fortification." These studies show that the tightening of the laws on modesty was a direct result of nationalism, since nationalism was described in terms of preserving the "purity" of the Jewish people. This link between modesty and nationalism has roots in classical Kabbalah, particularly in its latter incarnations, as in the *Shlah* by R. Isaiah Horowitz (see Garb, "On the Kabbalists of Prague").
64. See, for example, Kook, *Shmona Qevatzim*, vol. 1, pars. 87, 101, 105; vol. 6, par. 30.
65. Kook, *Shmona Qevatzim*, vol. 4, par. 3; vol. 1, par. 465. See also Rosenak, "Rav Kook's Hidden Treatises," p. 273.
66. I have discussed this issue elsewhere (Garb, "Fear and Power"). For the application of the representational-systems model to Jewish mysticism, see Garb, "Trance Techniques," pp. 55–56, and the professional hypnosis literature cited there. See also Garb, *Manifestations of Power*, p. 167. For a different approach to these texts, see Cherlow, "The Tzaddiq," p. 257.
67. For details, see his book *Qol Ha-Nevu'a* [The Voice of Prophecy], the name of which speaks for itself. See also Schwartz, *Challenge and Crisis*, pp. 156–158; Schwartz, *Religious Zionism*, pp. 156–160, 175, 177–178, 180–186. According to the passage quoted earlier, this applied to Ḥarlap, too.
68. Rosenak has aptly described his consciousness as that of "saintly silence." For a text that specifically links silence to hearing, see Schwartz, *Challenge and Crisis*, p. 180 (see also p. 84, n19). This issue needs to be clarified in its own right. Schwartz, on the basis of weighty evidence, claims (*Challenge and Crisis*, pp. 148–152, 158–159, 164) that Kook actually equated seeing with hearing, and perhaps even preferred hearing (see especially p. 169). However, despite the many contradictions in Kook's writings and the difficulty of forming some kind of "system" from them, I believe that some of the texts quoted by Schwartz himself (p. 149), as well as many other texts (for example, Kook, *Reish Milin*, p. 138), paint another picture: Kook focused on an experience that lay beyond the spoken or audible word. From this point of view, vision was closer to the amorphous experience that he wished to give expression to. In preferring sight, Kook continued the tradition of R. Elijah of Vilna and R. Shlomo Elyashiv, with whom he studied. See, for example, R. Elijah of Vilna's commentary on *Tiqqunei Zohar*; *Tiqqun* 40; and Elyashiv, *Leshem Shvo Ve-Aḥlama*, vol. 2 (at the end of page 4b). Evidently, we must qualify Ish-Shalom's description, which specifically emphasizes the sense of hearing in Kook's writings (*Rabbi Abraham Isaac Kook*, pp. 74–75). As stated, the entire subject

requires further clarification and research (see also Pedaya, *Name and Sanctuary*, p. 77n25). Thus, for example, Kook may have, generally speaking, equated vision with prophecy and hearing with the lower level of divine inspiration (unlike Schwartz's contention in *Challenge and Crisis*, p. 168). In any case, we only have the testimony of Kohen himself regarding the profound difference between Kohen and Kook on the question of hearing and seeing. For more on silence and the nebulous experience in Kook's doctrine, see Garb, "Rabbi Kook," pp. 83–84. For a more general discussion of language and silence in Jewish mysticism, see Garb, "Powers of Language."

69. Cited in Ish-Shalom, "R. Kook, Spinoza, and Goethe," p. 536. Cf. Schwartz, *Religious Zionism*, p. 155.
70. See Schwartz, *Religious Zionism*, pp. 198–233; Schwartz, *Challenge and Crisis*, pp. 159–160, 163, 168, 187. It appears, however, that Kook's doctrine is even more visual than Kohen's description implies. In *Shmona Qevatzim* (vol. 6, par. 205), Kook distinguishes between sound, hearing, silence, and seeing also within the Sefira of understanding itself.
71. On Kohen's fear of losing his independence, see Cherlow, "Modesty and Regeneration."
72. Kook, *Shmona Qevatzim*, vol. 1, pars. 412, 400; vol. 2, pars. 160, 34; vol. 1, par. 212. See also vol. 1, par. 410, on "great personalities" for whom the commandments no longer apply, but who observe them for the sake of the public at large. As well as the studies cited above, see Schwartz, *Israel in Religious Zionist Thought*, pp. 80–81; Abromovitz, "The Publication of the Notebooks," pp. 155–160. Although the antinomian elements declined greatly among the succeeding generations of the Kook circle, there is an antinomian connotation to Ratzia's claim (see Chapter 5 of the present book) that Eretz Israel has the power to convert the permitted into the proscribed.
73. Kook, *Shmona Qevatzim*, vol. 7, par. 208. See also Schwartz, *Challenge and Crisis*, p. 164; Cherlow, "The Tzaddiq," p. 130.
74. As noted earlier, there may be a silent visual element in the Sefira of understanding.
75. Kook, *Letters*, vol. 2, p. 555. On this letter in the context of the controversy on the contemporary observance of the Shmitta (agricultural sabbatical), see Malkiel, "Ideology and Halakha," pp. 185–186; Brown, "Sanctity of the Land," pp. 79–89.
76. See Efrati, *Ha-Sanegoria*; Ish-Shalom, "Tolerance in the Teachings of Rabbi Kook"; Ross, "Between Metaphysical and Liberal Pluralism"; Ross, "Rabbi Kook," pp. 68–69.
77. The idea of singularity itself is taken from earlier sources, such as the concept of "safwa" in R. Judah Halevi's *Sefer Ha-Kuzari* (vol. 1, section 95 [pp. 28–29 in the D. Z. Bennett edition, Jerusalem, 1977]). Kook's distinction is based on kabbalistic sources, especially on Luzzatto's doctrine (see *The Knowing Heart*, pp. 180–181, and the more kabbalistic-technical parallel, p. 280), and also the Kabbalah of R. Elijah of Vilna's disciples (see commentary *Be'er Yizḥaq* by R. Yizḥaq Ḥaver [the disciple of R. Menaḥem Mendel of Shklov, R. Elijah's disciple] on his rabbi's work, in his book *Mayim Adirim*, cited by Liebes, "The Vilner Gaon," p. 282; see also p. 277).
78. See Kook, *Ḥadarav*, pp. 187–188, concerning the toil necessary for clarifying "singularity."

79. For a general discussion of this issue, see Holzer, "Nationalism and Morality," pp. 49–53.
80. On dveiqut ha-maḥshava, see, for example, 'Azriel of Gerona, *Commentary*, p. 40.
81. Kook, *Ḥadarav*, pp. 23–24. See p. 127, where he describes communion with God (*deveiqut*) as an intrinsic part of his nature arising from the source of holiness in his soul.
82. See Rosenak, "Rav Kook's Hidden Treatises," pp. 265–266, 284.
83. See Kook, *Orot*, pp. 121–123. For use of the term *singularity* in an antinomian context, see Kook, *Shmona Qevatzim*, vol. 3, par. 336.
84. As well as being one of the great halakhic responders (*Meshivim*) of the twentieth century, Kook also wrote an entire book, *Ḥavash Pe'er* (Jerusalem, 1968), on the exact positioning of the phylacteries on the forehead. We are now in a position to demonstrate this tension around the issue of prayer alluded to in the aforementioned text. On the one hand, we know that Kook observed the order of prayer. He even wrote a two-volume commentary on the prayerbook (*'Olat Re'iah*), and it was the power of his prayer that led his disciple Kohen to choose him as rabbi and mentor (see Kohen's introduction to *Orot Ha-Qodesh*, p. 18). Yet, on the other hand, as Kook himself wrote in the introduction to *'Olat Re'iah* (vol. 1, p. 11), regular, routine prayer was actually a manifestation of the soul's constant spontaneous prayer and "served a purpose" for this reason only.
85. Kook, *Me'orot Ha-Re'iah*, pp. 27, 61, 100, 104, 106. These texts are accompanied by a fascinating psychological discussion of dreams as the main means for discovering one's singularity and destiny. For clear parallels to *Mei Ha-Shiloaḥ* in this 2004 anthology, see pp. 78, 81. See also Kook, *Shmona Qevatzim*, vol. 1, par. 147.
86. See Bar-Sella, "Hillel Zeitlin," pp. 116–120; see there also for Zeitlin's relatively sympathetic depiction of Jesus and the Sabbatians in this context.
87. For more detail, see Garb, "Rabbi Kook."
88. Kook, *Ḥadarav*, pp. 39–40 (see also pp. 38, 42). See also Rosenak, "Rav Kook's Hidden Treatises," p. 26. The term *roams* (*shata*) appears frequently not only in this text but also in Kook's writings in general, and his poems in particular. See Kook, *Orot Ha-Qodesh*, vol. 1, p. 183; *Ḥadarav*, p. 127; and texts cited by Rosenak in "Rav Kook's Hidden Treatises," pp. 264–266. Likewise, see Ofan, *Nafshi Taqshiv Shiro*, p. 53, on Kook's soul: "It roams, its soars above." Evidently, this is not merely poetic license but refers to a concrete mystical experience. See also *Ḥadarav*, p. 46: "It [Kook's soul] shall soar. . . . It shall fly rapidly and roam through the inner recesses of chambers and sanctuaries, it shall sing, it shall rejoice silently, it shall visit the holy sanctuary." This dense sentence, which is part of the passage on allowing the soul freedom, contains several themes relevant to our discussion, such as the freedom of the soul, and silence. In my opinion, this is a description of Kook's mystical experience of soaring to the higher sanctuaries.
89. 'Etzion, "Mi-Degel Yerushalayim," pp. 8, 24. See 'Etzion, "Psaq Halakha," for his incisive criticism of the chief rabbinate.

90. 'Etzion, "Mi-Degel Yerushalayim," p. 29. According to Kook, *Letters*, vol. 2, p. 878, "You, envoys of the Compassionate One . . . , by listening to the inner, Jewish, self . . .—with that holy power, the divine power . . . the power of the Guardian of Israel . . .—with this divine power your mission is entrusted to you."
91. 'Etzion, "Mi-Degel Yerushalayim."
92. 'Etzion cites Maimonides (*Guide to the Perplexed*, vol. 2, p. 45) on divine assistance to those who try to save the majority as the first step toward prophecy. In an interview I conducted, 'Etzion attempted to explain that he was referring only to the first level of prophecy as described by Maimonides, which corresponds to "divine inspiration" in other sources. In his opinion, Kook's prophetic consciousness, as reflected in *Shmona Qevatzim*, belongs to this level. He also explained that he aspired to the reinstatement of the Sanhedrin in the Lishkat Ha-Gazit (Chamber of Hewn Stone, former seat of the Sanhedrin), as a prelude to the rebuilding of the Temple. According to him, the halakhic authority of the Sanhedrin could innovate halakhic thinking.
93. See Segal, *Dear Brothers*, pp. 218–219.
94. Shapira, "Redemption and Temple," p. 434; Ari'el, "Authority in Halakha," p. 21. See also Yo'el Bin Nun's diatribe ("Derekh Ha-Orot," p. 11) against the "abominable arguments" legitimizing the "breaching" of Halakha and Mussar.
95. Cited in Segal, *Dear Brothers*, p. 216.
96. Zuckerman, "Interview," p. 9; Shapira, "Redemption and Temple," p. 436. On the place of Kabbalah in the "Underground" polemic, see also Segal, *Dear Brothers*, p. 234.
97. Zagdon, *Ilu Yeda'tiv*, pp. 9–10. See also Scholem, *Major Trends*, pp. 50–52, 81–82.
98. For references to the Torah of redemption, see Zagdon, *Or Ha-Ganuz*.
99. Ibid., p. 23. Zagdon quotes here two Talmudic sources: *Makkot* 24a and *Yoma* 72b. The former text, which may have been influenced by Jewish-Christian circles, already contains an antinomian potential. From one perspective, it appears to discuss the doctrine of the Tzaddiq, as the parallel in *Ḥagiga* 12b indicates. By identifying the Tzaddiq with the "one principle" of the Torah, Zagdon implies that the Tzaddiq symbolizes unity, while in the absence of the Tzaddiq, the Torah and even Kabbalah represents plurality (see *Or Ha-Ganuz*, p. 63). In practice, the Tzaddiq here replaces God as the symbol of unity.
100. Zagdon, *Or Ha-Ganuz*, pp. 21, 29, 67. See also p. 70, where Zagdon describes the *Shulḥan 'Arukh* and intricacies of Halakha as corresponding to the quality of divine justice. See Zagdon, *Ilu Yeda'tiv*, vol. 1, p. 14, on the messianic significance of the totally new Torah revealed by Zagdon.
101. Zagdon, *Ilu Yeda'tiv*, pp. 191–192, 194, 201; and cf. p. 199. However, Zagdon writes (p. 218) that there is also a need for action and connecting the inner world to the world of action.
102. See also Garb, "The Understandable Revival," p. 187n83.
103. Y. Sheleg, "Youngsters Outside the Fence," *Ha'aretz*, 27 Oct. 2002.
104. As opposed to numerous technical expositions of the details of the kabbalistic intentions of the commandments. This phenomenon exists in the Mussar move-

ment, too; among all four volumes of Dessler's *Mikhtav Me-Eliyahu*, only ten pages discuss the reasons for the commandments (vol. 4, pp. 169–179).

105. See Ḥayyim of Volozhin, *Nefesh Ha-Ḥayyim*, vol. 2, chap. 11. For a source in the Kabbalah of his teacher, see Elijah of Vilna, *Avnei Eliyahu*, p. 101. For earlier kabbalistic sources of this viewpoint, see Garb, *Manifestations of Power*, pp. 236–237, 265. For a rare contemporary espousal of this stance, see Tau, *Le-Emunat 'Itenu*, vol. 3, pp. 158–159, 284.

106. See also the important comment by Charvit, "Identity and History," pp. 109–110, on Kabbalah as an alternative to a Jewish identity based on Halakha among French Jewish thinkers in the twentieth century.

107. Gershom Scholem (*Explications and Implications*, p. 50) made a point of distinguishing between Zionism, on the one hand, and Sabbatianism and messianism, on the other. However, in his studies on Sabbatianism, Scholem himself evidently laid the foundation for the connection between Sabbatian and Zionist "anarchism." See his ambivalent formulation of the lesson of Sabbatianism for our generation in Scholem, *Shabbatai Zvi*, p. 11.

108. For a broader study of anomian trends in the Kabbalah of recent generations (including our generation), we must consider the nature of the ambient nomos. In other words, we must study the characteristics of Halakha in the twentieth century, with particular emphasis on the study processes that have evolved in Yeshivot, the influence of modernization and the establishment of the State on halakhic rulings, and the like.

109. Hence the relevance of the doctrine of the great Sufi poet Jalal Al-Din Rumi, who distanced himself from the world of the Shari'a. (On Rumi's popularity today, see Lewis, *Rumi*, pp. 564–646.)

110. Feild, *Last Barrier*, p. 77, and see also Taji-Farouki, *Beshara*. For similar perceptions in the thought of Inayat Khan, see Hammer, "Sufism for Westerners," pp. 134–135. Even though one can find similar formulations among classical Sufi thinkers—such as Ibn 'Arabi (see, for example, Chittick, *Sufi Path*, p. 171), who was, according to some, a Muslim legalist and zealot (see Hirtenstein, *Unlimited Mercifier*, p. 276)—this dialectic balance does not exist among contemporary Sufi masters.

111. See Wilson, *Sacred Drift*.

112. Al-Jamal, *Music of the Soul*, pp. 147–148.

113. On Gurdjieff and his school, see Needleman, "G.I. Gurdjieff and His School." On Steiner and his school, see McDermott, "Rudolf Steiner."

114. Robinson, *Honest to God*.

115. Trungpa, *Collected Works*, vol. 2, p. 19 of the editor's introduction. For the emphasis on psychology in Western Sufism, see Hermansen, "American Sufi Movements," pp. 47, 55; Hammer, "Sufism for Westerners," p. 142.

Chapter 7. The Upsurge of Mysticism as a Jewish and Global Phenomenon

1. See Eco, *Foucault's Pendulum*, which is also a critique of the new mysticism.
2. See Filc, "Israel Model 2000," p. 38. On the American cultural influence on Israel see T. Liebes, *American Dreams*. For the claim that Americanization is part of the identity of secular Israelis, see Shmaryahu, "Golden Arches of Macdonald's."
3. See Lyotard, *Post-modern Condition*. I will not discuss the "rationality" of modern Western culture, or even the definition of rationality itself, but will focus rather on the rhetoric of rationality, which contributed to the structuring of modernity.
4. See Forman, *Grassroots Spirituality*. To cite but one example, the Internet and similar information technologies played an important role in the globalization of Falun Gong, the Chinese mystical movement. This movement, which is a good example of the globalization of mysticism today, has a fair number of followers in Israel (who practice their techniques opposite the Knesset building in Jerusalem).
5. See Eliade, *Myths, Dreams, and Mysteries*, pp. 7–12. The books of Mircea Eliade, C. G. Jung, and Joseph Campbell reflect the new global spirituality that eclectically integrates mythical and mystical traditions from different cultures. On this theme, see Wasserstrom, *Religion after Religion*.
6. For a good example (studded, though, with inaccuracies) of this rearguard action, see Rachlevsky, *Messiah's Donkey*, especially chaps. 4 and 15.
7. See Boyarin, "Colonial Drag,"; Cuddihy, *Ordeal of Civility*, especially pp. 175–185. For a critical discussion of the tension between the identity of Jews from Arab countries and the Zionist hegemony, see Hever, Shenav, and Motzafi-Haller, *Mizrahim in Israel*.
8. On the territorial politics of language, see De Landa, *Non-Linear History*. Part 3 of this innovative book, in particular, outlines the connection between political control and linguistic "occupation" (in which one language is imposed on another).
9. For a summary of these processes from a slightly different perspective, see Mautner, Sagi, and Shamir, "Multiculturalism in Israel," pp. 68–69.
10. See, respectively, Bilu, "Sanctification of Place," p. 82; Koppel, "*Mamlakhtiut*," pp. 239–240.
11. Obviously this is less valid for the mystical current of the Kook school of Religious Zionism. For a further analysis of the relationship between modernity and innovation in Religious Zionism, see Sagi, "Religious Zionism," especially p. 139.
12. On religious opposition to globalization, see Robertson, "Anti-global Religion."
13. See Bar-Yosef, "Zionism and Redemption," and also Green, "Three Warsaw Mystics," p. 28, with reference to R. Hillel Zeitlin.
14. On clandestine yoga materials, see, for example, the report by I. Rotem-Zifroni, "Andrey Sikorsky: The Yoga Teacher from the Ukraine," *Yoga Be-Yisra'el* 2 (1995): pp. 25–26 [Hebrew].
15. See Weiss, "Torah Scholars."

16. Many thanks to Yishai Rosen-Zvi for his comments on this topic.
17. Therefore, I do not accept Sheleg's claim (*New Religious Jews*, p. 183) that this phenomenon substantially influenced ultraorthodox society.
18. See also Goodman, "Return to Orthodoxy." It should be noted that Kook was one of the first to call for the abolition of the distinction between orthodox and secular; see Kook, *Articles*, pp. 76–77. See also Brezovsky, *Kuntras Ha-Haruga 'Alayikh*, p. 30, for a kabbalistic explanation of the nature of those who return to orthodox Judaism: they are reincarnations of children who were murdered in the Holocaust.
19. Ginsburgh, *Ḥasdei David* (commentary on *Ḥasdei David* by R. David Majar). Ḥayyim Nativ, a close student of Ginsburgh's, informed me that Ginsburgh acquired his mystical training from Sephardic kabbalists.
20. See Sheleg, *New Religious Jews*, p. 261. This piece of journalism is a first attempt to document some of the changes orthodox society is currently undergoing.
21. In this sense, I predict a complementary trend to that documented in Kohen, "Knitted Kippa," p. 28 (at least as far as Religious Zionism is concerned)—a split into subsectors. In the postmodern social structure, which is composed of "networks," both phenomena may coexist. A large number of subsectors may arise that are connected to other sectors and subsectors in a variety of ways.
22. For studies on the newly religious, see, for example, Beit-Hallahmi, *Despair and Deliverance*, pp. 49–72; Davidman, "Accommodation and Resistance."
23. Kook, *Orot Ha-Teshuva*, p. 58; Kook, *Shmona Qevatzim*, vol. 2, par. 347. Kook is alluding to the fact that his statements are based on a kabbalistic tradition, presumably that of R. Elijah of Vilna's followers.
24. See Bar-Sella, "Hillel Zeitlin," pp. 109–111.
25. See the interview with R. Shagar, one of the main forces behind this process, in *De'ot* 3 (1999), pp. 9–13. (For more on him, see later in this chapter.)
26. S. Lev-Ari, "My brothers the poets of Palestine / come to me / strip my uniform from me," *Ha'aretz*, 26 Sept. 2003.
27. See Fischer, "Radical Religious-Zionist Thought."
28. See Goodman, "Return to Orthodoxy," pp. 133–135.
29. See Y. Mezuman, "Meditation with Tefillin," *Ha'aretz*, 15 Sept. 2004. The exposure of religious youths to the Indian experience, however, has brought about changes in religious society from halakhic to more mystical directions. See Assis, "Return from India"; Y. Sheleg, "The Congregations of the Far East," *Ha'aretz*, 15 Sept. 2002.
30. This phenomenon is not limited to Israel. Prestigious Western journals of this kind, such as *Parabola* or the erstwhile *Gnosis*, carry many articles written by Kabbalah scholars, such as Eli'ezer Shore or Ya'aqub Ibn Yusuf (who combines Kabbalah and Sufism in his teaching and runs a New Age bookstore in Jerusalem).
31. "El Ha-Tev'a—Judaism from a Holistic Perspective."
32. See Kamenetz, *Jew in the Lotus*. Rumor has it that R. Ya'aqov Aryeh Milikowsky, the Jerusalem rebbe of Amshinov, has ties with the famous (Jewish) neo-Buddhist

teacher Andrew Cohen. Rumor also has it that a kabbalist from a famous Hasidic family had (until the start of the present Intifada) ongoing contacts with a Sufi master. R. Menaḥem Fruman's ties with Sufi masters are also common knowledge.

33. Nir Malḥi-Zaltzman, the head of the Israeli Tai Chi Center, and Ilan Horovitz, author of *Torah Mi-Sin* (Torah from China), are only two of many examples.
34. This is part of the program of the El 'Ami movement, founded by members of the Kook circle, which advocates "converting" the secular through lectures on "faith."
35. Forman's claims (*Grassroots Spirituality*, pp. 12–16) on discrimination against those practicing New Age techniques testify to the consolidation of a sectorial consciousness, which is frequently characterized by a sense of "victimization." An exception to this rule is the Arab-Israeli sector, which has not yet been penetrated by the New Age, despite the recent publication of a popular work (*Medicine and the Seventh Sense*) on the "scientific" basis of alternative medicine by Nader Butto (an Arab-Israeli by birth).
36. Compare Eisenstadt, *Changes in Israeli Society*, pp. 67, 70–71. See also Tsur's important comment (*Torn Community*, p. 34) that "the criterion that determines affiliation to a sector is cultural and economic affinity, not political status." This definition fits the New Age perfectly.
37. See Touraine, *Return of the Actor*, pp. 104, 158; Castells, *Power of Identity*, pp. 356, 359–360; Bertens, *Idea of the Postmodern*, pp. 209–237; Van-Essen, *Digital Culture*; Eisenstadt, *Changes in Israeli Society*, p. 71.
38. For a classical work of this kind, see Capra, *Tao of Physics*. For the link between the new physics and Kabbalah, see Friedman, *Hidden Face*; Matt, *God and Big Bang*. This trend is also conspicuous in the works of Ginsburgh (for example, *Ḥasdei David*, vol. 1, p. 81) and in Bnei Barukh circles, based on statements by R. Yehuda Leib Ha-Levi Ashlag himself. See also Schechter, *Collection of Sayings*, vol. 1, pp. 31–32, for a discussion of the spiritual significance of the landing on the moon and the numerical value of the name of the spacecraft Apollo. In this context, note the classical works of Shem Tov Gefen on Kabbalah and physics dating back to the early century.
39. There have, however, been some advances. See Wexler, *Mystical Society*; Heelas, *The New Age Movement*, pp. 192–194; Wuthnow, *After Heaven*, pp. 168–198. In addition, as stated in the Introduction to the present book, there is a growing body of studies on the New Age in Israel. See Tavory, *Dancing in a Thorn Field*; Ruah-Midbar, "New Age Culture."
40. See Ram, *Globalization of Israel*.
41. A circular reciprocity evolves, since these workshops or therapies sometimes advertise products sold in these stores or by journals of this kind.
42. On the importance of the group in New Age spirituality, see Forman, *Grassroots Spirituality*, pp. 64–65. Hence the phenomenon—so frustrating to researchers—of internal publications and oral transmission.
43. Recently, *Ḥayyim Aḥerim* has even set up a spiritual center called Beit Ḥayyim Aḥerim—yet another stage in the process of institutionalization.
44. For a general review of new forms of identity emerging from the contemporary social

structure, see Castells, *Power of Identity*, pp. 355–346. On identity as a fluid process in contemporary society, see Maluchi, *The Playing Self*, p. 47.

45. To the best of my knowledge, no sociolinguistic study has yet been written on New Age jargon in Israel. For the time being, see Rapoport, Penso, and Garb, "Religious-Zionist Adolescent Girls."
46. There is room for using statistical tools to examine the contribution of these phenomena to the declining power of the Israeli left in recent years.
47. On the centrality of power in the New Age movement, see Maffesoli, *The Time of the Tribes*, p. 32.
48. On the various public committees that were set up in Israel to fight sects, see Beit-Hallahmi, *Despair and Deliverance*, pp. 11, 24, 39–44. See also Hervieu-Léger, *La Religionen Miettees.*
49. Clearly monarchist themes can also be found in the writings of Tolkien's colleague C. S. Lewis (author of the *Narnia* series), as well as in Susan Cooper's pagan-magical fantasy (the *Dark Is Rising* series). Philip Pullman's books, by contrast, are clearly antimonarchist.
50. See Kelner, *Pluralism*, p. 41, and also Chapter 3 of the present book, on criticism of democracy by national mystical circles. Thanks to Assaf Sharon for his insights on these topics. On the similarities between New Age circles and neo-Fascist movements, see Gardell, *Gods of the Blood*, and sources quoted there. In this context, it is worth noting Carl Jung's fascist period.
51. Danforth, *Firewalking.*
52. Essential oils and aromatherapies figure prominently in the cosmetic products market.
53. See especially Russell, *Barefoot Doctor's Handbook.* See also Carrette and King, *Selling Spirituality*, pp. 89–90.
54. See Bilu and Witztum, "Mystical Beliefs and Practices."
55. See Martin, Gutman, and Hutton, *Technologies of the Self*, and cf. Altglas, *Le Nouvel Hindouisme*, pp. 157–160.
56. Wexler, "Social Psychology" (but see also Carrette and King, *Selling Spirituality*, especially pp. 54–86). For the Israeli context, see Beit-Hallahmi, *Despair and Deliverance*, pp. 161–183. This study does not deal with developments since the 1990s and also tends to reduce mystical phenomena to psychological problems.
57. See, for example, Forman, *Grassroots Spirituality*, pp. 113–114.
58. See Chusman, "Why the Self Is Empty."
59. See Lasch, *Culture of Narcissism.* For an analysis of the New Age as an expression of regressive psychological impulses, see Faber's dogmatic Freudian argument in *New Age Thinking.*
60. See R. Ḥayyim of Volozhin, *Ruaḥ Ha-Ḥayyim*, p. 31b (on Tractate *Avot* 5:5); Garb, "Mystics' Critique," pp. 314–317, and sources cited there.
61. See, for example, Kook, *Shmona Qevatzim*, vol. 3, par. 290; vol. 4, par. 15; Cherlow, "The Tzaddiq," pp. 172–173, 189, 191. For a parallel in the Mussar literature, see, for example, Bloch, *Shi'urei Da'at*, vol. 2, pp. 51–52, and see also the statement by R.

Menaḥem Mendel Shneurson (*Ba'ti Le-Gani*, vol. 1, p. 85) on pleasure as "the interiority and essence" of spiritual powers. Note, however, that the Bnei Barukh circles are inclined toward asceticism.

62. An exception to this rule is Berland, head of the Shuvu Bonim Yeshiva and leader of one of the Bratzlav factions.
63. See Foucault, *History of Sexuality*, pp. 17–35.
64. Another influence of the New Age on contemporary culture is the infiltration of eastern movement techniques, especially the various improvisation techniques (such as "contact improvisation," which is very popular in Israel) in Western dance. Ohad Naharin and his Batsheva Dance Company are at the forefront of this phenomenon.
65. See also Chapter 3. On the great importance Théon attached to the body, see Argaman Circle, *Secrets of Contemplation*, p. 18: "The body plays the main role in the spiritual life of man."
66. See Csordas, *Sacred Self*.
67. See, for example, Shanon, *Antipodes of the Mind*, on the use of Ayahuasca.
68. See Bakan, *Sigmund Freud;* Schneider and Berke, *Sigmund Freud.*
69. See Jung, *Memories, Dreams, Reflections*, p. 274. Interestingly, Jung's doctrine was disseminated in Israel by his outstanding pupil Erich Neumann, who wrote a book (as yet unpublished) on Hasidism.
70. See Shecter, *Spiritual Intimacy;* Hoffman, *Way of Splendor.*
71. Halevi, *Kabbalah and Psychology;* Halevi, *School of Kabbalah.* The latter book was translated into Hebrew.
72. On the inflated prices of Kabbalah products, see, for example, M. Wagner, "Kabbalah for Cash," Business and Finance, *Jerusalem Post*, 8 Oct. 1994; D. Van Bienna, "Pop Goes the Kabbalah," *Time*, 24 Nov. 1997.
73. Movies have a special status in this context, inasmuch as they constitute a kind of shared cultural language. This trend intensified over the course of the twentieth century as the globalization process gained momentum.
74. It is rumored that Erison is going to finance a "mystical" channel on cable TV.
75. For an amusing description of a shift from spiritual to economic focus that took place in an organization set up by a famous Zen master, see Shainberg, *Ambivalent Zen*, pp. 257–295.
76. See Trungpa, *Collected Works*, vol. 3, pp. 15–17, 19.
77. Urban, "Cult of Ecstasy."
78. This debate was publicized mainly through the Internet.
79. Many of the kabbalists themselves come from a fairly low socioeconomic class, such as R. Kaduri or Ḥayyim Ha-Kohen, "the milkman" from Givatayim. For more on the role of Kabbalah among the residents of the impoverished town of Sderot, see R. Bar Simon, "The Sukkot of Doubt, Faith and Despair," *Ha'aretz*, 29 Sept. 2004.
80. Forman's comprehensive study *Grassroots Spirituality* (pp. 103–104) also showed that the New Age circles belong mainly to the middle or upper socioeconomic classes.

81. Hence the popularity of swift and easy techniques such as "affirmations" (changing one's internal and external reality through the repetition of positive statements).
82. See Danforth, *Firewalking.*
83. See, respectively, M. Odenheimer, "Yemima Is Gone but She Is Everywhere," *Ha'aretz,* 25 Feb. 2004; Rapoport-Albert, "Women in Sabbatianism," especially the introduction.
84. See Loewenthal, "Women and the Dialectic of Spirituality." On the role of women in the activity of the messianic faction of contemporary Habad, see Elior, "Messianic Resurgence," p. 400. See also Théon: "The redemption depends on the spiritual development of women" (Argaman Circle, *Secrets of Contemplation,* p. 18).
85. See Garb, *Manifestations of Power,* p. 13.
86. These issues were interestingly raised in the movie *Whale Rider* (dir. Niki Caro, 2003). Within the general context of the economic marginality of the Maoris in New Zealand, a drama unfolds at the end of which the elderly and conservative shaman is forced to accept his granddaughter's ability and potential for spiritual leadership.
87. Wexler, *Mystical Society,* pp. 69–73; Wexler, "A Secular Alchemy," pp. 24–25.
88. For a totally sympathetic description of this process, see Forman, *Grassroots Spirituality,* pp. 137–160. Forman's book in itself testifies to the penetration of New Age perceptions into the consciousness of veteran researchers of religion.
89. The report, "Jesus Christ, the Bearer of the Water of Life: Christian Reflection on the New Age," written by Father Michael Fitzgerald, can be found on the Vatican's sophisticated Web site. See also the report in *Ha'aretz,* 5 Feb. 2003. The identification with Gnosticism is partly true. Thanks largely to Jung's influence, there is today a significant revival of Gnosticism, and it is not an accident that one of the first (and more serious) New Age journals was called *Gnosis.*
90. See Forman, *Grassroots Spirituality,* pp. 118–122. This process was documented in the 1970s by Miller, *The New Polytheism.*
91. See, for example, Kristof and Emami, *Enlightenment.*
92. Žižek, *Puppet and the Dwarf,* pp. 38–39, and cf. Huss, "Contemporary Kabbalah." Heelas (*The New Age Movement,* p. 216), by contrast, questioned this relationship when writing up his research, although he allowed the possibility of such a development in the future. See his argument (p. 149) on the tendency toward mystical awakening in a period of transition (the transition from modernity to postmodernism is a case in hand). This last argument is developed even further by Tiryakian, "Sociology of Esoteric Culture," pp. 274–275.
93. Shagar, *Broken Vessels.* This book reveals some degree of awareness of postmodern theories. The book's editor, Odeya Tzurieli, is affiliated with New Age circles and is involved in mystical techniques originating from the Far East.
94. Ibid., p. 122.
95. Ibid., pp. 23, 119–122. See also ibid., p. 25, where Shagar cites Kook's thesis on the breakage of the vessels to support his claim that in the postmodern reality "breakage enables the reconstruction of reality." See also p. 26 on deconstruction as "a process of rupture that clears the way for a higher rectification."

96. Ibid., pp. 116–117. See p. 24 on the connection between Baudrillard's theory of postmodernist "simulation" (which had a strong influence on the movie *The Matrix*), science fiction, and the New Age. He claims that the common denominator of these phenomena is the replacement of a hard reality with a set of fabrications and images that create an "alternative reality," which can easily turn into a mystical reality.
97. Ibid., pp. 119–120. In another discussion on the use of drugs, Shagar "makes allowances" by referring to the fact that "the Old Hasidism were not averse to a glass of tipple, and sometimes even more than a glass" (p. 114). On antinomian tendencies among the hilltop youth, see Chapter 6 of the present book.
98. Ibid., p. 35.
99. See, for example, Zivan, *Religion without Illusion*. On this topic, see also Kepnes, *Interpreting Judaism*.
100. Kelner, *Pluralism*, pp. 5–7, 16, 32–33.
101. Ibid., p. 113.
102. See Shagar (*Broken Vessels*, p. 118) against the "rigid dogmas" of the third generation of the Kook circle who abandoned the mystical path. See also p. 36 on the "misuse" of Kook's ideas by an "obsessive ideology."
103. For an important discussion of the term *habitus* as bodily behavior, see Ostrow, *Social Sensitivity*, pp. 69–83. On the psychological stance that was shaped by modernity, see, for example, Ezrahi, "The Federalist," p. 208.
104. See *Le Monde*, 4 Aug. 2004.
105. The blurring of boundaries between the Jewish and non-Jewish worlds in contemporary mysticism is reflected in the phenomenon of Jubu, or Buddhist Jews (see Linzer, *Torah and Dharma*).
106. One could cite numerous examples. In Chapter 4, I mentioned Abulafia's influence on some members of the Kook circle. Ginsburgh also quotes at length Abulafia's works, which he read even before they were published. R. Aryeh Kaplan also gave Abulafia an important place in his book on Jewish meditation (Kaplan, *Meditation and Kabbalah*, pp. 57–114). An appeal by conservative ultraorthodox circles to the Court of the Eda Ha-Ḥaredit (Badatz) to ban publication of Abulafia's books failed in part because of the opposition of R. Moshe Shapira of the Mussar movement to this censorship. In this context, note the Bnei Ha-Nevi'im Yeshiva in Chicago, under the directorship of R. Ariel Bar-Tzadoq, whose pupils study mainly Abulafian techniques (see the Yeshiva Web site, www.koshertorah.com).
107. On Kook's pragmatism, see Ross, "R. Kook and Post-modernism." On Menaḥem Mendel's pragmatism, see S. Goldberg, "The Zaddik's Soul," p. 226.
108. On this issue, see Halbertal, *Concealment and Revelation*, p. 99.
109. For an example of internal material that was released in this circle, see Trungpa, *True Command*. These were talks that Trungpa gave to the "Dorje Kasung," a kind of private militia. This is an example of a movement reaching a stage of self-confidence that enables it to disclose material that had formerly been concealed for various reasons.

110. Trungpa, *Collected Works*, vol. 6, pp. 11–297.
111. See Green, "Three Warsaw Mystics," p. 5, and especially his argument that personalities such as Zeitlin wrote "in the period after Kabbalah had run its course." Cf. use of the term *neo-Sufism* by Hammer, "Sufism for Westerners."
112. See, for example, Ginsburgh, *Ḥasdei David*, vol. 3, p. 34.
113. On the persistence of magic as a cultural factor, see Harari, "Early Jewish Magic," p. 228; Garb, "New Age Kabbalah," p. 186.
114. Scholem, *Major Trends*, p. 350. On this statement, see also Idel, *Kabbalah*, p. 271.
115. See Huss, "Gershom Scholem," pp. 61–62.
116. One of the pioneering thinkers in this development was Joseph Schechter, who set up spiritual work groups without an affiliation to any religious faith. A similar vision lay behind Yosef Safra's group, currently operating in the settlement of Ne'ot Smadar. Schechter was one of the first to import mystical methods from the Far East to Israel (see Schechter, "Zen" and "Basic Values"). This issue will be discussed by my student Ruth Yosian in her PhD dissertation. For a discussion on the status of secularity in Schechter's thought, see Bursztein, "Revelation as a Psychological Phenomenon," p. 208.
117. Laitman, *Interview with the Future*, pp. 148, 63.
118. The organization Shambala, for example, is a secular front for the Buddhist organization set up by Trungpa. A group possibly matching the definition of a secular kabbalistic group is the Merkava movement, an esoteric group that is currently popular in Tel Aviv. One may add that a statistical review of the percentage of "dropouts" from orthodoxy in the New Age movement in Israel is in order.
119. See, for example, *Nehura De-'Eynin*, an interesting work by R. Arieh Reihanyan of Salford, England. R. Yizḥaq Maier Morgenstern, one of the most prominent Kabbalists in Jerusalem today, grew up in London. In this century, New Age–type communities of Israeli immigrants are emerging in Australia.
120. In my opinion, contemporary Kabbalah research could make use of tools offered by the science of futurology as regards extrapolations and forecasting trends. Although still in its infancy, I foresee a bright future for this field.
121. Dan, *Apocalypse*, p. 338.

POSTSCRIPT

1. See Bloom, *Omens of the Millennium*. The collapse of the World Trade Center towers matched these expectations. In this context, note the great acclaim of the *Rapture* series by Tim LaHaye and Jerry Jenkins, based on a radical Christian apocalyptic vision, which came about in part as a response to this pivotal event.

GLOSSARY

Abulafia, Abraham (1240–?)—Spanish kabbalist. Considered to be the founder of the ecstatic or prophetic stream of Kabbalah. Profoundly influenced Hasidism.

Ashkenazy, Yehuda Léon ("Manitou," 1922–1996)—Born in Morocco, immigrated to France, and became part of the Jewish intellectual circle in Paris. Eventually immigrated to Israel, established a close connection with the Kook circle, and obtained powerful influence within the local francophone community.

Ashlag, Barukh (1907–1991)—Founder of the Bnei Barukh kabbalistic circle in Bnei Brak, Israel. Comprehensively interpreted the doctrine of his father, Y. L. Ashlag.

Ashlag, Yehuda Leib Ha-Levi (1885–1954)—Polish kabbalist who immigrated to Israel in 1921 and founded a small circle in Jerusalem. Wrote extensive commentaries on canonical texts such as the Zohar, containing psychological and sociological interpretations.

Ben-Shushan, Yeshu'a—Israeli Sephardic kabbalist who served in an elite Israel Defense Forces unit and was a member of the Jewish Underground of the 1980s, which conspired to blow up the mosques on the Temple Mount in Jerusalem.

Brezovsky, Shalom Noaḥ (1911–2000)—Born in Belarus. Became the rebbe of Slonim Hasidism and founded its Yeshiva in Jerusalem in 1941. His writings, especially *Netivot Shalom*, are popular among other Hasidim as well as Religious-Zionist neo-Hasidic groups.

Carlebach, Shlomo (1925–1994)—Ex-Lubavitch Hasid who joined the counterculture of the 1960s and became famous for his songwriting. Was the source of inspiration for the Carlebach Prayer Groups ("Minyanim"), which are characterized by ecstatic worship.

Dessler, Eliyahu (1892–1953)—Prominent teacher of Mussar and ultraorthodox ideologue. Studied at the famous Kelm Yeshiva, then immigrated first to England and later to Israel. Most of his discourses were collected in the three-volume *Mikhtav Me-Eliyahu*. Succeeded by R. Ḥayyim Friedlander.

Elijah of Vilna ("The Gaon," "Hagra," 1720–1797)—Vastly learned kabbalist and halakhic expert. Lead the ban against the early Hasidic movement. Inspired both pre-Zionist immigration to Palestine as well as the Mussar movement.

Elyashiv, Shlomo (1839–1926)—Lithuanian kabbalist who immigrated to Israel after influencing Kook and Mussar authorities. Author of the four-volume *Leshem Shvu Ve-Aḥlama*. Grandfather of R. Shalom Elyashiv, the current leader of the non-Hasidic ultraorthodox world.

emunat ḥakhamim—Hasidic doctrine of belief in the rulings of rabbinical leaders even in nonhalakhic matters. Spread to the non-Hasidic world during the twentieth century under the rubric of "da'at Torah."

'Etzion, Yehudah (1952–)—One of the founders of the Gush Emunim settlement movement and a member of the Jewish Underground. Became a close student of Shabbetai Ben-Dov (ideologue of the pre-State LEḤI Underground) and edited his writings. Currently spearheads the attempt to restore Jewish presence on the Temple Mount.

Ginsburgh, Yitzchak (1944–)—Born in the United States. Follower of Lubavitch Hasidism who teaches in Israel and abroad. Author of dozens of books published in several languages that contain a psychological and radically nationalist interpretation of Kabbalah.

Haddaya, 'Ovadia (1891–1959)—Son of kabbalist Shalom Haddaya. Served as dean of the Bet El Sephardic kabbalistic Yeshiva. Sympathetic toward Religious Zionism.

Ḥarlap, Ya'aqov Moshe (1883–1951)—Student of Jerusalem kabbalist R. Yehoshu'a Tzevi Shapira. Became R. Kook's closest disciple and his partner in the aspiration to prophecy. His writings (especially *Mei Marom*) display a radical nationalistic stance.

Hillel, Ya'aqov Moshe—Dean of the Ahavat Shalom Yeshiva in Jerusalem and the most prominent Sephardic kabbalist today. Author of numerous halakhic responsa and kabbalistic commentaries. Fierce opponent of the popularization of Kabbalah.

Hutner, Yizḥaq (1906–1980)—Prominent and unconventional teacher of Mussar. After studying in major Yeshivas in Lithuania and Palestine, he headed the Ḥayyim Berlin Yeshiva in New York. Author of the multivolume work *Paḥad Yizḥaq*. Was succeeded by his son-in-law R. Jonathan David.

Kaduri, Yizḥaq (1889?–2006)—Born in Iraq and immigrated to Israel in 1922. Was reputed to possess magical powers and became a strong source of power for the Shas political party.

Kanievsky, Ya'aqov (1899–1985)—Known as "The Steipler." Born in the Ukraine and educated in Mussar Yeshivas. One of the prominent leaders of the Lithuanian ultra-orthodox world in the second part of the twentieth century. Author of the *Qehilot Ya'aqov* series of commentaries on the Talmud. His son Ḥayyim is to some extent considered his successor.

Kaplan, Aryeh (1934–1983)—Ex-physicist who became one of the leaders of the newly observant in the United States. Student of R. Zvi Aryeh Rosenfeld, one of the pioneers of the Bratzlav movement in the United States. Author of several pioneering works on the technique of Jewish meditation.

Kohen, David ("Ha-Nazir," 1887–1972)—Born in Lithuania and became a close student of R. Kook during the First World War. Author of *Qol Ha-Nevu'a* (The Voice of Prophecy). Practiced Abulafian techniques in an effort to attain prophetic inspiration.

Kook, Avraham Yizḥaq Ha-Kohen (1865–1935)—Born in Russia and immigrated to Palestine in 1904. Became chief rabbi of Palestine in 1921. Author of voluminous poetic, halakhic, and kabbalistic works. Considered to be the founder of the messianic wing of Religious Zionism.

Kook, Tzevi Yehudah Ha-Kohen ("Ratzia," 1891–1982)—Son of R. Kook who focused his doctrine on nationalist ideology. Became leading figure in the Merkaz Ha-Rav Yeshiva and from 1974 was spiritual mentor for the Gush Emunim settlement movement.

Laitman, Michael (1946–)—Born in Russia. After immigrating to Israel, became a close student of R. Barukh Ashlag and took over his Bnei Barukh circle, which he transformed into a worldwide empire through his use of sophisticated technology and marketing techniques.

Leibowitz, Yeruḥam (1875–1936)—Prominent Mussar teacher in pre-Holocaust Lithuania. Succeeded by R. Yechezkel Levenstein, who later became a leading Mussar figure in Israel. Taught R. Shlomo Wolbe, who continued his path into the twenty-first century.

Leiner, Mordekhai Yosef (1800–1854)—Student of the famous Menaḥem Mendel of Kotzk and founder of Izbicha Hasidism. Known especially for his radical and antinomian exegesis, collected in the two volumes of *Mei Ha-Shiloaḥ*.

Luzzatto, Moshe Ḥayyim ("Ramḥal," 1707–1747)—Italian kabbalist. Aroused severe controversy after his messianic and revelatory claims became known. Was subsequently rehabilitated and went on to markedly influence the school of Elijah, the Gaon of Vilna, and the R. Kook circle.

Mussar—Classical Jewish doctrine of self-scrutiny and self-improvement that was revived and propagated in northeastern Europe by R. Yisra'el Salanter and his followers. Although most of its adherents were killed in the Holocaust, it is currently undergoing a revival in Israel, in the United States, and on the Internet.

Naḥman of Bratzlav (1772–1810)—Great-grandson of the Ba'al Shem Tov, and founder of Bratzlav Hasidism. The subject of several hagiographies, which depict his psychological struggles as an inspiration for all seekers. His gravesite in Uman, Ukraine, is the site of a yearly mass pilgrimage.

Odesser, Yisro'el (1886–1994)—Israeli Bratzlav Hasid who supposedly received a written communication from R. Naḥman, which contained a mantra said to have redemptive powers. His followers form a small but distinctive sect within the Bratzlav community.

Rosenberg, Shimon Gershon ("Shagar," 1950–2007)—Founder and head of the Siach Yitzchak Yeshiva in the West Bank. Prominent among Religious-Zionist adherents of neo-Hasidism, he was especially famous for his partial espousal of postmodern and popular culture.

Roth, Aaron (1894–1946)—Born in Hungary. Author of *Shomer Emunim* and founder of a pietistic circle of the same name in Jerusalem, which later split into further subgroups (Toldot Aharon and Toldot Abraham Isaac). Known especially for his stringent rules on sexual purity and staunch opposition to Zionism.

Sefer Ha-Bahir (The Book of Illumination)—First known book-length kabbalistic treatise, edited in Provence in the twelfth century. Deals with theosophy, theurgy, myth, and the mystical rationale of the commandments. Author unknown.

Sefer Yetzira (The Book of Creation)—Cosmological and mystical treatise. Opinions as to its date of composition range from the beginning of the Common Era to the early Middle Ages. Subject of numerous later commentaries, including many works of kabbalistic exegesis (such as the commentary by Elijah, the Gaon of Vilna).

Shapira, Qalonymus Qalman (1889–1943)—Rebbe of Piasecszna. Wrote several books on Hasidic education and established a mystical fraternity dedicated to the cultivation of ecstatic states. Martyred in the Holocaust, which was also the subject of his sermons, published later as *Esh Qodesh*.

Shneurson, Menaḥem Mendel (1902–1994)—Seventh rebbe of Habad-Lubavitch Hasidism. Transformed Habad into a worldwide empire specializing in the dissemination of Hasidic doctrine. In his later years made messianic claims, which were upheld by some of his followers after his death.

Shneurson, Shalom Baer (1860–1920)—Fifth rebbe of Habad-Lubavitch. Began the redirection of this movement from contemplation to institution building, most notably the Tomkhei Tmimim chain of Yeshivas.

Shneurson, Yosef Yizḥaq (1880–1950)—Sixth rebbe of Habad-Lubavitch. Led Habad in the transition from Russia to the United States and intensified the propagation of messianic doctrines.

Tau, Tzevi Yisra'el (1936–)—Born in Vienna, grew up in Holland, and immigrated to Israel. Student of R. Tzevi Yehudah Ha-Kohen Kook. Broke off from the Merkaz Ha-Rav Yeshiva and became the spiritual mentor of the Har Ha-Mor Yeshiva and its satellites. Opposed to external political activism.

Teitelbaum, Yo'el (1887?–1979)—The rebbe of Satmar Hasidism. Born in Hungary. Moved to New York after being rescued from the Holocaust. Author of *Va-Yo'el Moshe* and several other halakhic and polemical works. Known for his fierce opposition to cooperation with Zionism.

Vital, Ḥayyim (1543–1620)—Kabbalist of Italian origin. Operated in the Galilee and Damascus. Became primary student of R. Yizḥaq Luria and edited his writings.

Wolbe, Shlomo (1914–2005)—Student of Lithuanian Mussar teacher R. Yeruḥam Leibowitz. Main preserver of the Mussar teachings in the late twentieth century. Author of the two-volume *'Alei Shur*. The most prominent of his successors is R. Reuven Leuchter of Jerusalem.

yiḥudim—Main mystical technique of Lurianic Kabbalah. Involves meditation on complex combinations of divine names. Practiced intensely by R. Luzzatto, certain Hasidic masters, and R. Kook.

Yosef, 'Ovadia (1920–)—Born in Iraq. Considered to be the leading halakhic authority in the Sephardic world. Erstwhile Sephardic chief rabbi and now the spiritual authority behind the Shas party.

Zadok Ha-Kohen of Lublin (1823–1900)—Born in Latvia. Converted to Hasidism and became a prime student of Mordekhai Yosef Leiner. Author of numerous Hasidic and halakhic works that are also popular outside the Hasidic world and developed kabbalistic historiosophy.

Zagdon, Avraham—Born in France, immigrated to Israel, and became leader of controversial subsect of Bratzlav Hasidism, which has recently gone through a schism.

Zeitlin, Hillel (1871–1942)—Writer and journalist active in Warsaw. Following transformative experiences, dedicated himself to popular Hasidic and kabbalistic writing. Martyred in the Holocaust.

BIBLIOGRAPHY

Primary Sources

Albotini, Yehuda. *Sulam Ha-'Aliya*. Jerusalem, 1989. [Hebrew]

Al-Jamal, Muhammad. *Music of the Soul: Sufi Teachings*. Petaluma, Calif., 1997.

Alush, Zvi. *The Amazing Story of the X-Ray Rabbi: R. Ya'aqov Israel Ifargan*. Omer, Israel, 2004. [Hebrew].

Argaman Circle. *A Gate for the Secrets of Contemplation*. Tel Aviv, 1977. [Hebrew].

Ari'el, Ya'akov. "Authority in Halakha." *Nequda* 74 (1984). [Hebrew]

——. "Rebellion in Halakha?" *Nequda* 75 (1984). [Hebrew]

Ashkenazy, Y. L. "And It Was in the Latter Days," *Shoresh Ha-Shoah* 2 (1983): pp. 22–31. [Hebrew]

——. *Eulogy for the Messiah?: Classes by Rabbi Y. L. Ashkenazy*. Kiryat Arba', Israel. 2006. [Hebrew]

——. "Jews in Exile in Moslem and Christian Countries," *Shevet Va'am*, second series, 1 (1970): pp. 85–92. [Hebrew]

——. *The Science of Kabbalah in the Works of R. Kook and R. Ashlag*, ed. S. Aviner. Jerusalem, 1991. [Hebrew]

——. *Secret of the Hebrew: The Foundations of Faith in Light of the Verses of the Torah*. Jerusalem, 2005. [Hebrew]

——. *Secret of the Holy Tongue*, vol. 1. Jerusalem, 2007. [Hebrew]

Ashlag, Barukh. *Sham'ati: Essays and Notes*, ed. M. Laitman. Bnei Brak, Israel, 1992. [Hebrew]

Ashlag, Y. L. *Introduction to the Science of Kabbalah*, with Barukh Ashlag's commentaries: *Or Barukh and Or Shalom*. Bnei Brak, Israel, 1994. [Hebrew]

——. *Or Ha-Bahir: On Kabbalah and Jewish Thinking*. Jerusalem, 1997. [Hebrew]

——. *Pri Ḥakham*. 2 vols. Bnei Brak, Israel, 1985. [Hebrew]

——. *Sefer Ha-Haqdamot*. Jerusalem, 1974. [Hebrew]

——. *Sefer Matan Torah*. Jerusalem, 1982. [Hebrew]

Aviner, Shlomo. "Alternative Medicine." *'Iturei Kohanim* 149 (1997): pp. 17–27. [Hebrew]

——. "Hasidim and Mitnagdim." *'Iturei Kohanim* 100 (1993): pp. 1–3. [Hebrew]

——. "Semi-mystical Complementary Medicine (Reiki and Healing)." *'Iturei Kohanim* 202 (2001): pp. 7–18. [Hebrew]

'Azriel of Gerona. *Commentary on Talmudic Aggadoth*, ed. I. Tishby. Jerusalem, 1983. [Hebrew]

Berkowitz, Dov. "Interview with R. Mordekhai Sheinberger." *Dimuy* 14 (1997): pp. 20–25. [Hebrew]

Bin-Nun, Yoel. "Derekh Ha-Orot versus the Path of Aberration." *Nequda* 91 (1985). [Hebrew]

——. "In Favor of Stocktaking." *Nequda* 75 (1984). [Hebrew]

Bloch, Yosef Leib. *Shi'urei Da'at* [lectures on Mussar]. Tel Aviv, 1953. [Hebrew]

Bonder, Nilton. *The Kabbalah of Envy*. Boulder, 1997.

——. *The Kabbalah of Money*. Boulder, 1997.

Brezovsky, S. N. *Kuntras Ha-Haruga 'Alayikh: Collection of Essays on the Holocaust*. Jerusalem, 1988. [Hebrew]

——. *Netivot Shalom*. Jerusalem, 1989. [Hebrew]

Butto, Nader. *Medicine and the Seventh Sense: A Revolutionary Approach to Treatment*. Ben Shemen, Israel, 2002. [Hebrew]

Capra, Fritjof. *The Tao of Physics: An Exploration of the Parallels between Modern Physics and Eastern Mysticism*. New York, 1977.

Commentary (magazine). *The Condition of Jewish Belief*. New York, 1966.

Dessler, Eliyahu. *Mikhtav Me-Eliyahu* [letters]. Jerusalem, 1983. [Hebrew]

Dorje, Rig'dzin. *Dangerous Friend: The Teacher-Student Relationship in Vajrayana Buddhism*. Boston, 2001.

Eco, Umberto. *Foucault's Pendulum*, trans. W. Weaver. New York, 1990.

Elijah of Vilna. *Avnei Eliyahu* [commentary on the Siddur]. Jerusalem, 1977. [Hebrew]

Elyashiv, Shlomo. *Leshem Shvo Ve-Aḥlama*. Vol. 1, *Haqdamot Ve-She'arim*. Petrakov, Russia, 1909. [Hebrew]

——. *Leshem Shvo Ve-Aḥlama*. Vol. II, *Drushei 'Olam Ha-Tohu*. Petrakov, Russia, 1912. [Hebrew]

'Etzion, Yehuda. "Mi-Degel Yerushalayim Li-Tnuat Ha-Ge'ula." *Nequda* 94 (1985): pp. 8–9, 28–29. [Hebrew]

——. "Psaq Halakha 'Al-Pi Hazmana." *Nequda* 235 (2000): pp. 32–37. [Hebrew]

Ezraḥi, Ohad. " 'Al Da'at Ha-Maqom." *De'ot* 5 (1999): pp. 12–16. [Hebrew]

Feild, Reshad. *The Last Barrier: A Sufi Journey*. Shaftesbury, England, 1976.

Fisch, A. B. *Points of Light and Knowledge in the Torah of R. Y. L. Ashlag*. Bnei Brak, Israel, 1996. [Hebrew]

Friedlander, Ḥayyim. *Treasures of Ramḥal*. Bnei Brak, Israel, 1986. [Hebrew]

Ginsburgh, Yitzchak. *The Aleph-Beit: Jewish Thought Revealed through the Hebrew Letters*. London, 1995.

——. *Be'Itah Aḥishenah: The Secrets of the Last Redemption as a Means for Understanding the Redemption of Our Generation*. Kfar Habad, Israel, 2003. [Hebrew]

——. *Bekhol Derakhekha Da'ehu*. Rehovot, Israel, 1997. [Hebrew]

——. *A Chapter in Divine Worship*. Jerusalem, 1987.

——. *Face to Face: The Foundations of the Inner Education according to Kabbalah and Hasidism*. Rehovot, Israel, 2000. [Hebrew]

——. *Ha-Hitqashrut Le-'Aḥar Gimel Tammuz*. Rehovot, Israel, 1998. [Hebrew]

——. *Ḥasdei David Ha-Ne'emanim: Introduction to Kabbalah and Contemplation*. Kfar Habad, Israel, 2004. [Hebrew]

——. *Kingdom of Israel*, 4. Rehovot, Israel, 1988. [Hebrew]

——. *Kingdom of Israel*, I. Rehovot, Israel, 1999. [Hebrew]

——. *Kuntras Barukh Ha-Gever*, ed. Y. Ariel. Kiryat Arba', 1995. [Hebrew]

——. *Le-Lamed Bnei Yehuda Qeshet*. Rehovot, Israel, 1994. (Reprinted in *Ruḥo Shel-Mashiaḥ*. Kfar Habad, Israel, 2004.) [Hebrew]

——. *Shekhina among Them*. Jerusalem, 1986. [Hebrew]

——. *Sod Hashem Li-Yer'eav*. Jerusalem, 1985. [Hebrew]

——. *The Spirit of the Messiah: The Current Period from a Hasidic Viewpoint*. Kfar Habad, Israel, 2004. [Hebrew]

——. *Transforming Darkness into Light: Kabbalah and Psychology*. Jerusalem, 2002.

——. *Ve-Tzaddiq Yesod 'Olam*. Jerusalem, 1989. [Hebrew]

——. *Yesod She-Ba-Yesod*. Jerusalem, 1998. [Hebrew]

Glazerson, Mattityahu. *The Mystery of the Hebrew Language*. Bnei Brak, Israel, 1984. [Hebrew]

Goldberg, Myla. *Bee Season: A Novel*. New York, 2001.

Gottlieb, A. M. *Ha-Sulam: The Lives and Teachings of Our Holy Rebbes of the Ashlagian Dynasty and Their Disciples*. Jerusalem, 1997. [Hebrew]

Gottlieb-Zornberg, Avivah. *Genesis: The Beginning of Desire*. Philadelphia, 1995.

——. *The Particulars of Rapture: Reflections on Exodus*. New York, 2001.

Grienberg, Yehoshu'a. *Almost a Bride*. Tel Aviv, 1999. [Hebrew]

Haddaya, 'Ovadia. *Va-Yiqaḥ 'Ovadyahu*. 4 vols. Jerusalem, 1962. [Hebrew]
——. *Yaskil 'Avdi*, vols. 2, 4, 5, 6, and 8. Jerusalem, 1981–1983. [Hebrew]
Halevi, Ze'ev Ben Shimon. *Kabbalah and Psychology*. Bath, England, 1986.
——. *School of Kabbalah*. London, 1983.
Ḥarlap, Y. M. *Ḥed Harim* [letters to R. Kook]. Jerusalem, 1971. [Hebrew]
——. *Ma'yanei Ha-Yeshu'a*. Jerusalem, 1979. [Hebrew]
——. "Opposition and Hasidism." *'Iturei Kohanim* 100 (1993): pp. 7–9. [Hebrew]
——. *Pure Sayings: Articles on the Generation and the Hour*. Jerusalem, 2002. [Hebrew]
——. *Yishlaḥ Mi-Marom: A Collection of Letters*. Jerusalem, 2003. [Hebrew]
Ḥayyim of Volozhin. *Nefesh Ha-Ḥayyim*. Bnei Brak, Israel, 1989. [Hebrew]
——. *Ruaḥ Ha-Ḥayyim*. Jerusalem, 1973. [Hebrew]
Ḥaver, Yizḥaq. *Treasures*, ed. S. Weiden. Jerusalem, 1990. [Hebrew]
Hillel, Y. M. *Shorshei Ha-Yam*, vol. 1. Jerusalem, 1999. [Hebrew]
——. *Faith and Folly (Tamim Tiyhe)*. Jerusalem, 1996. [Hebrew]
Israeli, Shula. *You Shall Enter through New Gates: Lessons with the Holy Ari*. Rishon Le-Zion, Israel, 2004. [Hebrew]
James, Tad, and David Shephard. *Presenting Magically: Transforming Your Stage Presence with NLP*. Carmarthen, Wales, 2001.
Jones, D. W. *The Chronicles of Chrestomanci*, vol. 1. New York, 2001.
Kaplan, Aryeh. *Meditation and Kabbalah*. York Beach, Maine, 1982.
Kelner, Yoseph. *Pluralism, Fanaticism and Totality: The Criteria of Truth and Morality*. Jerusalem, 2001. [Hebrew]
Kohen, David. *Nezir Eḥav*, ed. S. Y. Ha-Kohen, vol. 1. Jerusalem, 1978. [Hebrew]
——. *Qol Ha-Nevu'a: Ha-Higayon Ha-'Ivri Ha-Shim'i*. Jerusalem, 2002. [Hebrew]
Kook, Avraham Yizḥaq. *'Arphilei Tohar*. Jerusalem, 1983. [Hebrew]
——. *Articles*. Jerusalem, 1984. [Hebrew]
——. *Ḥadarav: Personal Chapters*, ed. R. Sarid. Expanded second edition. Ramat Gan, Israel, 2002. [Hebrew]
——. *Letters*. Jerusalem, 1985. [Hebrew]
——. *Me'orot Ha-Re'iah*. Jerusalem, 2004. [Hebrew]
——. *Mishpat Kohen*. Jerusalem, 1985. [Hebrew]
——. *Mussar Avikha*. Jerusalem, 1971. [Hebrew]
——. *'Olat Re'iah* [commentary on the prayerbook]. 2 vols. Jerusalem, 1978–1983. [Hebrew]
——. *Orot*. Jerusalem, 1985. [Hebrew]
——. *Orot Ha-Qodesh*. Jerusalem, 1964. [Hebrew]
——. *Orot Ha-Teshuva*. Jerusalem, 1985. [Hebrew]
——. *Orot Ha-Torah*. Jerusalem, 1985. [Hebrew]
——. *Pinkas Yud-Gimel*. Jerusalem, 2004. [Hebrew]
——. *Reish Milin: Rishmei Maḥsava Le-Midrash Ha-Otiot, Ha-Tagin, Ha-Nequdot Ve Ha-Te'amim*. Jerusalem, 2003. [Hebrew]
——. *Shmona Qevatzim Mi-Ktav Yad Qodsho*. Jerusalem, 1999. [Hebrew]

Kook, Tzevi Yehuda. "Hasidim Ve-Mitnagdim." *Shana Be-Shana* 40 (2000): pp. 290–303. [Hebrew]

——. *Li-Ntivot Yisra'el*. Vol. 1: Jerusalem, 1989. Vol. 2: Beit El, Israel, 2003. [Hebrew]

——. *Or Li-Ntivati*. Jerusalem, 1989. [Hebrew]

——. *Zemaḥ Tzevi*, vol. 1. Jerusalem, 1991. [Hebrew]

Kristof, Aziz, and Houman Emami. *Enlightenment beyond Traditions*. Delhi, India, 1999.

Laitman, Michael. *An Interview with the Future*. Ramat Gan, Israel, 2003. [Hebrew]

——. *The Kabbalah Experience*. Toronto, 2005.

Leet, Leonora. *The Kabbalah of the Soul: The Transformative Psychology and Practices of Jewish Mysticism*. Rochester, N.Y., 2003.

Leibowitz, Yeruḥam. *Da'at Ḥokhma U-Mussar*, vol. 1. Tel Aviv, 1972. [Hebrew]

Leiner, M. Y. *Mei Ha-Siloaḥ*, 2 vols. Bnei Brak, Israel, 1995. [Hebrew]

Luzzatto, Moshe Ḥayyim. *The Knowing Heart: Da'at Tevunot*, trans. S. Silverstein. Jerusalem, 1982.

Maman, Pinḥas, ed. *The Torah of the Messiah: A Collection of Talks and Commentaries on Matters of Messiah and Redemption*. New York, 1993. [Hebrew]

Menaḥem Mendel of Shklov. *Derekh Ha-Qodesh*. Jerusalem, 1999. [Hebrew]

——. *Mayim Adirim*. Jerusalem, 1984. [Hebrew]

Nathan of Nemirov. *Life of Moharan*. Jerusalem, 1998. [Hebrew]

Nov, Devora. "The Body in Movement as Spiritual Practice." *Mizraf: Journal of the Center for Creative Judaism* 1 (2000): pp. 51–80. [Hebrew]

Ofan, Boaz, ed. *Nafshi Taqshiv Shiro*. Ramat Gan, Israel, 1998. [Hebrew]

Piercy, Marge. *He, She and It*. New York, 1991.

Remer, Avraham. *Gadol Shimusha: From the Torah and Deeds of Our Rabbi R. Zevi Yehuda Kook*. Jerusalem, 1994. [Hebrew]

Robinson, John. *Honest to God*. Philadelphia, 1963.

Russell, Stephen. *Barefoot Doctor's Handbook for Heroes: A Spiritual Guide to Fame and Fortune*. London, 1999.

Ryback, Tzevi. *'Al Qetz Ha-Tiqqun: Amazing Revelations towards the End of the Sixth Millennium: The Future of Humanity and the Necessary Preparations for Survival*. Tel Aviv, 2000. [Hebrew]

Schechter, Josef. "Basic Values of the Far East." *Molad* 23 (1965): pp. 681–693. [Hebrew]

——. "Zen, Yoga and Meditation: Paths of the Far East." *Molad* 30 (1976): pp. 386–394. [Hebrew]

Schechter, Y. M. *Collection of Sayings*, vol. 1. Jerusalem, 1998. [Hebrew]

——. *Ve-Nikhtav Ba-Sefer: A Collection of Discourses to Awaken One to the Worship of the Creator and the Rectification of One's Traits*, vol. 1. Jerusalem, 1987. [Hebrew]

Schecter, Z. S. *Spiritual Intimacy: A Study of Counselling in Hassidism*. Northvale, N.J., 1991.

Segal, Israel. *Ne'ila*. Jerusalem, 1990. [Hebrew]

Shagar (Shimon Gershon Rosenberg). *Broken Vessels: Torah and Religious Zionism in a Post-modern Environment*. Efrat, Israel, 2004. [Hebrew]

Shapira, A. A. "Redemption and Temple (Interview)." *Teḥumin* 5 (1984): pp. 431–436. [Hebrew]

Shapira, Qalonymus Qalman. *Derekh Ha-Melekh*. Jerusalem, 1998. [Hebrew]

——. *Esh Qodesh*. Jerusalem, 1960. [Hebrew]

Shneurson, Menaḥem Mendel. *Ba'ti le-Gani: Articles*, vol. 1. New York, 1977. [Hebrew]

——. *Heikhal Menaḥem*. Jerusalem, 1984. [Hebrew]

Silverthorn, Julie, and John Overdurf. *Dreaming Realities: A Spiritual System to Create Inner Alignment through Dreams*. Carmmarthen, Wales, 2000.

Soloveitchik, J. B. *Family Redeemed: Essays on Family Relationships*, ed. D. Shatz and J. Wolowolsky. New York, 2000.

Steinsaltz, 'Adin. *The Candle of God: Discourse and Chasidic Thought*. Northvale, N.J., 1998.

Stroud, Jonathan. *The Golem's Eye*. New York, 2004.

Sussman, Yosef, ed. "Letters concerning the Biography of Our Teacher Rabbi Avraḥam Yizḥaq Ha-Kohen Kook: The Saintly Gaon R. Yosef Leib Sussman." *Me-Avnei Ha-Maqom: From the Fruits of Our Study* [Beit El Yeshiva] 14 (2002): pp. 14–35. [Hebrew]

Tau, Z. I. *Le-Emunat 'Itenu*, vols. 1, 3, 4, and 5. Jerusalem, 1994–2004. [Hebrew]

Trungpa, Chögyam. *The Collected Works of Chögyam Trungpa*, ed. C. G. Gimian, vols. 2–6. Boston, 2003–2004.

——. *True Command: The Teachings of the Dorje Kasung*, vol. 1. Halifax, 2004.

Vital, Ḥayyim. *Sha'ar Ha-Gilgulim*. Jerusalem, 1981.

Wilson, P. L. *Sacred Drift: Essays on the Margins of Islam*. San Francisco, 1993.

Winkler, Gershon. *The Place Where You Are Standing Is Holy: A Jewish Theology on Human Relationships*. Northvale, N.J., 1995.

Wolbe, Shlomo. *'Alei Shur: Gates of Guidance*. Vol. 1: Beer Ya'aqov, Israel, 1975. Vol. 2: Jerusalem, 1986. [Hebrew]

Yosef, 'Ovadia. *Yaḥve Da'at*, vol. 4. Jerusalem, 1981. [Hebrew]

Zagdon, Avraham. *Ilu Yed'ativ Haitiv*. Beitar 'Ilit, Israel, 2001. [Hebrew]

——. *Or Ha-Ganuz: Mavo Le-Torah De-'Atika Satimah*. Beitar 'Ilit, Israel, 2001. [Hebrew]

Zeitlin, Hillel. *The Book of the Few*. Jerusalem, 1979. [Hebrew]

Zuckerman, Yehoshu'a. "Interview with R. Yehoshu'a Zuckerman." *Nequda* 73 (1984). [Hebrew]

Secondary Sources

Abromovitz, Udi. "The Publication of the Notebooks." *'Alon Shvut* 156–157 (2000): pp. 135–161. [Hebrew]

Agnon, S. Y. *Book, Writer, Story*. Tel Aviv, 1978. [Hebrew]

Aḥituv, Yosef. "Between Haredi and National-Haredi Modesty." *De'ot* 4 (1999): pp. 13–16. [Hebrew]

——. "Modesty: Myth and Ethos." In *A Good Eye: Dialogue and Polemic in Jewish Culture (A Jubilee Book in Honor of Tova Ilan)*, ed. Y. Aḥituv et al., pp. 224–263. Tel Aviv, 1999. [Hebrew]

——. "Rav Ashlag and Levinas on Commitment to the Other." In *Be-Darkhei Shalom: Studies in Jewish Thought Presented to Shalom Rosenberg*, ed. B. Ish Shalom, pp. 464–483. Jerusalem, 2007. [Hebrew]

——. "The Strange Revival of Mysticism Today." In *Dvarim: A Collection of Articles Marking the First Decade of the Yaakov Herzog Center*, ed. Y. Aḥituv et al., pp. 37–42. Ein Zurim, Israel, 1999. [Hebrew]

Alfasi, Yizḥaq. "Hasidism and Proto-Zionism (1861–1882)." *Shragai* 2 (1985): pp. 65–73. [Hebrew]

Altglas, Véronique. *Le Nouvel Hindouisme Occidental*. Paris, 2005.

Aran, Gideon. "From Pioneering to Torah Study: Background to the Growth of Religious Zionism." In *A Hundred Years of Religious Zionism*, vol. 3, ed. A. Sagi and D. Schwartz, pp. 31–81. Ramat Gan, Israel, 2003. [Hebrew]

Ashkenazi, Y. L. "The Use of Kabbalistic Concepts in Rav Kook's Teaching." In *The World of Rav Kook's Thought*, ed. B. Ish-Shalom and S. Rosenberg, trans. J. Carmy and B. Casper, pp. 149–155. Avi Chai, Israel, 1991.

Assaf, David. *Bratzlav: An Annotated Bibliography*. Jerusalem, 2000. [Hebrew]

Assis, 'Amit. "The Return from India: Religious Travelers on a Spiritual Journey." *De'ot* 9 (2001): pp. 7–9. [Hebrew]

Aveni, Anthony. *Behind the Crystal Ball: Magic, Science and the Occult from Antiquity through the New Age*. New York, 1996.

Aviad, Janet. *Return to Judaism: Religious Renewal in Israel*. Chicago, 1983.

Avivi, Joseph. "History as a Divine Prescription." In *Rabbi Mordechai Breuer Festschrift: Collected Papers in Jewish Studies*, ed. M. Bar-Asher, pp. 709–771. Jerusalem, 1992. [Hebrew]

——. *The Kabbalah of the Gra*. Jerusalem, 1993. [Hebrew]

——. "The Source of Lights: R. Kook's Shemonah Kevatsim." *Tzohar* 1 (2000): pp. 93–111. [Hebrew]

——. *Zohar Ramḥal*. Jerusalem, 1987. [Hebrew]

Bakan, David. *Sigmund Freud and the Jewish Mystical Tradition*. Princeton, N.J., 1958.

Barabasi, A. L. *Linked: How Everything Is Connected to Everything Else and What It Means for Business, Science and Everyday Life*. London, 2003.

Barak, Uriel. "The Development of the Doctrine of Redemption of Rabbi Ya'akov Moshe Charlap." M.A. thesis, Hebrew University. Jerusalem, 1997. [Hebrew]

Bar-Asher, Shalom. "Eretz Israel in the Thought of North African Sages, 1830–1977." In *The Land of Israel in 20th Century Jewish Thought*, ed. A. Ravitzky, pp. 210–232. Jerusalem, 2004. [Hebrew]

Barnai, Jacob. *Historiography and Nationalism*. Jerusalem, 1996. [Hebrew]

——. *Sabbateanism: Social Perspectives*. Jerusalem, 2000. [Hebrew]

Bar-Sella, Shraga. *Between the Storm and the Quiet: The Life and Works of Hillel Zeitlin*. Tel Aviv, 1999. [Hebrew]

——. "Hillel Zeitlin's Prophetic-Messianic Approach to Judaism." *Da'at* 26 (1991): pp. 109–124. [Hebrew]

Bartal, Israel. *Exile in the Homeland: Essays*. Jerusalem, 1994. [Hebrew].

Bar-Yosef, Ḥamutal. "An Introduction to Mysticism in Modern Hebrew Literature." *Kabbalah* 11 (2004): pp. 369–399. [Hebrew]

——. "Zionism and Messianic Redemption: The Russian Background and its Reverberations in Hebrew Literature." In *Renewing Jewish Commitment: The Work and Thought of David Hartman*, vol. 2, ed. A. Sagi and Z. Zohar, pp. 773–800. Tel Aviv, 2001. [Hebrew]

Baumgarten, Eli'ezer. "History and Historiosophy in the Doctrine of R. Shlomo Elyashiv." M.A. thesis, Ben Gurion University. Beer Sheva, Israel, 2006. [Hebrew]

Beit-Hallahmi, Benjamin. *Despair and Deliverance: Private Salvation in Contemporary Israel*. New York, 1992.

Belcove-Shalin, J. S. *New World Hasidism: Ethnographic Studies of Hasidic Jews in America*. Albany, 1995.

Ben-Shlomo, Joseph. "Perfection and Perfectibility in Rabbi Kook's Theology." *'Iyyun: A Hebrew Philosophical Quarterly* 33 (1984): pp. 289–309. [Hebrew]

——. "The Sacred and the Profane in R. Kook's Philosophy." *Jerusalem Studies in Jewish Thought* 13 (1996): pp. 491–524. [Hebrew]

Berger, David. *The Rebbe, the Messiah and the Scandal of Orthodox Indifference*. London, 2001.

Bergman, S. H. *Men and Ways: Philosophical Essays*. Jerusalem, 1967. [Hebrew]

Bertens, Hans. *The Idea of the Postmodern: A History*. New York, 1995.

Biale, David. *Power and Powerlessness in Jewish History*. New York, 1986.

Bick, Abraham (Shauli). *Hem U-Mishnatom: Essays and Memories*. Jerusalem, 1982. [Hebrew]

Bilu, Yoram. "The Making of Modern Saints: Manufactured Charisma and the Abu-Hatseiras of Israel." *American Ethnologist* 19 (1992): pp. 672–687.

——. "The Sanctification of Place in Israel's Civil and Traditional Religion." *Jerusalem Studies in Jewish Folklore* 19–20 (1998): pp. 65–84. [Hebrew]

——. "Studying Folk Culture in the Postmodern Era: A Personal Story." *Theory and Criticism—An Israeli Forum* 10 (1997): pp. 37–54.

Bilu, Yoram, and Eli'ezer Witztum. "Heẓiz ve-Nifga': On Mystical Beliefs and Practices among Psychological Patients and Clinical Applications." *Alpayim* 9 (1994): pp. 21–43. [Hebrew]

Bishop, Peter. *Dreams of Power: Tibetan Buddhism and the Western Imagination*. London, 1993.

Bloom, Harold. *The American Religion: The Emergence of the Post-Christian Nation*. New York, 1992.

——. *Kabbalah and Criticism*. New York, 1975.

——. *Omens of the Millennium: The Gnosis of Angels, Dreams and Resurrection*. New York, 1996.

Bowman, Alan, and Greg Woolf. "Literacy and Power in the Ancient World." In *Literacy and Power in the Ancient World*, ed. A. Bowman and G. Woolf, pp. 1–16. Cambridge, England, 1996.

Boyarin, Daniel. "Colonial Drag: Zionism, Gender and Mimicry." *Theory and Criticism: An Israeli Forum* 11 (1997): pp. 123–143. [Hebrew]

Breuer, Mordechai. *Oholei Torah (The Tents of Torah): The Yeshiva, Its Structure and History*. Jerusalem, 2003. [Hebrew]

Brill, Alan. *Thinking God: The Mysticism of Rabbi Zadok of Lublin*. New York, 2003.

Brown, Benjamin. "The Hazon Ish: Halakhic Philosophy, Theology and Social Policy in His Prominent Later Rulings (1933–1953)." PhD diss., Hebrew University. Jerusalem, 2003. [Hebrew].

——. " 'Primal Faith' and 'Final Faith' in the Views of Three Haredi Thinkers." *Aqdamot: A Journal of Jewish Thought* 4 (1998): pp. 46–58. [Hebrew]

——. "The Sanctity of the Land of Israel in Light of the Shemittah Controversy." In *The Land of Israel in 20th Century Jewish Thought*, ed. A. Ravitzky, pp. 71–103. Jerusalem, 2004. [Hebrew]

Bursztein, Ari. "Revelation as a Psychological-Existential Phenomenon—The Place of the Bible in the Thought of Joseph Schechter." *Hagut: Jewish Educational Thought* 5–6 (2003–2004): pp. 199–217. [Hebrew]

Carrette, Jeremy, and Richard King. *Selling Spirituality: The Silent Takeover of Religion*. London, 2005.

Castells, Manuel. *The Power of Identity*, vol. 2. Oxford, England, 1997.

Charvit, Yossef. "Identity and History: The Cultural Heritage of R. Yehouda Léon Ashkenazi (Manitou)." *Pe'amim* 91 (2002). pp. 105–122. [Hebrew]

Cherlow, Smadar. "Boldness and Modesty: R. Kook's Ethical System versus the Power Morality of Nietzsche." In *Nietzsche, Zionism and Hebrew Culture*, ed. Jacob Golomb, pp. 347–374. Jerusalem, 2002. [Hebrew]

——. "The Circle of Rav Kook as a Mystical Fraternity." *Tarbiz* 74 (2005): pp. 261–303. [Hebrew]

——. " 'Ha-Ahavah Be-Ta'anugim': An Analysis of Rav Kook's World of Religious and Mystical Experience." *Da'at* 57–59 (2006): pp. 355–382. [Hebrew]

——. "Messianism and the Messiah in the Circle of Rav Kook," *Moreshet Israel: Journal of Judaism, Zionism and Eretz-Israel* 2 (2005): pp. 42–87. [Hebrew]

——. "Rav Kook's Mystical Mission." *Da'at* 49 (2002): pp. 99–136. [Hebrew]

——. "The Tzaddiq Is the Foundation of the World: Rav Kook's Esoteric Mission and Mystical Experience." PhD diss., Bar Ilan University. Ramat Gan, Israel, 2003. [Hebrew]

Cherlow, Yuval. "On Modesty and Regeneration: An Exchange of Letters between R. Kook and R. David Cohen." *'Iyyun: The Jerusalem Philosophical Quarterly* 46 (1998): pp. 441–450. [Hebrew]

Chittick, William. *The Sufi Path of Knowledge: Ibn 'Arabi's Metaphysics of Imagination*. Albany, N.Y., 1989.

Chusman, Philip. "Why the Self Is Empty: Towards a Historically Situated Psychology." *American Psychologist* 45 (1990): pp. 599–611.

Clarke, J. J. *The Tao of the West: Western Transformations of Taoist Thought*. London, 2000.

Clifford, James, and George Marcus. *Writing Culture*. Berkeley, Calif., 1986.

Csordas, Thomas. *The Sacred Self: A Cultural Phenomenology of Charismatic Healing*. Berkeley, Calif., 1994.

Cuddihy, J. M. *The Ordeal of Civility: Freud, Marx, Levi-Strauss and the Jewish Struggle with Modernity*. Boston, 1974.

Cuppit, Don. "Post-Christianity." In *Religion, Modernity and Post-Modernity*, ed. P. Heelas et al., pp. 232–218. Oxford, England, 1998.

Dan, Joseph. *Apocalypse Then and Now*. Tel Aviv, 2000. [Hebrew]

Danforth, Loring. *Firewalking and Religious Healing: The Anastenaria of Greece and the American Firewalking Movement.* Princeton, N.J., 1999.

Davidman, Lynn. "Accommodation and Resistance to Modernity: A Comparison of Two Contemporary Orthodox Jewish Groups." *Sociological Analysis* 51 (1990): pp. 35–51.

De Landa, Manuel. *One Thousand Years of Non-linear History.* New York, 1997.

Deutsch, S. S. *Larger Than Life : The Life and Times of the Lubavitcher Rebbe Rabbi Menachem Mendel Schneerson.* New York, 1995.

Don-Yehiya, Eli'ezer. "The Book and the Sword: Nationalist Yeshiva's and Political Radicalism in Israel." In *A Hundred Years of Religious Zionism*, vol. 3, ed. A. Sagi and D. Schwartz, pp. 187–228. Ramat Gan, Israel, 2003. [Hebrew]

Efrati, Benjamin. *Ha-Sanegoria Be-Mishnat Ha-Rav Kook.* Jerusalem, 1959. [Hebrew]

Eisenstadt, S. N. *Changes in Israeli Society.* Tel Aviv, 2004. [Hebrew]

Eliade, Mircea. *Myths, Dreams and Mysteries: The Encounter between Contemporary Faiths and Archaic Realities*, trans. P. Mairet. New York, 1975.

Elior, Rachel. "The Innovation of Polish Hasidism." *Tarbiẕ* 62 (1993): pp. 381–432. [Hebrew]

——. "The Lubavitch Messianic Resurgence: The Historical and Mystical Background." In *Towards the Millennium: Messianic Expectations from the Bible to Waco*, ed. P. Schäfer and M. R. Cohen, pp. 383–408. Leiden, The Netherlands, 1998.

——. "Messianic Expectations and Spiritualization of Religious Life in the 16th Century." *Revue Des Etudes Juives* 145 (1986): pp. 35–49.

——. *The Mystical Origins of Hasidism.* Oxford, England, 2006.

——. "Yesh and 'Ayin as Fundamental Paradigms in Hasidic Thought." In *Massu'ot: Studies in Kabbalistic Literature and Jewish Philosophy in Memory of Prof. Ephraim Gottlieb*, ed. M. Oron and A. Goldreich, pp. 53–74. Jerusalem, 1994. [Hebrew]

Etkes, Immanuel. *Rabbi Israel Salanter and the Beginning of the Mussar Movement.* Jerusalem, 1984. [Hebrew]

Even-Ḥen, Ya'aqov. *Rabbi and Leader.* Jerusalem, 1998. [Hebrew]

Ezrahi, Yaron. "The Federalist: On Democracy and Political Wisdom." *Theory and Criticism—An Israeli Forum* 21 (2002): pp. 205–210. [Hebrew]

——. *Rubber Bullets: Power and Conscience in Israeli Society.* Berkeley, Calif., 1997.

Faber, M. D. *New Age Thinking: A Psychoanalytic Critique.* Cardiff, Wales, 1996.

Faierstein, Morris. *All Is in the Hands of Heaven: The Teachings of Rabbi Mordecai Joseph Leiner of Izbica.* New York, 1989.

——. "The Friday Night Incident in Kotsk: History of a Legend." *Journal of Jewish Studies* 34 (1983): pp. 179–189.

Farbstein, Esther. "The Voice of God in Fire: The Sermons of R. Qalonymus Qalman Shapira, the Rebbe of Pietezna in the Warsaw Ghetto." In *The Broken Chain: Polish Jewry through the Ages*, vol. 2, ed. I. Bartal and I. Gutman, pp. 143–157. Jerusalem, 1997. [Hebrew]

Fields, Rick. *How the Swans Came to the Lake: A Narrative History of Buddhism in America.* Boston, 1992.

Filc, Dani. "Israel Model 2000: Post-Fordian Neo-Liberalism." In *The Power of Property: Israeli Society in the Global Age*, ed. D. Filc and U. Ram, pp. 34–56. Jerusalem, 2004. [Hebrew]

Fine, Lawrence. *Physician of the Soul, Healer of the Cosmos: Issac Luria and His Kabbalistic Fellowship*. Stanford, Calif., 2003.

——. "Rabbi Abraham Isaac Kook and the Jewish Mystical Tradition." In *Rabbi Abraham Isaac Kook and Jewish Spirituality*, ed. L. Kaplan and D. Shatz, pp. 23–40. New York, 1995.

Fischer, Shlomo. "Nature, Authenticity and Violence in Radical Religious-Zionist Thought." In *Generations, Locations, Identities: Contemporary Perspectives on Culture and Society in Israel: Essays in Honor of Shmuel Noah Eisenstadt*, ed. H. Herzog, T. Kohavi, and S. Zelniker, pp. 421–454. Jerusalem, 2007. [Hebrew]

——. "The Shas Movement." In "Fifty to Forty-Eight: Critical Moments in the History of the State of Israel," a special issue of *Theory and Criticism*, vols. 12–13 (1999), pp. 329–337. [Hebrew]

Forman, Robert. *Grassroots Spirituality: What It Is, Why It Is Here, Where Is It Going*. Exeter, England, 2004.

Foucault, Michel. *The Archeology of Knowledge*, trans. A. Sheridan. New York, 1972.

——. *The History of Sexuality*, vol. 1, trans. R. Harley. New York, 1980.

Friedman, Menaḥem. "Messiah and Messianism in Habad-Lubavitch Hasidism." In *The War of Gog and Magog: Messianism and Apocalypse in Judaism—Past and Present*, ed. D. Ariel-Yoel et al., pp. 174–229. Tel Aviv, 2001.

Friedman, Richard. *The Hidden Face of God*. San Francisco, 1996.

Gal-Or, Naomi. *The Jewish Underground: Our Terrorism*. Tel Aviv, 1990. [Hebrew]

Garb, Jonathan. " 'Alien Culture' in the Thought of Rabbi Kook's Circle." In *Study and Knowledge in Jewish Thought*, ed. H. Kreisel, pp. 253–264. Beer Sheva, Israel, 2006.

——. "Circumventions of Halakha: A Preliminary Study of Anomian Trends in the Twentieth Century." *Aqdamot: A Journal of Jewish Thought* 14 (2004): pp. 117–130. [Hebrew]

——. "The Concept of Power in the Circle of R. Kook." *Jerusalem Studies in Jewish Thought* 19 (2005): pp. 753–770. [Hebrew]

——. "Fear and Power in Renaissance Mediterranean Kabbalah." In *Fear and Its Representations: Arizona Studies in the Middle Ages and Renaissance*, ed. A. Scott and C. Kosso, pp. 137–151. Turnhout, Belgium, 2002.

——. "The Joy of Torah in the Thought of David Hartman: A Critical Study of the Phenomenology of Halakhic Experience." In *Renewing Jewish Commitment: The Work and Thought of David Hartman*, vol. 1, ed. A. Sagi and Z. Zohar, pp. 73–105. Tel Aviv, 2001. [Hebrew]

——. "Kabbalah outside the Walls: The Response of Rabbi Haddaya to the State of Israel." In *The Sephardic Sages in Israel (1948–1967): Creativity, Thought and Leadership*, ed. S. Ratzabi and Z. Zohar. Tel Aviv, forthcoming. [Hebrew]

——. *Manifestations of Power in Jewish Mysticism from Rabbinic Literature to Safedian Kabbalah*. Jerusalem, 2005. [Hebrew]

——. "Messianism, Antinomianism and Power in Religious Zionism: The Case of the 'Jewish Underground.' " In *Religious Zionism: An Era of Changes (Studies in Memory of Zvulun Hammer)*, ed. A. Cohen, pp. 323–363. Jerusalem, 2004. [Hebrew]

——. "Models of Sacred Space in Jewish Mysticism and Their Impact in the Twentieth Century." In *The Land of Israel in 20th Century Jewish Thought*, ed. A. Ravitzky, pp. 1–25. Jerusalem, 2004. [Hebrew]

——. "Mysticism and Magic: Opposition, Deliberation and Adaption." *Maḥanayim* 14 (2002): pp. 97–110. [Hebrew]

——. "Mystics' Critique of Mystical Experience." *Revue de l' histoire des religions* 221 (2004): pp. 293–325.

——. "The NRP Young Guard and the Ideological Roots of 'Gush Emunim.' " In *Religious Zionism: An Era of Changes (Studies in Memory of Zvulun Hammer)*, ed. A. Cohen, pp. 171–200. Jerusalem, 2004. [Hebrew]

——. "On the Kabbalists of Prague." *Kabbalah* 14 (2006): pp. 347–383. [Hebrew]

——. "Power, Ritual and Myth: A Comparative Methodological Proposal." In *Myths in Judaism: History, Thought, Literature*, eds. M. Idel and I. Gruenwald, pp. 53–71. Jerusalem, 2004. [Hebrew]

——. "Powers of Language in Kabbalah: Comparative Reflections." In *The Poetics of Grammar and the Metaphysics of Sound and Sign*, ed. S. De La Porta and D. Shulman, pp. 230–269. Leiden, The Netherlands, 2007.

——. "Prophecy, Halakhah and Antinomianism in the 'Shemonah Kevatsim' by Rabbi Kook." In *Shef'a Tal: Studies in Jewish Thought and Culture Presented to Bracha Sack*, eds. Z. Gries, H. Kreisel, and B. Huss, pp. 267–277. Beer Sheva, Israel, 2004. [Hebrew]

——. "Rabbi Kook: Nationalist Thinker or Mystical Poet." *Da'at* 54 (2004): pp. 69–96. [Hebrew]

——. "Rabbi Kook and His Sources: From Kabbalistic Historiosophy to National Mysticism." In *Studies in Modern Religions, Religious Movements and the Babhi-Bahai Faiths*, ed. M. Sharon, pp. 77–96. Leiden, The Netherlands, 2004.

——. "The Power and the Glory: A Critique of 'New Age' Kabbalah.' " *Zeek* (April 2006). Available at http://zeek.net/604garb. (Originally published in Hebrew in *Eretz Aḥeret* 26 [2005]: pp. 30–34.)

——. "Trance Techniques in the Kabbalistic Tradition of Jerusalem." *Pe'amim* 70 (1997): pp. 47–67. [Hebrew]

——. "The Understandable Revival of Mysticism Today: Innovation and Conservatism in the Thought of Joseph Aḥituv." In *Jewish Culture in the Eye of the Storm: Festschrift in Honor of Joseph Aḥituv*, ed. A. Sagi and Z. Zohar, pp. 172–199. Tel Aviv, 2002. [Hebrew]

——. "Working Out as Divine Work." In *Sport and Physical Education in Jewish History*, ed. G. Eisen et al., pp. 7–14. Netanya, Israel, 2003.

Gardell, Mattias. *Gods of the Blood: The Pagan Revival and White Separatism*. Durham, N.C., 2003.

Gellman, Jerome. "Aesthetics." In *The World of Rav Kook's Thought*, ed. B. Ish-Shalom and S. Rosenberg, trans. J. Carmy and B. Casper, pp. 195–206. Jerusalem, 1991.

——. *The Fear and Trembling and the Fire: Kierkegaard and Hasidic Masters on the Binding of Issac*. Beer Sheva, Israel, 1994.

——. "Teshuva in Kabbalah: Rav Kook's Sources." In *Shef'a Tal: Studies in Jewish Thought and*

Culture Presented to Bracha Sack, ed. Z. Gries, H. Kreisel, and B. Huss, pp. 261–266. Beer Sheva, Israel, 2004. [Hebrew]

Goldberg, Amos. "The Rebbe of Piesetzna as Hero and Anti-hero." *Bi-Shvilei Ha-Zikaron* 20 (1997): pp. 18–23. [Hebrew]

Goldberg, Sheli. "The Zaddik's Soul after His 'Histalkut' (Death): Continuity and Change in the Writings of 'Nesiey' (Presidents of) Habad." PhD diss., Bar Ilan University. Ramat Gan, Israel, 2003. [Hebrew]

Goldreich, Amos. "Investigations of the Self-Image of the Author of 'Tikunnei Zohar.' " In *Massu'ot: Studies in Kabbalistic Literature and Jewish Philosophy in Memory of Prof. Ephraim Gottlieb*, ed. M. Oron and A. Goldreich, pp. 459–496. Jerusalem, 1994. [Hebrew]

Gonen, Rivka (ed.). *To the Graves of the Righteous: Pilgrimage and Hilulot in Israel*. Jerusalem, 1998. [Hebrew]

Goodman, Yehuda. "Return to Orthodoxy and New Religious Identities in Twenty-First Century Israel." In *Hard to Believe: Rethinking Religion and Secularism in Israel*, ed. A. Kleinberg, pp. 98–117. Tel Aviv, 2004. [Hebrew]

Goshen-Gottstein, Alon. "The Land of Israel in the Thought of Rabbi Nahman of Braslav." In *The Land of Israel in Modern Jewish Thought*, ed. A. Ravitzky, pp. 276–300. Jerusalem, 1998. [Hebrew]

Grader, Chaim. *The Yeshiva*, vol. 2, trans. C. Leviant. New York, 1977.

Green, Arthur. "Three Warsaw Mystics." *Jerusalem Studies in Jewish Thought* 13 (1996): pp. 1–58.

——. *Tormented Master: A Life of Rabbi Nahman of Bratslav*. Tuscalusa, Alabama, 1979.

Greenberg, Gershom. "The Death of History and the Life of Akeda: Voices from the War." In *The Death of God Movement and the Holocaust: Radical Theology Encounters the Shoah*, ed. S. Haynes and J. Roth, pp. 99–109. London, 1999.

——. "Redemption after Holocaust according to Mahane Israel-Lubavitch, 1940–1945." *Modern Judaism* 12 (1992): pp. 61–84.

Gurevitch, Zali, and Gideon Aran. "On Place (Israeli Anthropology)." In *On Israeli and Jewish Place*, ed. Z. Gurevitch, pp. 22–73. Tel Aviv, 2007. [Hebrew]

Hadari, Ḥayyim Isaiah. "Two High Priests." In *Rabbi Avraham Yizḥaq Ha-Kohen Kook: A Collection of Articles*, ed. Y. Raphael, pp. 154–168. Jerusalem, 1966. [Hebrew]

Halbertal, Moshe. *Concealment and Revelation: The Secret and Its Boundaries in Medieval Jewish Tradition*. Jerusalem, 2001. [Hebrew]

Hallamish, Moshe. "The Concept of the Land of Israel in Hillel Zeitlin's World." In *A Hundred Years of Religious Zionism*, vol. 1, ed. A. Sagi and D. Schwartz, pp. 203–212. Ramat Gan, Israel, 2003. [Hebrew]

——. "Hasidism and the Land of Israel—Two Models." In *The Land of Israel in Modern Jewish Thought*, ed. A. Ravitzky, pp. 225–255. Jerusalem, 1998. [Hebrew]

Hammer, Olav. "Sufism for Westerners." In *Sufism in Europe and North America*, ed. D. Westerlund, pp. 127–143. London, 2004.

Hand, Sean, ed. *The Levinas Reader*. New York, 1984.

Hanegraaff, Walter. *New Age Religion and Western Culture: Esotericism in the Mirror of Secular Thought*. Albany, N.Y., 1998.

Hansel, David. "The Origin in the Thought of Rabbi Yehuda Halevi Ashlag: Ṣimsum of God or Ṣimsum of the World." *Kabbalah* 7 (2002): pp. 37–46.

Harari, Yuval. "Early Jewish Magic: Methodological and Phenomenological Studies." PhD diss., Hebrew University. Jerusalem, 1998. [Hebrew]

Heelas, Paul. *The New Age Movement: The Celebration of the Self and the Sacralization of Modernity.* Oxford, England, 1996.

Heelas, Paul, and Linda Woodhead. *The Spiritual Revolution: Why Religion Is Giving Way to Spirituality.* Oxford, England, 2005.

Hermansen, Marcia. "What's American about American Sufi Movements." In *Sufism in Europe and North America*, ed. D. Westerlund, pp. 36–63. London, 2004.

Hervieu-Léger, Danièlle. *La religion en miettees, ou la question des sectes.* Paris, 2001.

Heschel, A. J. "Inspiration in the Middle Ages." In *The Alexander Marx Jubilee Volume*, ed. S. Liberman, pp. 175–208. New York, 1950. [Hebrew]

——. *A Passion for Truth.* New York, 1973.

Hever, Hannan, Yehouda Shenav, and Pnina Motzafi-Haller, eds. *Mizrahim in Israel: A Critical Observation into Israel's Ethnicity.* Jerusalem, 2002. [Hebrew]

Hirtenstein, Stephen. *The Unlimited Mercifier: The Spiritual Life and Thought of Ibn 'Arabi.* Oxford, England, 1999.

Hobsbawm, Eric. *Age of Extremes: The Short Twentieth Century, 1914–1991.* London, 1995.

Hoffman, Edward. *The Way of Splendor: Jewish Mysticism and Modern Psychology.* Northvale, N.J., 1992.

Holzer, Elie. "Nationalism and Morality: Conceptions of the Use of Force within Ideological Streams of Religious Zionism." PhD diss., Hebrew University. Jerusalem, 1998. [Hebrew]

Horowitz, Rivka. "Revelation and the Bible in Jewish Philosophy in the Twentieth Century." In *Shef'a Tal: Studies in Jewish Thought and Culture Presented to Bracha Sack*, ed. Z. Gries, H. Kreisel, and B. Huss, pp. 237–259. Beer Sheva, Israel, 2004. [Hebrew]

Hundert, G. D. *Jews in Poland-Lithuania in the Eighteenth Century: A Genealogy of Modernity.* Berkeley, Calif., 2004.

Huss, Boaz. "All You Need Is LAV: Madonna and Post-modern Kabbalah." *Jewish Quarterly Review* 95 (2005): pp. 611–624.

——. "Altruistic Communism: The Modernist Kabbalah of Rabbi Yehuda Ashlag." *'Iyunim Bi-Tqumat Israel* 16 (2006): pp. 109–130. [Hebrew]

——. " 'Authorized Guardians': The Polemics of Academic Scholars of Jewish Mysticism against Kabbalah Practitioners." In *Polemical Encounters: Esoteric Discourse and Its Others*, ed. K. von Stuckrad and O. Hammer, pp. 104–126. Leiden, The Netherlands, 2007.

——. "Holy Place, Holy Time, Holy Book: The Influence of the Zohar on Pilgrimage Rituals to Meron and the Lag Be-Omer Festival." *Kabbalah* 7 (2002): pp. 237–256. [Hebrew]

——. "The New Age of Kabbalah: Contemporary Kabbalah, the New Age and Postmodern Spirituality." *Journal of Modern Jewish Studies* 6 (2007): pp. 107–125.

——. "A Sage Is Preferable to a Prophet: R. Simeon Bar Yohai and Moses in the Zohar." *Kabbalah* 4 (1999): pp. 103–139. [Hebrew]

——. "To Ask No Questions: Gershom Scholem and the Study of Contemporary Jewish Mysticism." *Pe'amim* 94–95 (2003): pp. 57–72. [Hebrew]

Huyssen, Andreas. "Mapping the Post-modern." In *The Post-modern Reader*, ed. C. Jencks, pp. 40–72. London, 1972.

Idel, Moshe. *Absorbing Perfections: Kabbalah and Interpretation*. New Haven, 2002.

——. "Academic Studies of Kabbalah in Israel, 1923–1998: A Short Survey." *Studia Judaica* 8 (1999): pp. 91–114.

——. *Hasidism: Between Ecstasy and Magic*. Albany, N.Y., 1995.

——. *Kabbalah: New Perspectives*. New Haven, 1988.

——. *Messianic Mystics*. New Haven, 1998.

——. *The Mystical Experience in Abraham Abulafia*, trans. J. Chipman. Albany, N.Y., 1988.

——. "On the Land of Israel in Medieval Jewish Mysticism." In *The Land of Israel in Medieval Jewish Thought*, ed. M. Hallamish and A. Ravitzky, pp. 193–214. Jerusalem, 1991. [Hebrew]

——. *Studies in Ecstatic Kabbalah*. Albany, N.Y., 1988.

Ish-Shalom, Benjamin. "R. Kook, Spinoza and Goethe: Modern and Traditional Elements in the Thought of R. Kook." *Jerusalem Studies in Jewish Thought* 13 (1996): pp. 525–556. [Hebrew]

——. *Rabbi Abraham Isaac Kook between Rationalism and Mysticism*. Tel Aviv, 1990. [Hebrew]

——. "Tolerance and Its Theoretical Basis in the Teaching of Rabbi Kook." *Da'at* 20 (1988): pp. 151–168. [Hebrew]

Jung, C. G. *Memories, Dreams, Reflections*, ed. A. Jaffe, trans. R. and C. Winston. London, 1983.

Kahane, Menahem. "The Importance of Dwelling in the Land of Israel according to the Deuteronomy Mekhilta." *Tarbiz* 62 (1992–1993): pp. 501–515. [Hebrew]

Kamenetz, Roger. *The Jew in the Lotus: A Poet's Rediscovery of Jewish Identity in Buddhist India*. Northvale, N.J., 1998.

——. *Stalking Elijah: Adventures with Today's Jewish Mystical Masters*. San Francisco, 1997.

Kaplan, E. K., and S. H. Dresner. *Abraham Joshua Heschel: Prophetic Witness*. New Haven, 1988.

Katz, Jacob. *Halakhah and Kabbalah: Studies in the History of Jewish Religion, Its Various Faces and Social Relevance*. Jerusalem, 1986. [Hebrew]

Kepnes, Steven, ed. *Interpreting Judaism in a Post-modern Age*. New York, 1996.

Klein, Yitzḥaq. *The Master-Slave Dialectic*. Tel Aviv, 1978. [Hebrew]

Kohen, Asher. "The Knitted Kippa and What It Conceals: Plurality of Identities in Religious Zionism." *Aqdamot: A Journal of Jewish Thought* 15 (2005): pp. 9–30. [Hebrew]

Koppel, Moshe. "'*Mamlachtiut*' as a Tool of Oppression." *Democratic Culture* 3 (2000): pp. 133–147.

Kraus, Yitzchak. *The Seventh: Messianism in the Last Generation of Habad*. Tel Aviv, 2007. [Hebrew]

Kravel-Tovi, Michal. "Tishrei with the Rebbe: The Coping Mechanisms of the Messianic Faction of Chabad following the Death of Menachem Mendel Schneerson." M.A. thesis, Hebrew University. Jerusalem, 2002. [Hebrew]

Lanir, Michal. "Rabbi Kook and Zionism, an Adventure in Hope: Rabbi Kook's Conception of Zionism between 1887–1935 against the Background of the Jewish Community in Eretz Israel and Jewish Thought of the Time." PhD diss., Tel Aviv University. Tel Aviv, 2000. [Hebrew]

Lasch, Cristophe. *Culture of Narcissism: American Life in an Age of Diminishing Expectations*. New York, 1980.

Lau, Benjamin. *From 'Maran' to 'Maran': The Halachic Philosophy of Rav Ovadia Yossef*. Tel Aviv, 2005. [Hebrew]

——. "The Holy Land in the Works of Rabbis from the Oriental Countries in the Twentieth Century." *The Land of Israel in 20th Jewish Thought*, ed. A. Ravitzky, pp. 168–183. Jerusalem, 2004. [Hebrew]

Lavi Toni. "The Idea of Cosmogony in the Studies of Jehuda Leib Ha-Levi Ashlag." PhD diss., Bar Ilan University. Ramat Gan, Israel, 2002. [Hebrew]

——. "The Idea of Creation, the Construction and Reconstruction of Creation in the Thought of R. Judah Leib Ha-Levi Ashlag." *Kabbalah* 10 (2004): pp. 239–334. [Hebrew]

Levine, S. W. *Mystics, Mavericks and Merrymakers: An Intimate Journey among Hasidic Girls*. New York, 2003.

Lewis, Franklin. *Rumi: Past and Present, East and West—The Life, Teachings and Poetry of Jalal al-Din Rumi*. Oxford, England, 2001.

Liebes, Tamar. *American Dreams, Hebrew Subtitles: Globalization from the Receiving End*. Cresskill, N.J., 2003.

Liebes, Yehudah. "New Directions in the Study of the Kabbalah." *Pe'amim* 50 (1992): pp. 150–170. [Hebrew]

——. *Studies in the Zohar*, trans. A. Schwartz et al. Albany, N.Y., 1993.

——. "Towards a Study of the Author of Emek Ha-Melekh: His Personality, Writings and Kabbalah." *Jerusalem Studies in Jewish Thought* 11 (1993): pp. 101–137. [Hebrew]

——. "The Ultraorthodox Community and the Dead Sea Sect." *Jerusalem Studies in Jewish Thought* 3 (1982): pp. 137–152. [Hebrew]

——. "The Vilner Gaon School, Sabbateanism and Dos Pintele Yid." *Da'at* 50–51 (2003): pp. 255–290. [Hebrew]

Linzer, Judith. *Torah and Dharma: Jewish Seekers in Eastern Religions*. Northvale, N.J., 1996.

Loewenthal, Naftali. "Between Mysticism and Modernity: Habad Contemplative Prayer in the Twentieth Century." *Jerusalem Studies in Jewish Thought* 15 (1999): pp. 235–259. [Hebrew]

——. "Contemporary Habad and the Paradox of Redemption." In *Perspectives on Jewish Thought and Mysticism*, ed. A. Ivry et al., pp. 381–402. Amsterdam, 1998.

——. "Habad Approaches to Contemplative Prayer, 1790–1920." In *Hasidism Reappraised*, ed. A. Rapoport-Albert, pp. 288–300. London, 1996.

——. "Women and the Dialectic of Spirituality." In *Within Hasidic Circles: Studies in Hasidism in Memory of Mordecai Wilensky*, ed. Immanuel Etkes et al., pp. 26–65. Jerusalem, 1999.

Lorberbaum, Yair. *Image of God: Halakhah and Aggadah*. Tel Aviv, 2004. [Hebrew]

Luz, Ehud. *Wrestle at Jabbok River: Power, Morality and Jewish Identity*. Jerusalem, 1998. [Hebrew]

Lyotard, J. F. *The Post-modern Condition: A Report on Knowledge*, trans. G. Bennington and B. Massumi. Minneapolis, 1993.

Maffesoli, Michael. *The Time of the Tribes: The Decline of Individualism in Mass Society*, trans. D. Smith. London, 1996.

Magid, Shaul. "Deconstructing the Mystical: The Anti-mystical Kabbalism in Rabbi Hayyim of Volozhin's Nefesh Ha-Hayyim." *Journal of Jewish Thought and Philosophy* 9 (1999): pp. 21–67.

——. *Hasidism on the Margin: Reconciliation, Antinomianism and Messianism in Izbica/Radzin Hasidism*. Madison, Wis., 2003.

——. "Rainbow Hassidism in America—The Maturation of Jewish Renewal." *The Reconstructionist* 68 (2004): pp. 34–60.

Malkiel, Eli'ezer. "Ideology and Halacha in Rav Kook's Heter Mechirah." *Shenaton Ha-Mishpat Ha-Ivri: Annual of the Institute for Research in Jewish Law* 20 (1995–1997): pp. 169–211. [Hebrew]

Maluchi, Alberto. *The Playing Self: Person and Meaning in the Planetary Society*. Cambridge, England 1996.

Marcus, George, and Michael Fischer. *Anthropology as Cultural Critique: An Experimental Moment in the Social Sciences*. Chicago, 1986.

Margolin, Ron. *The Human Temple: Religious Interiorization and the Structuring of Inner Life in Early Hasidism*. Jerusalem, 2004. [Hebrew]

Mark, Zvi. "The Formulation of R. Nahman of Bratslav's Tikkunim, the Pilgrimage to His Tomb and Their Relationship to Messianism." *Da'at* 56 (2005): pp. 101–133. [Hebrew]

——. *Mysticism and Madness in the Work of R. Nahman of Bratslav*. Tel Aviv, 2003. [Hebrew]

Martin, Luther H., Huck Gutman, and Patrick Hutton, eds. *Technologies of the Self: A Seminar with Michel Foucault*. Amherst, Mass., 1988.

Matt, Daniel. *God and the Big Bang: Discovering Harmony between Science and Spirituality*. Woodstock, 1996.

Mautner, Menachem, Avi Sagi, and Ronen Shamir. "Reflections on Multiculturalism in Israel." In *Multiculturalism in a Democratic Jewish State: The Ariel Rosen-Zvi Memorial Book*, ed. M. Mautner, A. Sagi, and R. Shamir, pp. 67–76. Tel Aviv, 1998. [Hebrew]

McDermott, Robert. "Rudolf Steiner and Anthroposophy in Modern Esoteric Spirituality." In *Modern Esoteric Spirituality*, ed. A. Faivre and J. Needleman, pp. 288–310. New York, 1992.

Meir, Jonatan. "Hillel Zeitlin's Zohar: The History of a Translation and Commentary Project." *Kabbalah* 10 (2004): pp. 119–157. [Hebrew]

——. "Lights and Vessels: A New Inquiry into the 'Circle' of Rabbi Kook and the Editors of His Works." *Kabbalah* 13 (2005): pp. 163–247. [Hebrew]

——. "Longing of Souls for the Shekhina: Relations between Rabbi Kook, Zeitlin and Brenner." *Jerusalem Studies in Jewish Thought* 20 (2005): pp. 771–818. [Hebrew]

——. *Rabbi Nahman of Bratzlav: World Weariness and Longing for the Messiah: Two Essays by Hillel Zeitlin*. Jerusalem, 2006. [Hebrew]

——. "The Revealed and the Revealed within the Revealed: On the Opposition to the

'Followers' of Rabbi Yehudah Ashlag and the Dissemination of Esoteric Literature," *Kabbalah* 16 (2007): pp. 151–268. [Hebrew]

——. "The Status of the Mitzvot in the Thought of R. Yosef Lainer of Izbicha." *Mishlav* 35 (2000): pp. 27–53. [Hebrew]

——. "Wrestling with the Esoteric: Hillel Zeitlin, Yehudah Ashlag and Kabbalah in the Land of Israel." In *Judaism, Topics, Fragments, Faces, Identities: Jubilee Volume in Honor of Rivka*, ed. H. Pedaya and J. Meir, pp. 585–647. Beer Sheva, Israel, 2007. [Hebrew]

Mendes-Flohr, Paul. "Fin-de-Siècle Orientalism and the Aesthetics of Jewish Self-Affirmation." *Jerusalem Studies in Jewish Thought* 3 (1984): pp. 623–681. [Hebrew]

Midal, Fabrice. *Chögyam Trungpa: His Life and Vision*. Boston, 2004.

Miller, D. L. *The New Polytheism: Rebirth of the Gods and Goddesses*. New York, 1974.

Mopsik, Charles. *Les grands textes de la cabale: Les rites qui font dieu*. Paris, 1993.

Morgenstern, Aryeh. *Messianism and the Settlement of Eretz Israel*. Jerusalem, 1985. [Hebrew]

——. "The Place of the Ten Tribes in the Redemption Process." In *The Vilna Gaon and His Disciples*, ed. M. Hallamish, Y. Rivlin, and R. Shuchat, pp. 207–235. Ramat Gan, Israel, 2003. [Hebrew]

——. *Redemption through Return: Vilna Gaon's Disciples in Eretz Israel, 1800–1840*. Jerusalem, 1997. [Hebrew]

Nadler, Allan. *The Faith of the Mitnagdim: Rabbinic Responses to Hasidic Rapture*. Baltimore, 1997.

——. "The War on Modernity of R. Hayyim Elazar Shapira of Munkacz." *Modern Judaism* 14 (1994): pp. 234–264.

Needleman, Jacob. "G. I. Gurdjieff and His School." In *Modern Esoteric Spirituality*, ed. A. Faivre and J. Needleman, pp. 359–380. New York, 1992.

Neher, André. *Le puits de l'exil—Tradition et modernité: La pensée du Maharal de Prague*. Paris, 1991.

Nehorai, Michael. "Halakhah, Metahalakhah and the Redemption of Israel: Reflections on the Rabbinic Rulings of Rav Kook." In *Rabbi Abraham Isaac Kook and Jewish Spirituality*, ed. L. Kaplan and D. Shatz, pp. 120–156. New York, 1995.

Neria, M. Z. *Bi-Sde Ha-Re'iah*. Bnei Brak, Israel, 1991. [Hebrew]

——. *Siḥot Ha-Re'iah*. Kfar Ha-Ro'eh, Israel, 1998. [Hebrew]

Omer-Man, Jonathan. "Modern Manifestations of Jewish Mysticism." *Ptaḥim* 51–52 (1980): pp. 75–80. [Hebrew]

Ostrow, James. *Social Sensitivity: A Study of Habit and Experience*. New York, 1990.

Pachter, Mordechai. "The Kabbalistic Foundation of the Faith-Heresy Issue in Rav Kook's Thought." *Da'at* 47 (2001): pp. 69–100. [Hebrew]

Padoux, André. "The Tantric Guru." In *Tantra in Practice*, ed. D. G. White, pp. 41–51. Princeton, N.J., 2000.

Pedaya, Ḥaviva. *Name and Sanctuary in the Teaching of R. Isaac the Blind: A Comparative Study in the Writings of the Earliest Kabbalists*. Jerusalem, 2001. [Hebrew]

——. "Space, Time, and Eretz Israel: Apocalypses of an End and Apocalypses of a Beginning." In *The Land of Israel in 20th Century Jewish Thought*, ed. A. Ravitzky, pp. 560–623. Jerusalem, 2004. [Hebrew]

——. *Vision and Speech: Models of Revelatory Experience in Jewish Mysticism.* Los Angeles, 2002. [Hebrew]

Picard, Ariel. *The Philosophy of Rabbi 'Ovadya Yosef in an Age of Transition: Study of Halakhah and Cultural Criticism.* Ramat-Gan, Israel, 2007. [Hebrew]

Piekarz, M. M. *The Beginning of Hasidism: Ideological Trends in Derush and Mussar Literature.* Jerusalem, 1978. [Hebrew]

——. *Ideological Trends in Hasidism in Poland during the Interwar Period and the Holocaust.* Jerusalem, 1990. [Hebrew]

——. *Studies in Braslav Hasidism.* Jerusalem, 1995.

Polen, Nehemia. *The Holy Fire: The Teachings of Rabbi Kalonymus Kalman Shapira.* Northvale, N.J., 1994.

Prell, R. E. *Prayer and Community: The Havurah in American Judaism.* Detroit, 1989.

Rachlevsky, Seffy. *Messiah's Donkey.* Tel Aviv, 1998. [Hebrew]

Rakover, Nahum. *Ends That Justify the Means.* Jerusalem, 2000. [Hebrew]

Ram, Uri. *The Globalization of Israel: McWorld in Tel Aviv, Jihad in Jerusalem.* Tel Aviv, 2005. [Hebrew]

Rapoport, Tamar, and Jonathan Garb. "The Experience of Religious Fortification: The Coming of Age of Religious Zionist Young Women." *Gender and Education* 10 (1998): pp. 5–20.

Rapoport, Tamar, 'Anat Penso, and Jonathan Garb. "Contribution to the Collective by Religious-Zionist Adolescent Girls." *British Journal of Sociology of Education* 15 (1994): pp. 375–388.

——. "Religious Socialization and Female Subjectivity: Religious-Zionist Adolescent Girls in Israel." *Sociology of Education* 68 (1995): pp. 48–61.

Rapoport-Albert, Ada. "On the Position of Women in Sabbatianism." *Jerusalem Studies in Jewish Thought* 16 (2001): pp. 143–327. [Hebrew]

Ratzabi, Shalom. "Rabbi Shalom Dov Baer Schneersohn and the Dilemma of Anti-Zionism and Messianic Tension." *Zionism: Studies in the History of the Zionist Movement* 20 (1996): pp. 77–101. [Hebrew]

Ravitzky, Aviezer. "Maimonides and His Students on Linguistic Magic and 'The Insanity of the Amulet Writers.'" In *Jewish Culture in the Eye of the Storm: Festschrift in Honor of Joseph Aḥituv*, ed. A. Sagi and N. Ilan, pp. 431–458. Tel Aviv, 2002. [Hebrew]

——. *Messianism, Zionism and Jewish Religious Radicalism*, trans. M. Swirsky and J. Chipman. Chicago, 1996.

——. "'Waymarks to Zion': The History of an Idea." In *The Land of Israel in Medieval Jewish Thought*, ed. M. Hallamish and A. Ravitzky, pp. 1–39. Jerusalem, 1991. [Hebrew]

Robertson, Ronald. "Anti-global Religion." In *Global Religions: An Introduction*, ed. M. Juergensmeyer, pp. 111–123. Oxford, England, 2003.

Rosenak, Avinoam. "The Babylonian and Jerusalem Talmud in Rabbi Kook's Conception of 'The Prophetic Torah of Eretz Israel.'" In *The Land of Israel in 20th Century Jewish Thought*, ed. A. Ravitzky, pp. 26–70. Jerusalem, 2004. [Hebrew]

——. "Between Prophetic Halakhah and Reality in the Halakhic Rulings of Rabbi A. I. Kook." *Tarbiẓ* 69 (2000): pp. 591–618. [Hebrew]

——. "Education and Meta-Halakhah in Rav Kook's Teaching." *Da'at* 46 (2001): pp. 99–123. [Hebrew]

——. "Halakhah, Aggadah and Prophecy in the Concept of the Land of Israel in the Light of Rabbi Kook's Theory of 'the Unity of Opposites.'" In *A Hundred Years of Religious Zionism*, vol. 1, ed. A. Sagi and D. Schwartz, pp. 261–287. Ramat Gan, Israel, 2003. [Hebrew]

——. "Individualism and Society, Freedom and Norm: A New Reading of the Writings of R. Kook." *Aqdamot: A Journal of Jewish Thought* 14 (2004): pp. 89–116. [Hebrew]

——. *The Prophetic Halakhah—Rabbi A. I. H. Kook's Philosophy of Halakhah*. Jerusalem, 2007. [Hebrew]

——. "Who's Afraid of Rav Kook's Hidden Treatises?" Book review. *Tarbiz* 69 (2000): pp. 257–291. [Hebrew]

Rosenak, Michael. "'Normative Deliberation': Exile and Eretz Israel in the Thought of Eliezer Berkovitz." In *The Land of Israel in 20th Century Jewish Thought*, ed. A. Ravitzky, pp. 539–559. Jerusalem, 2004. [Hebrew]

Rosenberg, Shalom. *Good and Evil in Jewish Thought*. Tel Aviv, 1985. [Hebrew]

——. "Introduction to the Thought of Rav Kook." In *The World of Rav Kook's Thought*, ed. B. Ish-Shalom and S. Rosenberg, trans. J. Carmy and B. Casper, pp. 16–127. Jerusalem, 1991. [Hebrew]

——. "R. Kook and the Blind Serpent (The Lights of Holiness and the Doctrine of Schopenhauer)." In *Be-Oro: Studies in the Thought of R. Kook and the Ways of Its Teaching*, ed. C. Hamiel, pp. 317–352. Jerusalem, 1986. [Hebrew]

Rosen-Zvi, Ishay. "The Creation of Metaphysics: The Debate in the 'Mercaz Harav Yeshiva'—A Critical Study." In *A Hundred Years of Religious Zionism*, vol. 3, ed. A. Sagi and D. Schwartz, pp. 421–445. Ramat Gan, Israel, 2003. [Hebrew]

——. "Justifying the Holocaust in the School of Rabbi Zvi Yehuda Kook." *Democratic Culture* 6 (2002): pp. 165–209. [Hebrew]

Ross, Tamar. "Between Metaphysical and Liberal Pluralism: A Reappraisal of Rabbi A. I. Kook's Espousal of Toleration." *Association of Jewish Studies Review* 21 (1996): pp. 61–110.

——. "The Cognitive Value of Religious Truth Statements: Rabbi A. I. Kook and Post-modernism." In *Hazon Nahum: Studies in Jewish Thought and History Presented to Dr. Norman Lamm*, ed. Y. Elman and J. S. Gorock, pp. 479–528. New York, 1997.

——. "The Elite and the Masses in the Prism of Metaphysics and History: Harav Kook on the Nature of Religious Belief." *Journal of Jewish Thought and Philosophy* 8 (1999): pp. 355–367.

——. "On Rabbi Kook's Concept of God." In *Studies in Jewish Thought*, ed. S. Heller-Wilensky and M. Idel, pp. 154–172. Jerusalem, 1989. [Hebrew]

——. "Rav Kook's Concept of God." *Da'at* 9 (1982): pp. 39–70. [Hebrew]

Roszak, Theodore. *Making of a Counter-Culture: Reflections of the Technocratic Society and Its Youthful Opposition*. Berkeley, Calif., 1995.

Ruah-Midbar, Marianna. "The New Age Culture in Israel: Methodological Introduction and 'The Conceptual Network." PhD diss., Bar Ilan University. Ramat Gan, Israel, 2006. [Hebrew]

Sagi, Avi. "Religious Zionism: Between Enclosure and Openness." In *Judaism: A Dialogue Between Cultures*, ed. A. Sagi, D. Schwartz, and Y. Stern, pp. 124–168. Jerusalem, 1999. [Hebrew]

Sassen, Saskia. "Globalization or Denationalization." *Review of International Political Economy* 10 (2003): pp. 1–22.

Schindler, Pesach. *Hassidic Responses to the Holocaust in the Light of Hassidic Thought*. New Jersey, 1995.

Schneider, Stanley, and Joseph Berke. "Sigmund Freud and the Lubavitcher Rebbe." *Psychoanalytic Review* 87 (2000): pp. 39–59.

Scholem, Gershom. *Explications and Implications: Writings on Jewish Heritage and Renaissance*. Tel Aviv, 1975. [Hebrew]

——. *Major Trends in Jewish Mysticism*. New York, 1941.

——. *On the Kabbalah and Its Symbolism*, trans. R. Manhcin. New York, 1974.

——. *Shabbatai Zvi: The Mystical Messiah, 1626–1676*, trans. R. J. Z. Werblowsky. Princeton, N.J., 1973.

——. *Studies and Texts concerning the History of Sabbetianism and Its Metamorphoses*. Jerusalem, 2004. [Hebrew]

Schuchat, Raphael. "The Doctrine of Redemption of the Vilner Gaon, Its Sources and Influence." PhD diss., Bar Ilan University. Ramat Gan, Israel, 1998. [Hebrew]

——. "The Historiosophy of the Vilna Gaon and the Influence of Luzzatto and His Disciples." *Da'at* 40 (1998): pp. 125–152. [Hebrew]

——. "Lithuanian Kabbalah as an Independent Trend of Kabbalistic Literature." *Kabbalah* 10 (2004): pp. 181–206. [Hebrew]

Schwartz, Dov. "A Theological Rationale for National-Messianic Thought: Rabbi Zvi Yehuda Kook." *Zionism: Studies in the History of the Zionist Movement and of the Jewish Community in Palestine* 22 (2000): pp. 61–81. [Hebrew]

——. *Challenge and Crisis in Rabbi Kook's Circle*. Tel Aviv, 2001. [Hebrew]

——. *The Land of Israel in Religious-Zionist Thought*. Tel Aviv, 1997. [Hebrew]

——. "Methods of Research on Religious-Zionist Thought." In *A Good Eye: Dialogue and Polemic in Jewish Culture (A Jubilee Book in Honor of Tova Ilan)*, ed. Y. Aḥituv et al., pp. 564–581. Tel Aviv, 1999. [Hebrew]

——. *The Philosophy of Rabbi J. B. Soloveitchik*, vol. 1. Alon Shvut, Israel, 2004. [Hebrew]

——. *Religious Zionism between Logic and Messianism*. Tel Aviv, 1999. [Hebrew]

——. "The Spiritual-Intellectual Decline of the Jewish Community in Spain at the End of the Fourteenth Century." *Pe'amim* 46–47 (1991): pp. 92–145. [Hebrew]

——. *The Theology of the Religious-Zionist Movement*. Tel Aviv, 1996. [Hebrew]

Schweid, Eli'ezer. *From Ruin to Salvation*. Tel Aviv, 1994. [Hebrew]

——. *Prophets for Their People and Humanity: Prophecy and Prophets in 20th Century Jewish Thought*. Jerusalem, 1999. [Hebrew]

——. "Renewed Prophecy in the Face of Beginning of Redemption." *Da'at* 38 (1997): pp. 83–103. [Hebrew]

Segal, Haggai. *Dear Brothers*. Jerusalem, 1987. [Hebrew]

Selzer, Michael, ed. *Zionism Reconsidered: The Rejection of Jewish Normalcy*. London, 1970.

Shainberg, Lawrence. *Ambivalent Zen: One Man's Adventures on the Dharma Path*. New York, 1995.

Shanon, Benny. *The Antipodes of the Mind: Charting the Phenomenology of the Ayahuasca Experience*. Oxford, England, 2002.

Shapira, Anita. *Land and Power*. Tel Aviv, 1996. [Hebrew]

Shapiro, Marc. "A Note on Practical Kabbalah in Early 20th-Century Jerusalem." *Kabbalah* 7 (2002): pp. 47–49.

Shashar, Michael. *Talks with Yeshayahu Leibowitz on the World*. Jerusalem, 1987. [Hebrew]

Shatil, Jonathan. *A Psychologist in a Braslav Yeshiva: Jewish Mysticism in Actual Practice*. Tel Aviv, 1993. [Hebrew]

Sheleg, Yair. *The New Religious Jews: Recent Developments among Observant Jews in Israel*. Jerusalem, 2000. [Hebrew]

Shemesh, Aharon. "Halakhah and Prophecy: The False Prophet and the Rebellious Elder." In *Jewish Culture in the Eye of the Storm: Festschrift in Honor of Joseph Aḥituv*, ed. A. Sagi and Z. Zohar, pp. 923–941. Tel Aviv, 2002. [Hebrew]

Shmaryahu, Maoz. "The Golden Arches of McDonald's." *Panim* 5 (1998): pp. 23–28. [Hebrew]

Shragai, S. Z. "The Letters of R. Aharon Shmuel Tamrat." *Shragai* 2 (1985): pp. 39–64. [Hebrew]

Smith, Jonathan. *Taking Place: Towards Theory in Ritual*. Chicago, 1987.

Stampfer, Shaul. *The Lithuanian Yeshiva*. Jerusalem, 2005. [Hebrew]

Taji-Farouki, Suha. *Beshara and Ibn 'Arabi: A Movement of Sufi Spirituality in the Modern World*. Oxford, England, 2007.

Tavory, Ido, ed. *Dancing in a Thorn Field: The New Age in Israel*. Tel Aviv, 2007. [Hebrew]

Tiryakian, Edward. "Towards the Sociology of Esoteric Culture." In *On the Margin of the Visible: Sociology, the Esoteric and the Occult*, ed. E. Tiryakian, pp. 257–280. New York, 1974.

Tishby, Isaiah. *Studies in Kabbalah and Its Branches*. Vol. 1, *Researches and Sources*. Jerusalem, 1982. [Hebrew]

——. *The Wisdom of the Zohar*, vol. 1, trans. D. Goldstein. Oxford, England, 1989.

Tobi, Yosef. "Settlement of Eretz Israel in the Philosophical and Exegetical Writings of North African Rabbis." In *The Land of Israel in 20th Century Jewish Thought*, ed. A. Ravitzky, pp. 184–209. Jerusalem, 2004. [Hebrew]

——. "Who Was the Author of Emunat Ha-Shem." *Da'at* 49 (2002): pp. 87–98. [Hebrew]

Touraine, Allan. *The Return of the Actor: Social Theory in Postindustrial Society*, trans. M. Godzich. Minneapolis, 1988.

Tsur, Yaron. *A Torn Community: The Jews of Morocco and Nationalism, 1943–1954*. Tel Aviv, 2001. [Hebrew]

Tuchman, Barbara. *The Proud Tower: A Portrait of the World before the War, 1890–1914*. New York, 1996.

Urban, Hugh. "The Cult of Ecstasy: Tantrism, the New Age and the Spiritual Logic of Late Capitalism." *History of Religions* 39 (2000): pp. 268–304.

Van-Essen, Y. A., ed. *Digital Culture: Virtuality, Society and Information.* Tel Aviv, 2002. [Hebrew]

Victoria, B. D. *Zen War Stories.* London, 2003.

Wacks, Ron. "Chapters of the Kabbalistic Doctrine of Rabbi Shlomo Elyashiv." M.A. thesis, Hebrew University. Jerusalem, 1995. [Hebrew]

——. "Emotion and Enthusiasm in the Educational Theory of Rabbi Kalonymus Kalman Shapira of Piacezna." *Hagut: Jewish Educational Thought* 5–6 (2003–2004): pp. 71–88. [Hebrew]

Wasserstrom, Steven. *Religion after Religion: Gershom Scholem, Mircea Eliade and Henry Corbin.* Princeton, N.J., 1999.

Weiner, Herbert. *Nine and a Half Mystics: The Kabbala Today.* New York, 1971.

Weinstein, Roni. "Religious Forums on the Internet." *De'ot* 15 (2003): pp. 6–10. [Hebrew]

Weiss, Tamar. "Torah Scholars without Fear of God." *De'ot* 6 (2000): pp. 10–14. [Hebrew]

Wexler, Philip. *Mystical Society: An Emerging Social Vision.* Boulder, Colo., 2000.

——. "A Secular Alchemy of Social Science: The Denial of Jewish Messianism in Freud and Durkheim." *Kabbalah* 12 (2004): pp. 7–26.

——. "Social Psychology, the Hassidic Ethos and the Spirit of the New Age." *Kabbalah* 7 (2002): pp. 11–36.

Williams, Raymond. *Keywords: A Vocabulary of Culture and Society.* Oxford, England, 1976.

Wolfson, E. R. *Abraham Abulafia—Kabbalist and Prophet: Hermeneutics, Theosophy and Theurgy.* Los Angeles, 2000.

——. *Venturing Beyond: Law and Morality in Kabbalistic Mysticism.* Oxford, England, 2006.

Wuthnow, Robert. *After Heaven: Spirituality in America since the 1950s.* Berkeley, Calif., 1998.

Zevin, S. Y. *Ishim Ve-Shitot.* Jerusalem, 1957. [Hebrew]

Zivan, Gili. *Religion without Illusion: Facing a Post-modern World—An Inquiry into the Thought of Soloveitchik, Leibowitz, Goldman and Hartman.* Jerusalem, 2005. [Hebrew]

Žižek, Slavoj. *The Puppet and the Dwarf: The Perverse Core of Christianity.* Boston, 2003.

Zohar, Zvi. "Zionism and the State of Israel as Viewed by Leading Sephardic-Oriental Rabbis (1948–1967)." In *On Both Sides of the Bridge: Religion and State in the Early Years of Israel*, ed. M. Bar-On and Z. Zameret, pp. 320–349. Jerusalem, 2002. [Hebrew]

Zorotzkin, David. "Building the Earthly and Destroying the Heavenly: The Satmar Rabbi and the Radical Orthodox School of Thought." In *The Land of Israel in 20th Century Jewish Thought*, ed. A. Ravitzky, pp. 133–167. Jerusalem, 2004. [Hebrew]

Index